Confucius

Confucius

The Man and the Way of Gongfu

Peimin Ni

ROWMAN & LITTLEFIELD
Lanham • Boulder • New York • London

Published by Rowman & Littlefield
A wholly owned subsidiary of The Rowman & Littlefield Publishing Group, Inc.
4501 Forbes Boulevard, Suite 200, Lanham, Maryland 20706
www.rowman.com

Unit A, Whitacre Mews, 26-34 Stannary Street, London SE11 4AB

Confucius: The Man and the Way of Gongfu is a refined and enriched edition of the material that first appeared as *Confucius: Making the Way Great* by Shanghai Translation Publishing House in 2010.

British Library Cataloguing in Publication Information Available

Library of Congress Cataloging-in-Publication Data

Names: Ni, Peimin.
Title: Confucius : the man and the way of gongfu / Peimin Ni.
Description: Lanham : Rowman & Littlefield, 2016. | Includes bibliographical
   references and index.
Identifiers: LCCN 2015034326| ISBN 9781442257412 (hardcopy) | ISBN
   9781442257436 (ebook) | ISBN 9781442257429 (pbk.)
Subjects: LCSH: Confucius. | Kung fu—Miscellanea.
Classification: LCC B128.C8 N477 2016 | DDC 181/.112--dc23 LC record available
   at http://lccn.loc.gov/2015034326

ISBN 978-1-4422-5741-2 (hardcover)
ISBN 978-1-4422-5742-9 (paperback)
ISBN 978-1-4422-5743-6 (ebook)

∞™ The paper used in this publication meets the minimum requirements of American National Standard for Information Sciences—Permanence of Paper for Printed Library Materials, ANSI/NISO Z39.48-1992.

Printed in the United States of America

Confucius can be a teacher to us today—a major teacher, not one who merely gives us a slightly exotic perspective. He was "ahead of our times" until recently, and this is an important reason for his having been pretty much neglected in the West for several centuries.

—Herbert Fingarette

~

Contents

~

Preface

As I was completing the first draft of this book, the US House of Representatives passed a resolution (October 28, 2009) to honor the 2,560th anniversary of the birth of Confucius, recognizing his invaluable contributions to philosophy and social and political thought. The resolution nicely captured two major reasons why we should pay special attention to this ancient Chinese thinker. One reason is that "Confucius, who is one of the greatest thinkers, teachers, and social philosophers in history, developed a philosophy that has deeply influenced, and continues to influence, the social and political thought of countries around the world." No one can understand the history of China and its close neighboring countries, including Korea, Japan, and Vietnam, without a good grasp of the major tenets of Confucianism. Today, with drastic social and political changes in the recent two and a half centuries, the Confucian influence in these countries has been weakened to a significant degree, but its existence is still pervasive, and it is reviving. It is vital for understanding how the people from these regions live their lives and respond to changes.

Over the past two millennia, the Confucian influence in these regions has saturated deeply into political institutions, social customs, ways of life, and perspectives through which people view everything. One can hardly talk about characteristics of East Asian culture without making reference to their root in the Confucian tradition. In doing business with Chinese, for instance, one has to understand the importance of *guanxi* 关系, "relationships." In developing diplomatic relations with China, one has to understand where Sinocentrism came from and how it has evolved into a complicated sense of national identity. In making friends with Chinese, one has to be aware of the cultural roots of their attitudes. Studying Confucius is like doing a cultural genealogy, because this is where the culture took its early shape, though without doubt the culture has taken up new variations along the course of its history.

More importantly, however, is that Confucius's thought is a rich source of inspiration, enabling us to face numerous challenges in today's deeply troubled world. The unprecedented level of cruelty displayed by some of the most "advanced" nations during the two World Wars shocked the entire human population. After the two wars, the world continues to be a threatened, insecure place to live, despite the amazing achievements we have made in other areas. What happened in Kosovo, in Rwanda, in Khmer Rouge, on 9/11 in America, during the Stalin era of the Soviet Russia, and the Cultural Revolution in China, is still happening in the world constantly, though not necessarily on the same devastating scale. With threats from religious fundamentalism, destruction of the environment, and global financial crisis, we are forced to reflect on the very basic values and ways of life that we have taken for granted since the Enlightenment movement in the West.

It is not that Confucius anticipated all these problems and has provided ready solution to them. However, as the US House of Representative resolution recognizes, Confucius's teachings about introspection, self-cultivation, sincerity, and the observance of respect within social relationships as a means of achieving justice and attaining morality in personal and public life, reflect "a moral fiber of the highest degree," "is a model for ethical behavior and for the promotion of harmony among us," and "serves as a reminder to all of our duty to serve with the utmost honor and respect." As an approach to life profoundly different from the modern Western ideas prevalent in the world today, Confucianism provides us with a valuable alternative and a rich resource from which to draw inspiration.

This book is intended to offer a comprehensive introduction of Confucius to general readers. It tries to present Confucius as lucidly and readably as possible, and thus, many historical stories and examples are used to illustrate Confucius's thought. However, for anyone who wants to learn about Confucius more seriously than just satisfying the typical curiosity of a tourist, we have to get to the depth required by the profundity of Confucius's thought. This is exactly where most of the introductory books on Confucius fall short. Why would Confucius be so influential that he would above all others become a symbol of Chinese civilization and shape the culture of all of East Asia? What profound rationality exists behind his apparently fortune-cookie-like sayings? After two thousand years, and after having been proclaimed dead many times by its modern-minded critics, why is Confucianism reviving and being reappropriated today? These questions cannot be answered by simply repeating his life story and listing his major ideas.

For a modern reader of Confucius, the first disturbing difficulty one encounters is the apparent lack of logical order and articulation of the Master's teachings. Confucian classics, whether the *Analects* of Confucius or other works attributed to him, seem to contain mostly sayings and anecdotal records of the Master's life, randomly put together without context. They are often enigmatic or seemingly irrelevant to our lives today, or seem to be simply moral preaching that lacks any rational justification. To overcome this difficulty, adequate articulation of the teachings is necessary.

For the sake of achieving comprehensiveness with a systematic outlook, the book is divided into the following chapters, each aiming at introducing and articulating one aspect of Confucius and his teachings: Confucius as a historical figure, Confucius as a spiritual leader, Confucius as a philosopher, Confucius as a political reformer, Confucius as an educator, and Confucius as a person. However, this method of systematic introduction and articulation runs the risk of arbitrarily separating what was originally intertwined. The whole Confucian system is more like a crystal, with every single side of it reflecting all the other sides. It does not really matter from which side one starts. Sometimes one saying in the *Analects* reveals as much about the Master's view of spirituality as it does his views on politics or education, and his approach to education reflects as much his philosophy as it reveals his personality.

Deep understanding of Confucius is therefore in part dependent on seeing the connection between its multiple dimensions. To retain this important feature in the current introduction, a certain amount of overlap between different chapters is not only inevitable, but also necessary and desirable. One and the same passage from the *Analects* may be quoted several times in various contexts, as its content may be relevant to multiple subject matters. To help the reader see the connections, the book offers an index of quotes from the *Analects*, as well as a name and subject index, so that readers can navigate through and across the chapters more easily, and use the book as a reference guide for reading the *Analects* itself.

Beyond the abovementioned difficulty, however, there is a more substantial obstacle that cannot be eradicated by simple tactics of composition. While the prevalence of the modern Western intellectual framework has allowed current-day readers of Confucius to see him in a new light, it has also prevented many, including even learned scholars, from understanding and appreciating Confucius on his own terms. Generations of modern Confucius scholars have tried hard to interpret Confucianism as a serious philosophical theory, like its Western counterparts, yet since Confucianism is very different from mainstream Western philosophy, their efforts to interpret it according to the Western philosophical conceptual framework have often ironically reinforced the impression of its irrelevance.

Confucius's basic approach is oriented toward the transformation of the person and guiding people's lives, which the Song-Ming neo-Confucians have insightfully called *gongfu* 功夫. It would be misleading to treat it as a system of philosophical theory that aims to either obtain descriptive truths about reality or to justify certain universal moral principles.

Nowadays the term *gongfu* is known mostly through its connection to the martial arts. Whether in the West or in China, most people think of skilled acrobatic fighters like Bruce Lee, Jackie Chan, and Jet Li when they first hear the term. This conception is associated with a double misunderstanding. It first misconceives of *gongfu* as nothing but martial arts, and then takes martial arts to mean simply the skills of fighting and killing. As a matter of fact, *gongfu* is much more than the martial arts, and real martial arts involve far more than fighting skills. Originally used to describe human labor during the third to fourth centuries, the term *gongfu* was later developed into a locus from which a cluster of meanings emerged, referring to the time and effort spent on something, the ability to accomplish intended results, and the result of such effort and abilities. Consequently it came to be used broadly for all the arts of life that require cultivated abilities and effective skills, be it the arts of cooking, speaking, dancing, dealing with human relationships, or the art of living in general.

The Song-Ming neo-Confucians, as well as the Daoists and the Buddhists, all unequivocally spoke of their learning as *gongfu*. This broad understanding of *gongfu* is a lens, though by no means the only one, through which we can understand traditional Chinese philosophy. Through this lens we shall see that the apparent lack of logical order in Confucius's teachings exists because they were not offered as theoretical discourses in the first place. This does not mean that Confucius's teachings have no logic of their own. While a theory typically starts by laying out the premises and, through reasoning, gradually reaching the conclusion, a *gongfu* system starts from the existing condition of the practitioner and, through step-by-step guidance and practice, gradually reaches higher levels of artistic perfection. Different constituents within a theoretical discourse are linked together through their logical connections; hence, their order could only be linear. But different constituents of a *gongfu* system are linked together through their practical implications, which is much more dynamic. They are not so much synthesized in the brain and manifested in the space of words as they are synthesized in a person's embodied dispositions and abilities and manifested in the space of actual life.

Similarly, we shall realize that statements in a *gongfu* system are often used as other than mere descriptions. As British philosopher J. L. Austin has pointed out, we can use words to *perform* actions, such as to promise, to apologize, to acknowledge, to mobilize, to set up a stage, to adjust attitude, and to even transform a life. The ancient Chinese had a special term for this: *yiming zhishi* 以名制实, which means "using names to affect the reality." The *gongfu* reading of Confucius equips us with sensitivity toward the context in which a statement is made and the "language game" it plays. As we shall see, this sheds important light on how, for example, we should understand Confucius's claims about his relationship with heaven (7.23 and 9.5, see pp. 37–38), and how he teaches his students (see p. 125).

Likewise, when viewed through this lens, we shall realize that as a *gongfu* system, Confucius's teachings have to be evaluated differently from theoretical discourse. The convincing power of *gongfu* instructions ultimately lies not in logical proof of conclusions but in the efficacious results they generate. Consequently, contradictory statements in a *gongfu* system may each be valid within their own respective contexts (see the example of Confucius offering opposite answers to the same question brought up by different disciples, on pp. 126–27). Although for the sake of being effective an instruction may appear to be a universal rule, ultimately it may still be subject to the use of discretion (see the example of the Confucian "Golden Rule," on pp. 60–61). Furthermore, since this "effectiveness" is open to alternative visions of excellence, *gongfu* systems are non-exclusivist. Unlike truth claims, they do not have to assert themselves as the only correct form of art. This is different from having no right or wrong or good and bad, however; it is just like any form of art—subject to the judgment of people's cultivated experiences.

Through the lens of *gongfu* perspective one shall further realize that as a way of *gongfu*, Confucius's teachings are ultimately aimed not at setting up moral rules to constrain people, but rather at providing guidance to enable people to live good, artistic lives. In other words, Confucianism is more aesthetic than it is moralist. Confucius is obviously concerned about morality, but our common conception of morality today is too narrow to capture the Master's aim, which goes far beyond moral obligations into the realm of mastering the art of living. Moral norms are *imposed* (whether by an external authority, or, as in the case of Kantian ethics, by self) to *constrain* a person as *responsibilities*, but *gongfu* instructions are *recommended* for *enabling* a person to live *artistically*. Moral norms allow no exception, but *gongfu* instructions are like protocols, which can allow flexibility. Norms are recognized by the brain as principles, yet *gongfu* abilities must be embodied as one's dispositions or habits. While the former is taught by using abstract concepts, the latter has to engage embodied imitation of masters or exemplars (hence, the relevance of lots of "tedious" records of Confucius's lifestyle in the *Analects*). From the moral point of view, the Confucian virtue of *ren* (human-heartedness) is what makes a person morally good, but from the *gongfu* point of view, it is directly a person's *gongfu* of enacting cosmic energies.

Last but not least, *gongfu* perspective reminds us that, like any form of art, the Confucian Way of *gongfu* can only be appreciated through practice. A person who has never actually been immersed in water cannot fully understand what it is like to swim, regardless of how much he knows *about* swimming. Similarly, without associating the learning of Confucianism with actual life experience and practice, one will have trouble understanding what makes Confucius and his disciple YAN Hui happy in their materially impoverished life (6.11 and 7.16), and how YAN Hui can be so fascinated about learning that he would be unable to stop his pursuit even if he wanted to (9.11).

Traditionally the Confucian classics were first memorized and followed before people tried to comprehend them, because it takes practical experience and repeated rehearsal to develop the virtuosity required for true understanding. As Song dynasty Confucian CHENG Yi says: "Nowadays people no longer know how to read. When they read the *Analects*, for instance, they are the same kind of people before they read the book and after they read the book. This is no different from not having read the book" (Zhu, 1992, 4). In an article about how to read the *Analects* and *Mencius*, ZHU Xi says:

> In reading the *Analects* and the *Mencius* one should not merely aim at understanding the theory and the meanings of the texts. One should make careful reflection and put the teachings into practice. . . . If a reader can relate the sages' sayings to his own person and examine them through his own embodied practice, his effort will surely not be spent in vain. Every day will bring him the result (*gong* 功) of the day. If one only takes the books as collections of sayings, it would be merely the learning of the mouth and the ears. (Zhu, "*Du Lunyu Mengzi Fa*," 3)

Cheng and Zhu have both pointed out the difference between two approaches to reading—one is intellectual, and the other is the *gongfu* approach. The former requires only intellectual understanding, while the latter requires self-reflection of what is learned and application of it in practice. The former leads only to bookish knowledge, while the latter leads to embodied understanding and holistic growth. The former reader passively receives information from the text, but the latter interacts with the text, making it come alive through personal engagement with it. Given the difference in orientation between the propositional and the instructional, it might not be too far-fetched to say that using the intellectualist approach to read Confucius is like eating the menu instead of the food.

One special feature of this book is its comparative approach. In addition to the contrast between the Confucian Way of *gongfu* and the predominantly Western intellectual discourses, it also engages major modern Western values such as freedom, equality, dignity, human rights, democracy, justice, rule of law, and science in direct dialogue with Confucianism. In the wake of the modern West, these values have been upheld by critics of Confucianism as the bar with which to measure its backwardness. Defenders of Confucianism have also taken these values for granted, but try to argue that Confucianism is somehow not incompatible with them, or even has rudiments of the same ideas. With special attention to what Confucianism can offer to the contemporary reader, this book differs from these previous positions. It highlights the points in which Confucianism can pose challenges to these core modern Western values, and tries to reveal how Confucianism can be a constructive resource for the postmodern transformation of these values.

Associated with the problem of reading Confucius with a Western perspective is the problem of using a Western language to introduce Confucius. People commonly consider writing about Confucius in any language other than classic Chinese as a disadvantage, for the language barrier creates a need for additional interpretation, thus introducing a greater likelihood of misinterpretation. Indeed, the words to describe many concepts crucial to Confucianism are nonexistent in English, and using English terms to interpret them would lead directly to such a risk. For the sake of avoiding misinterpretation, we have to sometimes transcribe the pronunciation of Chinese words together with extensive articulation in order to clarify their meaning. Careful readers will find that occasionally the same passage can appear slightly different in translation when it is quoted in different contexts, as the multiple meanings entailed in the passage can require different renderings in different contexts. The linguistic distance from the original texts, however, is not necessarily a disadvantage. As the Chinese saying states, "You don't see the true face of Mount Lu exactly because you are inside the mountain." The linguistic space created by the use of a non-Chinese language could actually offer the reader a chance to see it more clearly from a distance, and more comprehensively from multiple angles. The same is true for engaging Western ideas in comparison to Confucian ideas.

One note regarding the technical treatment of Chinese names in this book: Chinese people typically put family names first and given names last, although some Chinese switch the order to fit the Western custom. Given this variation, Westerners may get confused about which is the family name and which is the given name. The proper use of names is a significant aspect of traditional Confucian ritual. How a person is addressed contains important information about the relationship between the relevant people. To avoid such confusion, I use small capital letters for Chinese family names when they are placed before given names. For instance, "Zhu Xi" means "Zhu" is the family name and "Xi" is the given name. When not capitalized in this way, the order would be just like the Western custom. So in the case of "Chenyang Li," "Li" is the family name. There are also cases in which a historical person is only known through a given name or a style name. In these cases, I will simply put the name in its normal case, with no space between the Romanization of multiple Chinese characters (e.g., "Nanzi"). One more important note here is that ancient names often come with "Zi," an honorary way of addressing the person as a "Master" (e.g., Lao Zi, Xun Zi, Mo Zi). Since few Chinese people have "Zi" as a family name, it is safe to assume that in all of these cases, it means "Master," as "Xun Zi" means "Master Xun."

Translation of Chinese texts in this book is either my own or based on the English books listed in the bibliography at the end, sometimes with modifications. Citations from the Analects of Confucius will be given simply in parentheses, with the chapter number and the section number. For example, "(2.1)" means chapter 2, section 1, from the book of the Analects.

This book was originally published through Shanghai Translation Publishing House in China (2010) under the title Confucius: Making the Way Great. Since its publication, I have received many critical yet constructive comments, as well as compliments, on the basis of which I was able to make some significant improvements to this edition. Among those who contributed in this way, I would like to especially thank Professor Huaiyu Wang, whose book review (published in the Journal of Chinese Philosophy, 39:3) was particularly helpful.

Professor Henry Rosemont Jr. and Fred R. Dallmayr deserve special thanks, because their encouragement resulted more directly in the birth of this newer version. Of course I must reiterate my indebtedness to Zhao Yuese, Ma Sheng, Stephen Rowe, Patrick Shan, Jennifer Lechy, and Anthony Bergman, for their various contributions to the earlier version of the book. I want to further thank Natalie Mandziuk, editor at Rowman & Littlefield, for her enthusiasm for this project and her guidance in bringing this new version into print.

Last but not least, my deep gratitude goes to my beloved teachers, Professor Henry Rosemont Jr. and Professor Joel J. Kupperman, for having led me to a deeper appreciation of my own cultural heritage, and for showing me living examples of junzi, an exemplary person!

—P. N.

~

Chronology

Antiquity

ca. 24th–22nd c. BCE	Sage Kings Yao, Shun, and Yu
ca. 21st–17th c. BCE	Xia dynasty
ca. 17th–11th c. BCE	Shang dynasty
ca. 11th c. BCE	King Wen, King Wu, and the Duke of Zhou laid the foundation of the culture of the Zhou dynasty.
ca. 11th–8th c. BCE	Western Zhou dynasty

Confucius's Life

551 BCE	Confucius was born on September 28.
549 BCE?	Confucius's father died.
537 BCE	"At the age of fifteen, I set my heart on learning."
533 BCE?	Married to Jiguan 丌官 from the state of Song.
532 BCE	His son Kong Li 孔鲤 (Boyu 伯鱼) was born.
531 BCE	Said to be managing herds of cows and sheep.
522 BCE	"At the age of thirty I was able to take my stand."
518 BCE	Lu noble Mengxizi 孟僖子, before his death, told his two sons to study with Confucius.
517 BCE	Duke Zhao of Lu was defeated in an attempt to get his power back from the three families and fled to Qi. Confucius went to Qi as well.

516 BCE   Probably during this time Duke Jing of Qi asked Confucius about government (12.11), and Confucius heard the music of Shao (7.14).

515 BCE?   Left Qi and went back to Lu.

512 BCE   "At the age of forty, I am free from perplexities."

510 BCE   Duke Zhao of Lu died, succeeded by Duke Ding.

504 BCE?   The Ji family chief administrator YANG HUO, who became powerful in politics, wanted to see Confucius, but Confucius refused to see him (17.1).

502 BCE   "At the age of fifty, I knew the mandate of heaven."

            GONGSHAN Furau 公山弗扰 took hold of the Bi 费 stronghold against the Ji family and summoned Confucius to join him. Confucius was tempted but did not go (17.5).

501 BCE   YANG HUO 阳货 failed in an attempt to overthrow the three families and fled to Qi, and then to Jin.

            Said to be appointed by Duke Ding as the governor of Zhongdu 中都 and brought the area to peace within one year.

500 BCE   Said to be appointed as the minister of justice of Lu.

497 BCE?   Ji Huanzi accepted dancing girls from Qi and did not hold court for three days. Confucius resigned and started on his travels (3.1).

            First visit to Wei; stayed there for about ten months.

            On the way from Wei to Chen, besieged by the people of Kuang, who mistook him to be YANG HUO (9.5, 11.23).

496 BCE   Returned to Wei, met Nanzi, the wife of Duke Ling of Wei (6.28).

495 BCE   Returned to Lu. Duke Ding died, succeeded by Duke Ai.

493 BCE   Went to Wei again. Duke Ling of Wei asked about military formations (15.1). Confucius left the next day.

492 BCE   "At sixty, my ears were attuned."

            Passed through Song on the way to Chen, when Huantui made an attempt on his life (7.23).

            Ji Huanzi died.

            Left Chen and went to Cai.

490 BCE   Went from Cai to She 叶. The governor of She asked about governing and about uprightness (13.16, 13.18).

490 BCE   Tempted by Bixi's 佛肸 summon, but did not go (17.7).

489 BCE   Ran out of provisions in the region between Chen and Cai during the invasion of Chen by Wu (15.2).

488 BCE?   Confucius returned to Wei.

485 BCE	Wife died.
484 BCE	Returned from Wei to Lu.
483 BCE	His only son KONG Li died.
482 BCE	"At the age of seventy, I can follow my heart's wishes without overstepping the boundaries."
	YAN Hui died.
480 BCE	Zilu was killed during a coup in Wei.
479 BCE	Confucius died in the spring. Duke Ai of Lu wrote a eulogy.
478 BCE	Lu set three rooms of his former residence as a Confucian temple.

Other Major Philosophers during the First Epoch of Confucianism

6th c. BCE?	Lao Zi, founder of philosophical Daoism
483–402 BCE?	Zisi, Confucius's grandson, who allegedly authored the "Great Learning" and the "Zhongyong"
470–391 BCE?	Mo Zi, founder of Moism
372–289 BCE	Mencius, who is later honored as "the Second Sage" in the Confucian tradition
369–286 BCE	Zhuang Zi, Daoist philosopher
325–238 BCE?	Xun Zi, Confucian philosopher
280–233 BCE?	HAN Fei, major Legalist philosopher

First Sweeping Attack on Confucianism

259–210 BCE	Qin Shi Huang—the First Emperor of the Qin
213 BCE	Qin Shi Huang ordered book burning.
212 BCE	Qin Shi Huang buried 460 scholars alive.

Confucianism Became Official Ideology

202–157 BCE	Emperor Wen of the Han
194–114 BCE?	DONG Zhongshu, who contributed greatly to the making of Confucianism as an official ideology
156–87 BCE	Emperor Wu of the Han, who accepted DONG Zhongshu's suggestion to "Denounce all other schools, uphold Confucianism only."

141 BCE	Books hidden in the wall by KONG FU 孔鮒 (eighth-generation descendant of Confucius) during the Qin discovered.
146–86 BCE?	SIMA Qian, author of the first biography of Confucius
48 BCE	The imperial court granted Confucius's descendant KONG Ba 孔霸 the tax income of eight hundred families to maintain annual rituals to honor Confucius.
8 BCE	Confucius's descendant KONG Ji 孔吉 was given a dukedom.
1 CE	Confucius was posthumously given the title of *Baocheng Xuanni Gong* 褒成宣尼公, "Honorable Consummate Duke of Xuanni," marking the beginning of imperial conferring of honorary titles to the Master.
72	Emperor Ming of the Han offered a sacrificial ritual at Confucius's hometown of Qufu to honor Confucius and his seventy-two disciples.
79	Emperor Zhang of the Han 汉章帝 called for a conference at the White Tiger Temple to discuss Confucian classics.
285	Korean Confucian scholar brought the *Analects* to Japan.
581	The first Emperor of the Sui dynasty addresses Confucius as *Xianshi Nifu* 先师尼父, "Foremost Teacher and Forefather Ni."
628	Tang Emperor Taizong 唐太宗 honored Confucius as *Xiansheng* 先圣, "the Sage of Antiquity," replacing the position held by the Duke of Zhou.
630	Emperor Taizong issued an edict to build Confucian temples all over the country.
666	Emperor Gaozong 唐高宗 and Empress Wu 武后 went to Qufu to pay tribute to Confucius.
710	Japan had its first official ritual ceremony to honor the "Foremost Teacher," Confucius.
739	Confucius was conferred the title of *Wenxuan Wang* 文宣王, "King of Culture Manifestation," and started the tradition of conferring an inheritable title, *Wenxuan Gong* 文宣公, "Duke of *Wenxuan*," to the eldest male descendant of every generation of the Kong family.
768	The Emperor of Japan honored Confucius as *Wenxuan Wang*.
963	The first Emperor of the Song dynasty, Taizu 宋太祖, ordered the expansion of the Imperial Academy of Learning (*guozijian* 国子监), with a statue of Confucius enshrined in it, and wrote articles to praise Confucius and YAN Hui.

1011	The imperial court of the Song issued an edict to build Confucian temples all over the country.

The Second Epoch of Confucianism

1017–1073	ZHOU Dunyi 周敦颐, who infused Daoist ideas into Confucianism; also, the beginning of the "School of Principle" interpretation of Confucianism.
1073	First Confucian temple built in Vietnam.
1032–1085	CHENG Hao and
1033–1107	CHENG Yi. The Cheng brothers marked the upsurge of the "School of Principle."
1130–1200	ZHU Xi, who brought the "School of Principle" to the highest peak, and established the "Four Books" as part of the Confucian canon.
1139–1193	LU Xiangshan; the "School of Heart-mind" interpretation of Confucianism.
1289	Cheng-Zhu School of Principle spread to Korea.
1308	Emperor Wu of the Yuan dynasty 元武宗 ordered the honorary title of Confucius to be changed to *Dacheng Zhisheng Wenxuan Wang* 大成至圣文宣王, "The Great Consummative Supreme Sage King of Culture Manifestation."
1368	The first Emperor of the Ming dynasty ordered to continue to confer Confucius's direct descendants the inheritable title of *Yansheng Gong* 衍圣公, "Duke of Broadening Sageliness," and appointment as the governor of Qufu County.
1472–1528	WANG Yangming; marked the high peak of the "School of Heart-mind."
1501–1570	Korean Confucian Scholar YI Hwang 李滉.

Modern Encounters with Confucianism

1552–1610	Matteo Ricci, an Italian Jesuit, translated basic Confucian classics, the "Four Books," into Latin.
1644	The first Emperor of the Qing dynasty held a ceremony to honor Confucius.
1704	The Vatican issued a proclamation forbidding Catholic missionaries and Chinese converts from taking part in Confucian rituals—The "Rites Controversy."

1815–1897 British Sinologist James Legge translated numerous Confucian classics into English.

1866–1925 Sun Zhongshan (Sun Yat-sen), the first president of the Republic of China

1881–1936 Lu Xun, a leading intellectual in the New Culture Movement, who criticized institutionalized Confucianism as a form of cannibalism.

1915–1919 The New Culture Movement launched widespread criticism of Confucianism.

1939 The Nationalist government of China announced that Confucius's birthday would be called "Teachers' Day."

1942 The Nationalist Party of China proclaimed Confucius's birthday as a national memorial day.

The Third Epoch of Confucianism

1948 Mou Zongshan and other scholars first used the concept of "The Third Epoch of Confucianism."

United Nations Declaration of Human Rights added the Confucian clause that all men "should act towards one another in a spirit of brotherhood."

1958 Tang Junyi 唐君毅, Mou Zongshan, Xu Fuguan, and Carsun Chang 张君劢 jointly published "A Manifesto for a Reappraisal of Sinology and Reconstruction of Chinese Culture."

1966–1976 The Cultural Revolution in China. Pro-Confucian national leader, Liu Shaoqi, was ousted from office and openly criticized nationwide.

1973 "Denounce Lin Biao and Denounce Confucius" movement.

1984 China Confucius Foundation established.

1986 Inaugural issue of the journal *Confucius Studies* published.

2004 The Chinese government set up "Establishing a harmonious society" as its strategic goal.

2014 China's new president Xi Jinping spoke at an international conference commemorating the 2565th anniversary of Confucius's birth, placing China's peaceful development in the context of the long tradition of Confucianism, and holding the Chinese Community Party up as the "successor to and promoter of fine traditional Chinese culture.

CHAPTER I

~

Confucius as a Historical Figure

"Confucius" is the Latinized name of Kong Fuzi 孔夫子, "Master Kong" (551–479 BCE), or, in its abbreviated form, Kong Zi 孔子. Kong is his family name. His given name is Qiu 丘, and his style name is Zhongni 仲尼.[1] Although Confucius's life does not appear extraordinary in comparison with many other historical figures, Confucius exerted unparalleled influence on Chinese history and culture. He is known as China's first and foremost teacher, a supreme sage, and as a "king without a crown." His teachings laid the foundation for a philosophy that became China's guiding principle in morality, law, government, education, and life in general. Throughout much of Chinese history in the last two thousand years, everyone, from the emperors down to the commoners, was supposed to follow Confucius's teachings. When some Western Enlightenment thinkers encountered the teachings of Confucius through Jesuit missionaries who had traveled to China, they were astonished and excited by the fact that a humanitarian philosophy had already served as the backbone of Chinese civilization for almost two millennia.

At the same time, however, Confucianism suffered serious distortions and negative stereotypes. It was associated with being impractical, pedantic, and excessively conservative. In the awakening of modern China, Confucianism was criticized as elitist, sexist, nepotistic, repressive, and authoritarian; it was taken to be responsible for everything backward and benighted in China, including political corruption, suppression of women, concubinage, female infanticide, and illiteracy. In Lu Xun's 鲁迅 (1881–1936) famous short novel, *Madman's Diary*, it is even portrayed as a form of cannibalism.

Indeed, various accounts of Confucius and Confucianism have been created and re-created throughout history, both inside and outside of China, so much so that it is hard to recognize the original, historical Confucius. Someone even argued that the image we have today of the Master and his teachings was to a large degree "manufactured" (see Jensen, 1997). Exactly because of this, however, the "real" Confucius has extended far beyond the confinement of the individual person, and therefore the full discovery of Confucius can only come from continuously reappropriating his resourceful teachings. Just as one is in a better position to understand fireworks after they explode, the unfolding of different interpretations of Confucianism actually helps to reveal what was in the original texts.

Long, Long Ago, There Was a Time

Confucius was born during the latter part of the Zhou dynasty known as "Spring and Autumn 春秋" (770–476 BCE), when China's civilization had already existed for more than two thousand years. Even though knowledge about remote antiquity was passed down through legends and songs, the cultural messages contained within them were also quite rich. Stories about ancient sage kings Yao 尧, Shun 舜, and Yu 禹 were quoted by Confucius and others during that time, without suspicion of their reliability. It was believed that these sage kings were all exemplary persons, and both Yao and Shun selected their successors according to moral integrity and ability, not simply choosing their own descendants. Succession of power by direct descendants began after Yu passed away and his son Qi 启 took the throne, which marks the beginning of the Xia 夏 dynasty (ca. twenty-first to seventeenth century BCE). If the existence of Xia is still questionable because of the lack of direct archaeological evidence, the existence of the succeeding Shang 商 dynasty (ca. seventeenth to eleventh century BCE) has been confirmed by abundant bronze vessels, tortoiseshells, and animal bones discovered during the last one hundred years or so in Anyang, Henan Province, and other ancient ruins. Written records found on these materials show that during the Shang dynasty, China had already developed sophisticated methods of agriculture and techniques for working with pottery, bronze, and silk.

The Shang dynasty lasted for six hundred years, until it was overthrown by the revolt of the Zhou 周 people in the Wei River valley in today's Shaanxi Province. In contrast to the last king of the Shang, who was notoriously cruel, the founders of the Zhou dynasty (founded in 1122 BCE), King Wen 文王 and his son, the Duke of Zhou 周公, laid the foundation of a humanitarian government in emulation of the ancient sage-kings, Yao, Shun, and

Yu, refining the traditional ritual system. They justified their overturning of the Shang dynasty as a revolution to liberate the people from oppressors.

This revolution, so they claimed, was carried out under the *tian ming* 天命, the "mandate of heaven," which was exemplified through the will of the people. The founding King of the Zhou is said to have declared that "Great heaven has no affections;—it helps only the virtuous" (*Shu Jing*, 490). Their mission therefore became not only legitimate, but also sacred. The difference between a mere rebel and a heaven-appointed new ruler was that the latter had the support of the people. The victory of the Zhou in overthrowing the Shang certainly reinforced the claim that the new rulers had a special tie with heaven, and this religious dimension played an important role in allowing subsequent leaders throughout the Zhou to effectively control the vassals across the vast territory of central China for hundreds of years. It added a sacred layer to their conferring limited sovereignty over portions of the land to members of the royal lineage, which made the tie between the central power and the vassals both religious and familial.

Moreover, the Zhou retained traditional ritual services to natural and ancestral spirits and developed new forms of ritual proprieties in all aspects of human life. The music and dances performed in ceremonies started to gain a special significance in maintaining social order—so much so that the spirits themselves became secondary in importance. The rituals themselves became exemplifications of the order of heaven. From this tradition, Confucius developed his own account of humanism and ritual propriety, which subsequently became the mainstream of traditional Chinese culture for over two millennia.

By the Spring and Autumn period, the social order of the Zhou was already crumbling. Whereas possessing the mandate of heaven had to be earned through manifesting one's virtues, which therefore suggests the mandate of heaven would not belong to one dynasty forever, the edicts of the kings during this period were less and less effective, as they demonstrated few virtuous deeds. The feudal lords became disobedient to their kings and increasingly hostile to each other, swallowing up territories of weaker neighbors, constantly shifting state boundaries. The kings eventually became little more than puppets manipulated by powerful vassals.

Similarly, some clans of principal ministers inside the states grew stronger and in turn threatened the power of the rulers. Confucius's home state of Lu, for instance, was largely controlled by "The Three Families," Meng 孟, Shu 叔, and Ji 季—the descendants of three sons of Duke Huan of Lu 鲁桓公 (who reigned from 711–697 BCE). They were involved in murdering two heirs of the ducal throne and setting up one who had their own favor in 609, and, in 562, they divided the state, leaving the Duke of Lu only a fraction of the revenues.

In a time when material might equaled right, religion and morality inevitably weakened, and the lives of the people were often extremely unstable and miserable. There was no concept of law other than that which was conducted through the whims of the mighty ones. Subordinates risked their lives in remonstrating their superiors; friends and relatives became enemies overnight; the job of assassin was a hot profession; and rulers of states frequently became detainees of other states. In 593 BCE, the capital of the state of Song was under siege for so long that the residents had no choice but to "exchange their children to eat," since they could not bear to eat their own (see *Zuo Zhuan*, Duke Xuan, Year 15).

Even though there were sporadic stories of great fidelity, loyalty, courage, and respect for dignity, on what grounds could these virtues be justified and prevail? Or, more crudely, in such a society, were these virtues or mere stupidity? Obviously, there were deep problems with the society. What way could be found to solve the problems? Or, even more fundamentally, what was *the* problem?

Questions about the right way of life and what to believe in, as well as the search for answers to profound social problems, naturally occupied the most reflective minds of the time. These reflective minds were usually from a social class known as *shi* 士, sometimes translated as "scholar-apprentice," but I prefer to use "educated person" instead, as this seems closer to the way Confucius interpreted the term. Somewhat akin to the old European knights and the Japanese samurais, *shi* originally referred to the ancient warrior caste, but gradually evolved into a term referring to those who had a noble family background and a good education, but had fallen to the middle or lower social status due to the unstable social climate. They were ambitious, discontented with the status quo, and often had their own ideas about how to make their life and society better.

It was against such a historical backdrop that China experienced its most glorious period in philosophy. Confucianism, Daoism, Moism, Legalism, and numerous other schools of thought emerged and competed with each other. This is known as the period of "[a] hundred schools of thought," and it is comparable to the golden age of ancient Greek philosophy both in terms of the importance to their respective civilizations and in terms of their philosophical and spiritual profundity. Indeed, the time in which these schools of thought emerged coincides with the emergence of Greek philosophers, such as Socrates, Parmenides, Heraclitus, Archimedes, Plato, Aristotle, and other major thinkers in the world, such as Siddhartha Gautama (the Buddha) and the authors of *Upanishads* in India, and Elijah, Isaiah, and Jeremiah in the Near East. These thinkers all had a profound influence on future philosophies and religions. The striking parallel development of these philosophies and schools of religious thought in light of the lack of any clear and direct transmission of ideas from one region to the other triggered the German philosopher Karl Jaspers to coin the term "the axial age" to describe this period (ca. 800 to 200 BCE).

A Man from a Humble Background

Confucius was born in 551 BCE in a town near today's Qufu city in Shandong Province, China. In ancient times, Qufu belonged to the state of Lu, which was known for its preservation of early Zhou rituals and music. According to the *Zuo Zhuan* 左传, a narrative history book dated around the fourth century BCE, Confucius was a descendant of a noble family in the state of Song, who, fearing political implications, fled to the state of Lu. It is said that his family line could be traced all the way back to the royal family of the Shang dynasty. Scholars have disputed whether this story is based on historical facts or on the assumption that a great man like Confucius must have had a noble ancestry. It is said in *Kong Zi Jiayu* 孔子家语, "*Confucius Family Discourse,*" and *Shi Ji* 史记, the "*Historical Records,*" written by the Han dynasty historian Sima Qian 司马迁 (145–90 BCE), that Confucius's father was a low-ranking military officer named Shuliang-He 叔梁纥 ("Shuliang" is his style name, and "He" is his given name), or Kong He 孔纥.

Since Shuliang-He had nine daughters but no son with his first wife, he acquired a concubine, who consequently gave birth to a crippled son named Mengpi 孟皮. Wishing to have a healthy son, in his sixties he married the youngest of the three daughters of the Yan family, Yan Zhengzai 颜徵在. Yan got pregnant after they went to Mount Ni 尼山 to pray for a son, and subsequently gave birth to a boy with a big forehead like a small hill. This is how Confucius got his given name, Qiu, and his style name, Zhongni. As *qiu* 丘 means hill, *zhong* 仲 signifies that he was the second son, and *ni* 尼 was for Mount Ni. Confucius's father died when Confucius was only three. He was brought up by his mother, who died when he was about seventeen. Presumably for the same reason that a sage must have a noble ancestry, his mother was also said to be a descendant of the Zhou royal family, all the way from the Duke of Zhou!

Confucius himself never bragged about having "noble" ancestry. "I was poor when I was young, and that is why I acquired many humble skills" (9.6), says the Master. "Confucius was once a minor keeper of stores, and he said, 'All I had to do was to keep correct records.' He also served as a minor official in charge of sheep and cattle, during which, he said, 'All I had to do was to see to it that the sheep and cattle grew up to be strong and healthy'" (*Mencius*, 5B:5). Of course, this does not mean that Confucius was literally from the bottom rungs of society. His ancestors were probably aristocrats, and even though his family was poor, he was still able to get some education and learn arts such as archery and music.

What Confucius was most proud of was the fact that he had set his heart on learning at the age of fifteen (2.4), and he was a determined learner ever after. Unlike typical school-age children today, the young Confucius did not have a school to attend, nor did he have many books available to read. Back then education was conducted mostly in a private tutoring fashion, or governmental officials offered lessons to their subordinates, like an apprenticeship. The books available at the time were few in number and hard to get. They were hand-copied scripts written on bamboo strips, which were heavy to carry and easily fell apart. Nonetheless, Confucius seized every opportunity to learn. He never had a single and constant teacher, and the sources of his knowledge were not limited to books. He says, "Walking along with two others, I am certain there is my teacher among them. I select their good qualities to follow, and their bad qualities to rectify" (7.22). He learned also from traveling around, visiting historical sites, experiencing life, and reflecting on the things he encountered. Entering the Grand Temple, for instance, he inquired about everything, as this was the place where the culture of the Zhou was preserved. Upon climbing the Eastern Mount, he started to see how tiny the State of Lu was, and upon ascending Mount Tai, he came to an even broader realization—that the world he had previously known now seemed quite small (*Mencius*, 7A:24). This was an insight somewhat similar to the moral behind Plato's allegory of the cave: One's vision is dependent on where one stands.

Probably by the age of thirty, Confucius had already attracted a group of young people to study with him. A clear indication of his reputation as a teacher was that when he was thirty-four, a senior official of Lu and a member of the powerful "Three Families," Mengxizi 孟僖子, on his deathbed told his two sons to study with Confucius (*Zuo Zhuan*, Duke Zhao, Year 7). Confucius is believed to be the first in the history of China to set up a school and offer education in an institutional way, but the word *first* may actually mean "foremost," for according to the *Mencius*, there were schools long before Confucius's time (*Mencius*, 3A:3). There is no doubt that this is also the way that the Master has been revered—as China's foremost teacher.

According to a likely exaggerated account, Confucius had over three thousand students throughout his life, and seventy-two of them became conversant with the "Six Arts" that he taught—ritual, music, writing, arithmetic, archery, and charioteering. He taught them how to be *junzi* 君子, an "exemplary person," which includes (but is not limited to) being a talented statesman. Some of his disciples actually did end up playing significant roles in politics. Among the twenty-two disciples mentioned in the *Analects*, at least nine became officials of some importance. Three of them served successively as the steward to the Ji family, which was in virtual control of the state of Lu. This was the highest position in the state that could be attained without relying on inheritance.

The magic of the Master's success, however, lies not merely in the subjects he taught. Instead, it lies more in the humanitarian spirit of his teachings, together with his extensive knowledge, profound wisdom, personal integrity, and charisma. His disciples looked at him as a sage beyond comparison, and followed him with loyalty and devotion. It is said that after the Master passed away, many of his disciples mourned him for three years, a ritual that was typically applied only to one's parents. One of them, Zigong 子贡, even spent six years of his life mourning the Master by living in a hut next to the Master's grave!

Like Socrates, Confucius himself never seemed to have written any books. His teachings were recorded by his students and collected mostly into a book known as *Lunyu* 论语, the *Analects*, which contains his sayings, short descriptions of his encounters and his personality, conversations between him and his disciples, and the sayings of these disciples. Although there are controversies surrounding the authenticity of some of the sections of the book, the *Analects* is still considered the most reliable source of Confucius's teachings.

Confucius considered himself a transmitter rather than a creator. He claimed that the wisdom he taught was already contained in the ancient traditional rituals, history, music, poetry, and limited written works that were, while corrupted after surviving the turmoil of the ages, available at his time. In his teachings there are indeed traces of ideas from ancient texts such as the *Book of Changes*, the *Odes*, the *Book of Historical Documents*, and the *Zhou Rituals*. Because of this, Mencius calls Confucius a "great synthesizer." In fact, however, Confucius is also an innovative thinker of his time. His teachings are a creative reconstruction and reinterpretation of the tradition, and they contain deep insights about what is most valuable. He rationalized the humanitarian spirit of the early Zhou culture and its ritual tradition, brought both of these to a new level of significance, and succeeded in passing them on to his followers, significantly impacting and transforming their lives.

The Master is believed to have edited some of the most basic Chinese classics, including the *Book of Rites*, the *Book of Historical Documents*, the *Book of Odes*, the *Book of Music*, the *Spring and Autumn Annals*, and the *Book of Changes*. According to SIMA Qian, the author of the *Historical Records*, Confucius selected 305 of the best songs from the 3,000 known at that time and organized them into the *Book of Odes* (*Shi Jing* 诗经). Although the extent to which Confucius edited the *Odes* is questionable, the fact that he worked on editing them is beyond a reasonable doubt. The *Analects* tells us that the Master said, "After I returned from Wei to Lu, the *Music* was corrected, and the Ya 雅 and the Song 颂 (sections in the *Book of Odes*) each obtained their proper places" (9.15). It would be a mistake to take what Confucius did to the book as merely the technical work of a copy editor. From the way that Confucius quoted and interpreted the *Odes*, we can tell that his editorial work transformed it into a work full of hidden moral messages.

Similarly, even though the *Spring and Autumn Annals* apparently contains nothing but brief records of individual events, such as wars, political unifications, deaths, and even tedious natural events like "this spring there was no ice," "mynahs came and nested in trees," it is believed that Confucius artistically imbedded praises and condemnations in the book through his use of words, his arrangement of sentences, and his selection of which details to include and which to exclude, to subtly convey moral messages. The book is therefore more of an ethics canon than a book of history. The *Mencius* tells us that "Confucius completed the *Spring and Autumn Annals* and rebellious subjects and undutiful sons were struck in fear" (*Mencius*, 3B:9).

> When the world declined and the Way fell into obscurity, heresies and violence again arose. There were instances of regicides and parricides. Confucius was apprehensive and composed the *Spring and Autumn Annals*. Strictly speaking, this is the Emperor's prerogative. That is why Confucius said, "Those who understand me will do so through the *Spring and Autumn Annals*; those who condemn me will also do so because of the *Spring and Autumn Annals*." (*Mencius*, 3B:9)

Indeed, as far as the debate about whether it was written by Confucius as a covert ethics canon, or whether it merely preexisted as a poorly composed historical record, the very oddity and the apparent poor quality of it as a history book served exactly as evidence that it was not meant to be primarily a history book in the first place!

Even though Confucius was temperamentally more fitted to be a scholar and teacher than a politician, he took political reform as his lifelong pursuit. With a strong sense of mission and ambition to bring the world into harmonious order, the Master spent a considerable amount of his time trying to implement his visions in the political sphere. At one point (502 BCE), Confucius even seriously considered accepting an invitation from a person who betrayed his nominal overlord, the Ji family, by taking hold of a city and forming his own government. Confucius's disciple Zilu 子路 asked him bluntly: "If we have nowhere to go, so be it! Why must you go to this man?" The Master said, "Can one invite me for no reason? If anyone employs me, may I not make another Zhou of the East?" (17.5)

It was said that Duke Ding of Lu appointed Confucius the following year (501 BCE) as the governor of Zhongdu, and that he managed to bring the area to peace within one year. Subsequently, he was promoted to serve as Minister of Justice at Lu, during which he successfully defeated Duke Jing of Qi's attempt to coerce Duke Ding of Lu with an armed force in a summit meeting. However, scholars have questioned the reliability of these stories. Some believed that later Confucians fabricated them, for if they were true, the *Analects* of Confucius would not have remained entirely silent regarding these events.

Whether Confucius took the above-described offices or not, it is indisputable that he despised the Ji family for usurping the power of Lu from the Duke. Passage 18.4 in the *Analects* implies that he did hold an office under Ji Huanzi 季桓子, but resigned as a protest: "The men of Qi sent as a gift a group of female entertainers. Ji Huanzi accepted it, and for three days no court was held. Confucius took his departure." For Confucius, "When the Way is in the state, one receives a stipend of grain. But when the Way is lost in the state and one still receives a stipend of grain, this is shameful" (14.1).

With a deep disappointment in the political situation in Lu, Confucius resolved to leave the state at the age of fifty-five and embark on travels from one state to another, seeking to be appointed by a ruler who would allow him to implement his humanistic ideas in political affairs. According to SIMA Qian's biography of Confucius, before he left the state, he stayed at a place called Tun near the border of Lu over the first night, hoping that the Duke of Lu and Ji Huanzi might regret to see him leave and come to get him back. But they did not.

He visited many states, including Qi, Wei, Song, Chen, and Cai, and he met numerous rulers and their ministers. As Zigong said, "Here is a beautiful gem—should one wrap it up and store it in a cabinet? Or should one seek a good price and sell it?" The Master said, "Sell it! Sell it! I am one waiting for the right offer!" (9.13) However, none of the rulers would propose "the right offer."

Traveling during that time was by no means easy and safe. When they were passing through a place called Kuang on their way from Wei to Chen, the locals mistook the Master for a man named YANG Huo 阳货, who had just ravaged the place. During the incident, Confucius's disciple YAN Hui 颜回 was separated from the others. When they finally reunited, the Master exclaimed with relief, "I thought you had died!" YAN Hui replied, "While you are still alive, how could I dare to die?" (11.23)

On another occasion, when Confucius was passing the state of Song, a man named SIMA Huantui 司马桓魋 attempted to kill him. The Master had to dress in inconspicuous clothing to avoid further attempts on his life (*Mencius*, 5A:8). Historical records left us with no explanation for SIMA Huantui's attempt at taking Confucius's life. H. G. Creel, however, offers a plausible, though circumstantial, explanation: SIMA Huantui's brother, SIMA Niu 司马牛, was a disciple of Confucius who despised Huantui's notorious behaviors so much that he refused to live in the same state with Huantui. He even lamented that he had no brother, even though Huantui was still alive at the time. Creel writes, "It is easy to see that Confucius would have been guilty, in the eyes of Huantui, of the crime for which Socrates was executed: corrupting the young. And it may well be for this reason that he tried to assassinate him" (Creel, 45).

As they reached Chen, the group was once straitened by the shortage of food for seven days. The Master and his disciples were so weak that they could hardly stand up on their feet. At one point, Confucius was tempted by what seemed an attractive opportunity for employment, as a man named BI Xi 佛肸 in the state of Jin asked Confucius to join him. BI Xi had taken control of a city called Zhongmou in opposition to another group who had the Duke of Jin as their pawn. Zilu, the most meticulous and straightforward disciple, was once again the first to stand out against the idea. "I have heard you say, Master, that 'Exemplary persons will not enter the circle of those who do bad things.' Now BI Xi is holding possession of Zhongmou to stage a revolt. How do you justify going to him?" Confucius's reply shows the utmost pathos of his long series of disappointments: "Yes, I did make such a remark. But is it not said that if a thing is really hard, grinding will not make it thin? Is it not said that if a thing is really white, dyeing will not make it black? Am I a gourd [*paogua* 匏瓜]? How can I be hanging there, not being served as food?" (17.7) In the end, however, the Master did not go to Jin.

The Master was getting old. Meanwhile, some of his disciples, who had stayed in Lu and accomplished a great deal in their political careers, felt that it was embarrassing to let their Master go on traveling throughout other states, seeking employment. Zigong, for instance, successfully helped Ji Kangzi 季康子, who succeeded Ji Huanzi as the head of the Ji family after the latter died, to get over a crisis by attending a high-level diplomatic conference in Ji's place. RAN Qiu 冉求 had proved his military talent in a battle against a Qi invasion. The disciples were said to have persuaded Ji Kangzi to send a messenger with gifts to invite Confucius back to his home state. They said to Ji Kangzi, "It would be a shame that a sage from the state of Lu is traveling and seeking a position in other states." Upon such an invitation, Confucius finally returned home, at the age of sixty-eight.

During Confucius's remaining years, his son KONG Li 孔鲤 (also known by his style name, Boyu 伯鱼) and his favorite disciple, YAN Hui, both died, one shortly after the other. Two other disciples, SIMA Niu and Zilu, also died tragically. Upon YAN Hui's death, the Master cried, "Alas! Heaven ruins me! Heaven ruins me!" (11.9) The Master himself died in 479 BCE at the age of seventy-three, with no anticipation that people would later worship him so much that the age of seventy-three would be taken as a threshold for a life span, along with eighty-four—the age to which his famous later follower, Mencius, lived.

The Life Story Continues . . .

After the death of the Master, his teachings were carried on and developed through the persistent efforts of his followers. During the Warring State 战国 period (403–221 BCE), Confucius had already become the most influential thinker in China. The *Spring and Autumn Annals of Lü Buwei* 吕氏春秋, a book composed during the late Warring State period, quoted Confucius over fifty times, which was more than any other thinker quoted in the book. The book of *Zhuang Zi* 庄子, a Daoist work also composed during the Warring State period, used Confucius's name frequently to convey the author's own Daoist ideas, sometimes with sarcasm against Confucius, and other times simply as a mouthpiece for the author's own ideas. The founder of another contending school of thought, Mo Zi 墨子, Master Mo, included a whole chapter on "Against Confucians" in his major work, the book of *Mo Zi*.

At the same time, Confucius's teachings also started to be interpreted in many different ways. The *Historical Records* says that the school of *ru* 儒 (as Confucianism is commonly called) had developed into eight branches.

One of them was the lineage carried on by Confucius's disciple, Zeng Zi 曾子, who is said to have taught Confucius's grandson, Zisi子思, and through Zisi, reached its completion with Mencius (Latinized name for Meng Zi 孟子, Master Meng, 372–289 BCE), who was later recognized as a sage second only to Confucius in the Confucian tradition. Under the shadow of the Si (Zisi)-Meng (Mencius) influence, other branches gradually faded away, and most of them left us with no trace of record.

During Mencius's time, the teachings of Mo Zi were well-known and influential. His most distinctive view is love without discrimination. This view was attractive, but in opposition to the Confucian idea of love in gradation, which basically means that love should start from one's immediate family and then expand outwardly. At the other end of the extreme was the egoistic philosophy of Yang Zi 杨子, who claimed he was unwilling to lose a single hair from his shank in order to benefit the whole world.

Mencius vehemently defended Confucianism against these two rivals, and in doing so, made significant developments to Confucianism. He argues that Mo Zi's love without discrimination is no better than Yang Zi's egoism, because it entails treating one's own parents no differently than one would treat strangers, which is the same as denying one's own parents their special status, and hence would be virtually reducing humans to the level of wild beasts.

Of Mencius's contributions, the most well-known is his idealistic account of human nature. He believed that humans are all born with incipient good tendencies: the heart of compassion, of shame, of courtesy and modesty, and of right and wrong. These four tendencies are the root of human-heartedness, appropriateness, ritual propriety, and wisdom (*Mencius*, 2A:6). A person full of moral integrity will have a strong *qi* 气, or "vital energy," which can fill the space between the earth and heaven. Mencius emphasized that being morally virtuous is a ruler's most important quality. He saw the contrast between the way of a sage king, who unifies his people by the power of morality, and the way of a hegemon, who reigns through physical force and terror, and argued that the former path is not only morally superior, but also in the ruler's own best interest. Mencius is also the first one in the Confucian tradition to state clearly that people are justified in starting a revolution if the ruler is corrupt. Killing a bad ruler is not a crime of regicide, because by failing the people, the ruler has already disqualified himself, making himself a "mere fellow." He says, "The people are the most important, the spirits of the land and the grain are secondary, and the sovereign is the least" (*Mencius*, 7B:14).

Another great Confucian during the initial formation epoch of Confucianism is Xun Zi 荀子 (ca. 312–238 BCE). His more-realistic emphasis on publicly observable ritual propriety provided a contrast to Mencius's idealistic emphasis on internal moral goodness. Openly against Mencius, Xun Zi argued that humans are by nature bad, although through learning, everyone can become a sage. Exactly because humans have natural inclinations toward being bad, the ancient sage kings created ritual propriety and offered teachings about appropriateness to regulate people's behaviors and let them reform themselves. As Robert Neville puts it, to Xun Zi, this concern with propriety is far more important than a celebration of the original goodness of human nature, or attention to the stern stuff of obligation, which are preoccupations of Mencius. Rather, the Confucian focus is best directed, says Xun Zi, toward the stylized or conventional social forms that mediate people's relations with one another, with nature, and with institutions such as family, community order, government, and the arts and letters (Neville, 6).

Ironically, Xun Zi's two most famous students, HAN Fei 韩非 and LI Si 李斯, turned toward Legalism. Their thoughts served as the intellectual foundation for the most totalitarian regime in Chinese history: the Qin 秦. The state of Qin was located in the far western region of ancient China, where a harsh environment turned out to be fertile ground for militarism. Constant wars with neighboring states made the Qin people more disciplined and submissive to authorities. Xun Zi's theory that humans are by nature evil fitted the need for the justification of using external authority. His Legalist disciple HAN Fei argued that only an unchallenged supreme authority could bring the world back into order. Neither teachings of morality nor the use of ritual proprieties could regulate the people; only strict enforcement of laws and regulations, which instilled fear of punishment, could keep people from going astray.

HAN Fei was not covert about the anti-Confucian nature of his ideas. For Confucius, the legitimacy of a government lies in its good service to its people, and for that reason, education must be offered, and government must entrust its power to those who are most competent and most virtuous. But for HAN Fei, Confucian ideas are not only ineffective, they are also dangerous for the state, as they suggest the ruler should follow the will of ignorant people (see chapters "Wu Du 五蠹" and "Xian Xue 显学" in *Han Fei Zi* 韩非子).

The founder of Qin, who later became known as Qin Shihuang 秦始皇, "the First Emperor of the Qin dynasty," embraced Legalist ideas. He consolidated his direct control over the people by setting up strict laws, breaking up the unity of powerful clans, offering rewards to informers, and recruiting talents from everywhere. The state of Qin quickly rose to become a military giant, conquering all of the other states through bloody wars. On one occasion, the Qin army massacred 400,000 surrendered Zhao soldiers! By 221 BCE, the Qin brought the entirety of China under its control. The Emperor of Qin implemented Legalist ideas to everything: Laws and regulations were made uniform, and measures of weights, sizes, written characters, and even the space between cart wheels were all standardized. Following the advice of his Legalist minister, Li Si, he also tried to unify people's ideology by force so that no one would think differently and spread doubt about the emperor. He ordered that all books in the hands of the people be burned, except those on medicine, divination, and agriculture. Those who disobeyed the order were branded, sent to do forced labor, or even put to death.

According to a widespread story, when the First Emperor of the Qin ordered the burning of books, KONG Fu 孔鲋, a ninth-generation descendant of Confucius, sealed many Confucian classics into a wall, including the *Analects*, the *Book of Filial Piety* 孝经, the *Book of Rites* 礼记, and the *Book of Historical Documents* 书经. KONG Fu himself later became a consultant of CHEN Sheng 陈胜, the leader of the first peasant uprising forces against the Qin. The books hidden in the wall were rediscovered about sixty years later, when Han Emperor LIU Qi 刘启's son LIU Yu 刘馀 came to Qufu as the governor of Lu. He accidentally found the books when he was expanding his palace into the territory of the old Kong family dweller.

Not only did the First Emperor of the Qin burn books, in 212 BCE he also had 460 scholars, many of whom were Confucians, buried alive. Having eliminated rival voices, the emperor became even more ruthless. He drove hundreds of thousands of people to build his palaces; 270 of them were said to be in the area of the capital alone. He started building a massive tomb for himself, which, seen from the outside, is literally a small mountain. He also launched the first upsurge of massive construction of the Great Wall, linking the existing walls of the previous states together at the northern border of the kingdom.[2]

The short-lived Qin dynasty was quickly brought down by the uprising peasants. Out of rage toward the Qin, the invading army burned the Qin palaces. The fire is said to have kept the sky lit for three months!

The lesson behind the grand failure of the Legalist Qin government was obvious to the rulers of the subsequent dynasty, Han. They turned toward Huang-Lao Daoism, a version of Daoist theory attributed to the legendary ancient ruler, Huang Di 黄帝, "Yellow Emperor," and the author of the *Dao De Jing*, Lao Zi 老子, as their guiding principle. What the theory taught, mainly tranquility and nonaction, allowed the government to minimize its interference and taxation for the ordinary people, and to maintain a peaceful environment for their recovery from the damages of the previous turmoil. In only about seventy years, the Han reached an unprecedented level of prosperity during the reigns of Emperor Wen 汉文帝 (reigned 180–157 BCE) and Emperor Jing (reigned 157–141 BCE)—the famous Wen-Jing era of flourishing 文景之治.

The Huang-Lao Daoism adapted by the early Han rulers was in fact a mixture of many theories, including some elements of Legalism and Confucianism. It utilizes the ideas of these theories as strategies for effective rule of the empire. Emperor Wen, for instance, exemplifies both the Daoist idea of noninterference and the Confucian idea of human-heartedness. He reduced taxes, cut down his personal expenses, and avoided extravagant displays. He authorized funding for famine relief and pensions for the aged, issued an edict to free government slaves, abolished punishment by mutilation, regulated the administration of justice, and pardoned prisoners of war. He repealed laws that punished criticism directed toward the government, pointing out that the laws made subjects afraid of speaking their minds and rulers unable to hear about their mistakes and errors. He sought capable commoners to assist in governmental affairs, and he even seriously considered leaving his throne to the most worthy person rather than to his own son. He decreed in his will that, upon his death, mourning for him should be reduced to the absolute minimum. He said that instead of canceling weddings and other ceremonies while mourning him, people should instead feel happy for him, because during his twenty-some years of reign, there had been no wars, and the kingdom was in peace.

In comparison, his later successor, Emperor Wu 汉武帝 (reigned 141–87 BCE), was more a Confucian in appearance but Legalist in reality. However, Emperor Wu turned out to be a more important figure in turning Confucianism into a state ideology. He established the positions of *boshi* 博士 (official "Scholars of Broad Learning") for each of the Five Confucian Classics,[3] and he provided funding for fifty disciples to study with each of the scholars. Later, he established *Taixue* 太学, an Imperial Academy from which government officials would be selected.

One of the "Scholars of Broad Learning," Dong Zhongshu 董仲舒 (179–104 BCE), played a key role in molding Confucianism to fit the requirements of an official state ideology. Politically, he advised Emperor Wu to adhere to a policy of "denouncing all other schools and upholding Confucianism only." By establishing the Confucian authority, Dong aimed to simultaneously justify and limit the power of the emperor.

During the early Han, the school of *yin-yang* 阴阳 and *wuxing* 五行 (the "five agents" theory) had gained popularity in China. According to the school of *yin-yang*, there are two basic forces in the universe: the negative *yin* and the positive *yang*. *Yin* and *yang* work together in a process of mutual transformation and constitute the rhythm of the universe. The five-agents theory proposes that there are five basic agents in the universe, and the re-ciprocal relationships between them are the basis of all kinds of connections: Wood produces fire but overcomes soil; fire produces soil but overcomes metal; soil produces metal but overcomes water; metal produces water but overcomes wood; and water produces wood but overcomes fire.

Dong Zhongshu combined Confucianism with the *yin-yang* and five-agents theories. He created a cosmology in which individual human beings and the cosmos are seen as isomorphic in structure, capable of mutually affecting each other. Natural calamities would be interpreted as warnings sent by heaven to show its displeasure with the ruler. Natural forces such as *yin* and *yang* were given moral significance, on the basis of which norms of human relation-ships were justified. In so doing, Dong applied an important twist to early Confucianism: Not only did it become a mixture of mystic cosmology and moral doctrines, but reciprocal moral relationships were also made to be more one-directional, as demonstrated in Dong's creation of the so-called "Three Norms": The ruler (*yang*) is the norm of the minister (*yin*), the father (*yang*) is the norm of the son (*yin*), and the husband (*yang*) is the norm of the wife (*yin*). In addition, Dong contributed significantly in imbedding Confucian ritual propriety into the Han legal system, and thereby legalized Confucianism.

Another notable figure who played a key role in shaping the culture dur-ing Emperor Wu's reign was Sima Qian 司马迁 (ca. 145–90 BCE), author of *Shi Ji* 史记, the *Historical Records*. He was already a learned scholar when he succeeded his father to become the official court historian in his late thirties. Because he spoke out against Emperor Wu's opinions, he suffered humiliating castration and many years of imprisonment. The punishment, however, made him more determined to record history truthfully and to finish his ambitious writing project: a book of half a million words on the history of China up to his lifetime. He was the one who made the famous remark: "While everyone dies, some die as majestic as Mount Tai, and others die as insignificant as a feather." His book took the form of bibliographies of individuals, dealing not only with what the historical figures did, but also providing vivid portrayals of them as people. By imbedding moral praises and condemnations in the writing of history, he continued Confucius's legacy of editing the *Spring and Autumn Annals*, and established another landmark of the Confucian authority.

What happened during the early Han was an extremely significant chapter in the history of Confucianism. On the one hand, it marked a great triumph for Confucianism, as it was during this period that the Confucian principle of government was formally recognized by the state. According to this prin-ciple, the purpose of a government is to make the society harmonious and its people educated, happy, and prosperous. If the government is unable to serve this function, it may be criticized and even overthrown. The authority of the Confucian principle became even higher than the emperor, as even emperors must be judged accordingly. It was also during this time that Confucianism spread into Korea (early first century CE), and later, to Vietnam and Japan (before the fifth century CE).

On the other hand, the early Han was also the beginning of a series of misfortunes for Confucianism. Along with the official recognition and appointment of Confucian scholars to government positions, being a Confucian also became a way to gain position and wealth. Learning for the sake of transforming oneself was often replaced by learning for the sake of impressing others and for gaining material prosperity. Institutionalized Confucianism turned Confucianism into an official ideology, which started to compete with other schools of thought by denouncing them as heresies. Dong Zhongshu's high official position made his twist on Confucianism, most notably his "Three Norms" theory, an official interpretation of Confucianism, which was a typical example of the kind of deals between political power and "truth" that French philosopher Foucault tried to reveal.

The degree to which Confucianism was institutionalized is proportional to the degree that the Master became deified. More Confucian temples were built, and more and more legends about the Master were created. For instance, in the book titled Kong Zi Jiayu (Confucius Family Discourse), which was created over a long period of time but normally attributed to Wang Su 王肅 during the Three Kingdoms period (ca. 220–280 CE), there were numerous anecdotes portraying the Master as a prophet who could read mysterious codes like a fortune-teller.

In one of them, it is said that once a flock of one-legged birds flew around the palace of Qi and landed in front of the palace hall. The Marquis of Qi was surprised and asked Confucius about it. Confucius told him that the name of the bird was Shangyang, and that its appearance was an omen for water. He quoted a children's folk song, according to which the activity of Shangyang was an indication that a storm was coming. He predicted that there would be a flood, and advised the Marquis to mobilize the people to dig canals and build dams. Consequently, when the storms indeed came, other states were all devastated by floods, and only Qi was prepared and did not suffer massive loss. The author wrote, "The Marquis of Qi said, the sage's words are proven to be true!" (Kong Zi Jiayu, 3.14) Although folk songs were often the summation of people's empirical observations and wisdom, and thus, predictions made on the basis of them may not have been totally fabricated, the story obviously paints an image of the Master as mysterious and superhuman.

The deification of the Master continued, often sanctioned by political figures all the way up to the emperor. During the Tang dynasty, for instance, Emperor Taizong 唐太宗 (reigned 627–650) issued an edict (in 630) to build temples honoring Confucius throughout the country. The honorary title bestowed upon Confucius gradually went from *xiansheng* 先圣, "the Sage of the Antiquity," to *zhisheng wenxuan wang* 至圣文宣王, "the Supreme Sage King of Cultural Manifestation." Enshrined in these temples is a statue of Confucius sitting on a throne and wearing a crown. Next to him are usually statues of Mencius and several of Confucius's most distinguished disciples. The historical and cultural figures were turned into deities of a state religion that gave legitimacy to the government, and rituals held in honor of the sages and exemplary persons were transformed from personal means of tribute into state ceremonies.

The Confucian temples often had small schools attached to them, offering basic classes on the canonized Confucian texts. The establishment of the Imperial Examination System (*keju* 科举) made it mandatory for anyone who sought a governmental position to be conversant in Confucian classics. Confucius's private-school model began to be overshadowed by a government-sponsored education system, in which the ideas of the Master were no longer discussed and debated by freethinking individuals; instead, they were treated as unquestionable truth and rules of conduct to be accepted and followed rigidly.

The Second Epoch

Alongside Confucianism, the two other most prevalent schools of thought or religion in traditional China were Daoism and Buddhism. Daoism emerged roughly around the same time as Confucianism. Its founder, known as Lao Zi, remains a mystical and legendary figure in Chinese history. Of all the stories about him, the most famous is perhaps the one in which he appears on the back of an ox, surrounded with a purple aura, at the western border of China on his way out into the desert to become a hermit. At the request of the border keeper, he wrote down five thousand words of his teachings, which became the famous *Dao De Jing* 道德经, or the *Book of the Way and Its Power*. Around the fourth century BCE, Zhuang Zi, another great Daoist, left us with a landmark book, the *Zhuang Zi*.

Though Lao Zi and Zhuang Zi differed from each other in many subtle ways, together they shaped a Daoist culture that paralleled Confucianism in its influence on China. If Confucianism is overall the upper current of the cultural stream in China, Daoism can be thought of as the undercurrent of the stream. Although Daoism has always been an essential part of Chinese culture, it only occasionally became involved in the public or political realm. Daoists have typically been seen as hermits living invisibly on remote mountains and in forests, enjoying a simple, natural, and spontaneous lifestyle and reluctant to come forward to public service. These kinds of Daoist hermits are spotted in the *Analects* a number of times. On one occasion, a "madman of Chu" went past Confucius, singing:

> Oh Phoenix! Oh Phoenix!
> How your virtuosity has declined!
> No use to rebuke what has already past;
> But what is to come can still be chased.
> Give it up! Give it up!
> Peril awaits those who now engage in government!

Confucius, wanting to speak with this madman, got down from his carriage, but the madman disappeared too quickly (18.5).

The other main school of thought in traditional China is Buddhism. Unlike Daoism, Buddhism is not Chinese in origin. Originating from a northern region of South Asia, it is a philosophy and religion founded by a prince of the Sakya clan named Siddhartha Gautama (ca. 563–483 BCE). It was introduced in China during the first century CE, a little later than the time when Confucianism took the status of being a state ideology. At first, it came in with a low-key presence. It used Daoist terms to translate Buddhist concepts, and accepted Confucian ideas of filial piety and service to the state, promising that Buddhist practices would ensure better reincarnation, stability, and prosperity for the country.

But soon the religion revealed itself to be a much stronger rival than the Confucians had initially thought. Not only was its central idea of denouncing the human world and its encouragement of young people to leave their families for a monastic life alien to the Confucian tradition, but the fast spread of Buddhism also resulted in a large portion of the population and vast land resources being taken over by Buddhist monasteries. Buddhist influences also penetrated into the political realm, so much so that not only did Buddhist organizations become rival political powers, but sometimes even emperors themselves were converted. During the Southern dynasties, Emperor Wu of the Liang 梁武帝 (reigned 502–549) abandoned his throne several times to became a Buddhist monk. Each time the imperial court had to pay a huge amount of money to redeem him back!

The challenges from Buddhism and Daoism drastically weakened the dominant position of Confucianism. During the Song (960–1279) and Ming

(1368–1644) dynasties, Confucian scholars brought out another upsurge of Confucianism by responding to these challenges with creative interpretations of traditional Confucianism. CHENG Hao 程颢 (1032–1085) and CHENG Yi 程颐 (1033–1107), known as the Cheng brothers, and ZHU Xi 朱熹 (1130–1200) were the leading figures of *Lixue* 理学, "the School of Principle." Two other very influential figures were LU Xiangshan 陆象山 (1139–1193) and WANG Yangming 王阳明 (1472–1529), the leading figures of *Xinxue* 心学, "the School of Heart-mind."[4] Both schools left us with an enormous amount of literature and sophisticated theories. The Cheng-Zhu School of Principle developed a metaphysical theory, according to which the highest principle, *li* 理, is the heavenly given nature in everything. Just as the moon is reflected in all the waters, everything involves *li*. By cultivating and manifesting one's nature, humans can achieve unity with heaven and become co-creators of the universe. ZHU Xi singled out two chapters from the *Book of Rites*: *Da Xue* 大学 ("*Great Learning*") and *Zhongyong* 中庸 ("Centering the Commonality"), the most metaphysical work of all the Confucian classics. These two books, together with the *Analects* and the *Mencius*, became the "Four Books," upheld as the most canonical Confucian texts. Through careful reinterpretation of these texts around the doctrine of *li*, ZHU Xi completed a philosophical system with enough metaphysical sophistication to rival Buddhism and Daoism, and regained an upper-hand position for Confucianism.

The Lu-Wang School of Heart-mind significantly differed from the Cheng-Zhu School of Principle. Pointing out the danger of making the principle (*li*) an abstract metaphysical entity external to human subjectivity, Lu and Wang emphasized the point that *li* is nothing but the concrete human heart-mind itself. In turn, the School of Heart-mind was accused of being merely another form of Buddhism and Daoism in disguise.

These neo-Confucians established numerous colleges (*shuyuan* 书院) and attracted a large number of students. Sometimes they held open debates or conferences, presenting their views and arguing against each other in a direct and yet collegial manner. The debate between the two schools continued for centuries. It not only helped the permeation of the neo-Confucian theories, but also trained many Confucian scholar-officials.

The dialogue—externally with Buddhism and Daoism, and internally within different interpretations of Confucianism—brought Confucianism to a new level of sophistication, known in general as Neo-Confucianism. It is a synthesis of Daoist cosmology and Buddhist spirituality, with a core of Confucian values. Since the fall of the Mongols (the Yuan dynasty, during which the emperors were mainly Buddhists of the lama religion, which still prevails in Tibet and Mongolia), all the way to the end of imperial China (the beginning of the twentieth century), the Chinese imperial government uniformly favored Confucianism as the principal school of thought of the state.

While the literati were sensitive to the sophisticated debates within and between the schools of *li* and *xin*, the common people paid attention to the actual applications of the doctrines that most directly affected their lives. In the realm of actual social application, some lines of the Song and Ming neo-Confucian teachings were often singled out from their original context and strictly enforced. Among them the most remembered were "eliminating human desires and preserving the principle of heaven," and "It is a small matter to starve to death, but a large matter to lose one's chastity." These sayings became the focused target of criticism during the early-twentieth-century revolt against Confucianism, as they served the primary function of suffocating human freedom and natural desires.

The late Ming and Qing Confucian scholars were already critical to their Song and Ming predecessors, but they were not as radical as the twentieth-century critics. Through their own reinterpretation of early Confucian classics, "enlightenment"-minded scholars such as WANG Fuzhi 王夫之 (1619–1692) brought Confucianism back into a much more human-friendly shape. The ancient Master did not want people to eliminate their desires, they argued; instead, he just wanted to ensure that people satisfied their desires in a humane way. Politically, however, these late Ming and Qing Confucians' opinions remained largely inconsequential. The Song-Ming doctrine of *li* was still the orthodox view, and during the late Qing, it even had a short period of glorious revival, notably associated with the military accomplishments of a Confucian scholar-general, ZENG Guofan 曾国藩 (1811–1872).

During the seventeenth century, Western missionaries, mainly the Jesuits, encountered Confucius's teachings when they traveled extensively in China. They were the first ones to introduce the "Eastern wise man" to the West with relative completeness. For a while, Western enlightenment thinkers, including G. W. Leibniz, Christian Wolff, and Voltaire, were excited about the humanitarian ideas of the Master, and they used them as a weapon in their attack on European hereditary aristocracy. Leibniz, in particular, was fascinated by the fact that the binary arithmetic he invented was already contained in the *Yi Jing* 易经 (*I Ching*), or the *Book of Changes*, where the broken line, the symbol for *yin*, and the unbroken line, the symbol for *yang*, can replace 0 and 1, respectively. He wrote with excitement: "[T]his shows that the ancient Chinese have surpassed the modern ones in the extreme, not only in piety (which is the basis of the most perfect morality), but in science as well" (Cook and Rosemont, 133).

New Challenges and the Third Epoch

Ironically, while the Western Enlightenment thinkers were admiring the humanitarian spirit of Confucianism, in its home country, dogmatization of Confucianism developed to its extreme. Formalized rituals became not only mere pedantry, but also a hindrance to creativity and the acceptance of anything new. The idea that the Middle Kingdom (what the word for "China" literally means in Chinese) was the only civilized world made the imperial government unable to realize that revolutionary changes were taking place in Europe. They were curious about fancy machinery, such as Western clocks, yet remained totally imperceptive of the significance of the profound scientific innovations and other changes that were taking place.

It was not until the nineteenth century that the Chinese began to really feel the impact of the West and started to take the West seriously as a strong rival to their Confucian tradition. Unlike the Jesuits who came in the earlier times with a culturally conciliatory approach, the Europeans and the Japanese in the nineteenth century came wholly unconcerned about Chinese susceptibilities. Beginning with the Opium War in 1840, they launched continuous military assaults to force the Chinese to accept humiliating treaties, to open ports, and to let foreign powers establish settlements in China. This harsh reality forced the Chinese to reevaluate traditional Chinese thought, the Confucian ideas in particular. Seeing the impractical nature of the conservatives' position, a group of Confucian officials, most notably LIN Zexu 林则徐 (1785–1850) and ZHANG Zhidong 张之洞 (1837–1909), started a "self-strengthening" movement. They tried to retain the Chinese tradition as *ti* 体, "substance," and the Western culture as *yong* 用, "a function or utility for practical use." But this slogan proved to be little more than a face-saving self-deception. There was no way to keep the Confucian tradition intact as a superior belief system and selectively accept some Western elements condescendingly, just for "practical use." Indeed, the separation of substance and function seemed to be a fallacy to begin with.

At the beginning of the twentieth century, Chinese intellectuals of the "New Culture Movement" launched the largest anti-Confucianism movement ever since the time of the First Emperor of the Qin. Confucianism was criticized as the root of all the problems in China. "Down with the 'Kong family store'!" "Welcome 'Mr. De' [democracy] and 'Mr. Sai' [science]"! With these slogans, a group of scholars who were disillusioned with their cultural heritage, such as CHEN Duxiu 陈独秀 (1879–1942), CAI Yuanpei 蔡元培 (1868–1940), LI Dazhao 李大钊 (1889–1927), LU Xun 鲁迅 (1881–1936), and HU Shi 胡适 (1891–1962), led a revolt against the entire traditional

Confucian culture. These intellectuals also introduced a large amount of Western enlightenment ideas into China, including Rousseau's social contract theory, J. S. Mill's theory of liberty, Schopenhauer's idea of *Wille zum Leben* (will-to-life), Nietzsche's idea of *Übermensch* (superman, or over-man), Bergson's theory of creative evolution, Karl Marx's theory of communism, and John Dewey's pragmatism.

In 1949, the Communists took over China and Marxism became the dominant ideology in the country. One thing that most people outside of China do not know is that LIU Shaoqi 刘少奇 (1898–1969), the Chairman of the People's Republic of China from 1959 through 1968, wrote a small but influential book called *On the Self-Cultivation of a Communist Party Member*, or, as it is commonly translated, *How to Be a Good Communist*. In this book, Liu not only used the Confucian term "self-cultivation," but he also quoted Confucius and Mencius many times, showing that self-cultivation is a long process that requires enduring hardship and self-transformation, and to be a good Communist is to be faithful to the aim of eliminating all exploitation and corruption.

After Liu's tragic death during the Cultural Revolution, in which he was criticized for being reactionary, the supreme leader of the Communist Party of China, MAO Zedong (1893–1976), launched another wave of attack against Confucianism, with a campaign called "Denouncing LIN Biao 林彪 and Denouncing Confucius." In this campaign, LIN Biao, the previously chosen successor of Mao, was portrayed as a leader who, like Confucius, used the best interest of the people as a cover for keeping the privileged class in power.

The Cultural Revolution ended shortly after Mao's death in 1976. Having experienced the turmoil of the Cultural Revolution, Chinese people started to reevaluate Mao's ideas and to modernize the country. However, few would anticipate a revival of Confucianism at that time. In a book titled *Confucian China and Its Modern Fate: A Trilogy*, American sinologist Joseph Levenson wrote:

> In the beginning, their [the Confucian] idea was a force, the product and the intellectual prop of a living society. In the end it was a shade, living only in the minds of many, treasured in the mind for its own sake after the society which had produced it and which needed it had begun to dissolve away. . . . Confucianists had always been historical-minded; now they became historical themselves. (Levenson, x)

Levenson did not realize that what MOU Zongshan 牟宗三 and others called "Third Epoch Confucianism" had already arrived. The ever-deepening problems of the modernized, Westernized world in contrast to the success of the four "small dragons" in Asia, where Confucianism retained its strong hold—Hong Kong, Singapore, South Korea, and Taiwan—triggered critical reflections of the Western intellectual traditions. The interest in Confucianism revived. Along with a critical reappropriation and transformation, many contemporary Confucian scholars became increasingly convinced that Confucianism provided valuable philosophical resources for addressing disturbing situations in the postmodern world.

Seeing the danger of either having a "moral vacuum" after the Mao era, or total acceptance of the Trojan horse of Western ideas, as the country began to move in fast pace toward modernization, the Chinese government also started to reevaluate Confucianism, showing an increased appreciation for what it could offer. In the early 1980s, China had established a Confucius Foundation, which sponsored large-scale conferences on Confucianism and published a journal titled *Confucius Studies*. More recently the government advocated *he* 和, "harmony," and *yiren weiben* 以人为本, "take humanity as the foundation," as its fundamental principles. Both ideas bear clear marks of Confucianism. Books and public TV forums on Confucianism have become popular topics of discussion in culture salons, and even at family dinner tables. Indicative is the fact that a book published in 2006 that draws practical moral insights from the *Analects* sold four million copies in one year in China. The author of the book, though deemed by most scholars to be intolerably inaccurate in her interpretations of Confucius's teachings, became a celebrity, in the form of an "academic superstar," overnight.

Notes

1. A style name (*zi* 字) is traditionally given to Chinese (typically males) when they become adults. According to the *Book of Rites* 礼记, after a man becomes an adult, it is disrespectful for others of the same generation to address him by his given name.

2. The second and the third major constructions of the Great Wall were during the Han dynasty and the Ming dynasty.

3. The *Book of Odes*, the *Book of History*, the *Book of Rites*, the *Book of Changes*, and the *Spring and Autumn Annals*.

4. The Chinese word *xin* 心 is best translated as "heart-mind," because even though it literally means "heart," in Chinese it performs the function of both thinking and feeling.

CHAPTER II

~

Confucius as a Spiritual Leader

At Confucius's hometown of Qufu, located in China's Shandong province today, there is a large temple in honor of Confucius. Originally built only one year after Confucius's death (478 BCE), the temple has been rebuilt and expanded many times throughout many dynasties to reach its present scale. It covers about fifty acres at the center of Qufu, with a larger oblong walled enclosure structured like a down-scaled Imperial Palace in Beijing. The middle route links nine courtyards, divided by the major halls of the temple. The number "9" signifies "uttermost," as it is the highest single-digit number in the decimal system. The yellow-glazed tiles on the roofs of the halls and the flying dragons carved on the marble poles both symbolize highest authority, as the color yellow and the dragon were both symbols of emperor. On the outer wall there are four corner towers overlooking a canal that circles the wall. At the front gate there is a clear sign carved on a stone tablet that tells everyone to step down from carriages or horses and enter on foot as a way of showing respect to Confucius. Among the more than two thousand stone tablets inside the temple, many were set up by emperors throughout Chinese history who went there to pay homage to the sage. One of these tablets, known as *chenghua bei* 成化碑, "the Tablet of Consummation and Transformation," was erected in 1468 by Emperor Xianzong of the Ming dynasty 明宪宗. Engraved on the tablet are the emperor's words:

> Under heaven, not a single day can pass without the way of Confucius. Why is this so? Because when the way of Confucius is there, the society is orderly and the ethical principles are manifested; everything under heaven is placed

appropriately in their positions. Otherwise heresies will interfere and cults will arise. [If heresies interfere and cults arise,] how would the society be orderly? How would the ethical principles manifest? How would everything under heaven be placed appropriately in its position? Therefore Confucianism is where the weal and woe of the people and peace and chaos of the state depend on. Those who rule the land under heaven really cannot spare Confucianism even for just a single day.

A Wooden Bell-Clapper

The earliest recorded recognition of Confucius as a man with a spiritual mission comes from an episode recorded in the *Analects*: When Confucius was traveling with his disciples to the small border town of Yi, the border official asked for an interview with the Master, saying: "When superior persons come to this place, I have never been denied an interview." Confucius's followers then presented him to the Master. At that time, the disciples had already traveled with the Master for a long time, and were frustrated by the fact that no one seemed to be willing to keep them and offer the Master an official position. But the border official seemed to have a different observation. When he came out from the interview, he said to Confucius's disciples, "Why worry about the loss, you disciples? Long has all under heaven been without the Way. Heaven is going to use your Master as a wooden bell-clapper" (3.24).

A wooden bell-clapper is a bronze bell with a wooden tongue in it. It was used for announcing important civil affairs messages. A bell-clapper with a metal tongue in it would be used for military affairs. The comparison of the Master with a wooden bell-clapper shows that the border official saw the problems of the world as a matter not solvable by wars, but a matter of lacking the proper culture.

At the same time, Confucius himself had a strong sense of mission. When he was under siege in Kuang, for instance, he said: "With King Wen being gone, is civilization not lodged here? If heaven were to let the civilization perish, we latecomers would not have gotten such a relation to that civilization. If heaven does not let the civilization perish, what can the people of Kuang do to me?" (9.5)

While the words of the border keeper sound like nothing but empty encouragement to the disciples, the words of the Master appear to be like a silly self-deception, pompous and dangerous. In fact, the Master was warned several times by Daoist hermits about how dangerous and hopeless it was to continue his mission. But Confucius's determination was unyielding. He firmly believed that his mission was bestowed upon him by *tian* 天, "heaven"

(9.5). For this mission, one should be determined to travel a journey that is not supposed to end before one's death (8.7), and the aim is even more important than life itself (15.9).

Probably no story from Confucius's life has triggered more imagination than when he was stranded in Chen and Cai, during which the shortage of food left the Master and his accompanying disciples so weak that they could hardly rise to their feet. The *Analects* record a simple exchange between Zilu and his Master: Zilu said with resentment, "Even exemplary persons have such adversity?" The Master replied, "Exemplary persons may indeed have adversity, but when petty people encounter adversity, they become reckless" (15.2).

The story was rendered differently in at least nine expanded versions, and three in the book of *Zhuang Zi* alone! Most of them used the scenario as a basis upon which to elaborate on the Master's standpoint. In one of the versions, the Master was said to be singing and playing music continuously despite the dreadful situation. Zilu and Zigong were puzzled by the Master's apparent lack of a sense of embarrassment. The Master replied: "Exemplary persons are stranded only when they lose the Way. Now, upon reflection I find myself not without the sight of the Way, and facing difficulties, I find myself lacking no virtue. Now the cold season has arrived, and snow and frost have fallen, so that we can tell how enduring pines and cypresses are. Isn't it my fortune to have the narrow path at Chen and Cai?" Having said that, he picked up his lute and continued to play music. Inspired and encouraged by the Master, Zilu took up his shield and started to dance along with the rhythm, and Zigong said, "I did not realize how high is the sky and how low is the ground" (*Zhuang Zi*, 981).

In another version of the story, the Master is reported to have said to his disciples: "It is not merely my fortune; it is yours as well, my young friends. I heard that a ruler cannot become a king unless he endures hardship, and a hero cannot demonstrate his heroic deeds unless he faces danger. How do you know that this is not exactly where our determination will be generated and tested?" (*Kong Zi Jiayu*, 5.22)

Although the sources of the above-quoted versions of the story are not reliable for historical details, the spirit of the Master is well captured in them. The *Analects* tells us that the Master is so determined and idealistic that he kept trying, even though he knew that it was in vain (14.38).

Indeed, as H. G. Creel comments, "It would be easy to liken the travels of Confucius, which on the surface accomplished little or nothing, to those of the celebrated knight of La Mancha who tilted at windmills. But there are significant differences." Creel says:

Don Quixote was an echo of the past, imitating the knight-errantry that was at its last gasp. Confucius was a prophet of the future. . . . Assuredly his proper realm was that of ideas and of teaching them to others; he was incapable of the compromises necessary to put them into practice. But it was extremely important that he should *try*. The difference is that which distinguishes an officer who says, "Follow me!" from one who says "Advance!" If Confucius had stayed in Lu, enjoying a sinecure and strolling about with his pupils, he would have remained a preacher; by setting off on his hopeless quest he became a prophet. The picture of this venerable gentleman, in some respects still unsophisticated, setting off in his fifties to save the world by persuading the hard-bitten rulers of his day that they should not oppress their subjects, is in some ways ridiculous. But it is a magnificent kind of ridiculousness, found only in the great. (Creel, 51–2)

While these were necessary conditions, they are insufficient when it comes to explaining the long-lasting influence of Confucianism. Mo Zi (ca. 470–391 BCE), a Chinese philosopher who lived shortly after Confucius, had no less "futuristic" ideas, and tried even more tirelessly to implement his ideals. After a short period of prominence, however, the theory known as Moism was largely forgotten. Why was Confucianism able to become the major spiritual tradition in China for thousands of years, and is even reviving today in the twenty-first century? The answer has to be found in the content of Confucian spirituality.

Humans Are Part of Heaven

The spirituality contained in Confucius's teachings is quite different from being religious in the narrow, more-ordinary sense of the term, which implies belief or worship of a divine being, belonging to a monastic order, and so forth. Even though Confucius was deified as the Supreme King of Culture and enshrined in Confucian temples all over China, he is still largely conceived of as a model human rather than as a divine being. There is neither priesthood nor any religious ordination within the order of Confucianism. The Chinese have generally seen Confucius's temples more as memorials than monasteries.

Even the word *Confucianism* is unknown to most Chinese, because in China it is known as *rujia* 儒家—the school of *ru*—where "*ru*" refers not to Confucius, but originally and roughly to a class of people who performed rituals, taught the arts for rulers, and are familiar with the ancient classics. The term later became associated with the practices and the way of life most distinctively represented by Confucius. Yet on the other hand, the teachings of the school of *ru* established through Confucius are not ordinary moral principles. They certainly involve spirituality. Hence, Confucianism may be considered "religious" in a broader sense. The Way that Confucius advocates aims at transforming mundane human lives into manifestations of the Way of heaven, and yet since this Way of heaven is manifested exactly through ordinary human activities, it is utterly human. For this reason Confucian religiosity has been variously characterized as "immanent transcendence," "secular as sacred," or the "unity of heaven and human."

Confucius's own attitude toward issues regarding deities and the afterlife is partly skeptical and partly pragmatic. When the Master was gravely ill, his disciple Zilu asked if he might offer a prayer on his behalf. The Master queried, "Was such a practice ever done?" Zilu replied, "There was. In the *Eulogies* it is said, 'We pray for you to the spirits above and below.'" The Master said, "I have been praying for a long time" (7.35). He says, "To say you know when you know, and to say you do not when you do not. That is wisdom" (2.17). "The Master would not speak about mysterious phenomena, . . . or spirits" (7.21).

When his fellow villagers were performing the *nuo* ritual (a ritual dance wearing masks to exorcise hungry ghosts), he would dress himself in court robes and stand in attendance as host at the stair (10.14), for this is to "show respect for ghosts and spirits while keeping a distance from them" (6.22). When Zilu asked about serving spiritual beings, the Master replied: "Without being able to serve people, how can you serve spiritual beings?" Zilu then asked about death, but the Master replied: "Without understanding life, how can you understand death?" (11.12)

From these examples, it is evident that the Master did not conceal his lack of knowledge about matters related to spiritual beings or to life after death. He refrained from speculating or conjecturing about things of which he had no knowledge.

At the same time, he remains open to the possibility that there might be deities and an afterlife. When his disciple Zigong asked about whether those who were dead had consciousness, the Master is reported to have responded:

> If I were to say that they do have awareness, I am afraid that those who are filial to their parents and grandparents would send off the dead ones as if they were alive.[1] If I were to say that they don't have awareness, I am afraid that those who are not filial would discard the dead ones unburied. Ci [Zigong], do you want to know whether people have awareness after they die? When you die, you will eventually know. It will not be too late to know by then. (Sun & Guo: 21)

This response interestingly contains no direct answer to Zigong's question about the afterlife. He is primarily concerned with how those who are alive would behave. This suggests that for the Master, as long as one lives a decent human life in this world, one will have nothing to regret, whether or not there is an afterlife. "If upon internal reflection you find nothing to regret, what is there to be anxious about or to be afraid of?" (12.4) This attitude is also reflected in another passage in the *Analects*, when his disciple ZAI WO 宰我 inquired: "The three-year mourning period on the death of one's parents is already too long, . . . surely a year is enough." The Master replied: "Would you then feel at ease eating fine rice and wearing colorful brocade?" (17.21)

Clearly the Master's concern is not so much directed toward pleasing the spirits, and much less is his concern about knowledge pertaining to the existence of the afterlife. He is concerned primarily with the appropriateness of one's own feelings and disposition. Similarly, we can say that the reason for him to support the observance of ancestral ceremonies is more to act upon the power associated with reverence and to bring people together than to literally please the spirits. While we are not sure whether there are spirits, we know that sharing common ancestral ceremonies can bring people together and create a common bond.

What is particularly indicative is a passage in the *Analects* that says, "Sacrifice as if [they were] present. When sacrificing to the spirits, do it as if the spirits were present. The Master said, 'If I did not participate in a sacrifice, it is no different from not having done the sacrifice' " (3.12). This passage suggests a position that might be called "as-if-ism," which differs from theism, atheism, and skepticism (although it might be compatible with all of them). It does not focus on *believing* in the existence or presence of the spirits; instead, it guides one's mental disposition in the *practice*.

The purpose of having such a disposition is to make the internal state match the external ritual, so that the power of the ritual can be enlivened. Even an atheist may talk to a gravestone *as if* the deceased were present. The difference between as-if-ism and simple self-deception is subtle, but nothing short of substantial. A mental state may be self-deception if it is enacted as merely a belief, but it can be a practice of as-if-ism if it is enacted consciously as a way to do something.

In French writer Victor Hugo's great novel *Les Misérables*, Bishop Myriel treated Jean Valjean as if he were a noble, although the latter, a convicted criminal just released from the prison, stole the bishop's silverware after he had sheltered him with warmth and trust. Myriel lied to the police, saying that the silverware was his gift to Valjean, even handing him two additional silver candlesticks as if the convict had forgotten to take them! This practice of as-if-ism played a key role in transforming Valjean. The far-reaching implications of this difference are worth our deep reflection.

Confucian spirituality is more contained in the notion of *tian* 天, heaven, than in the Master's attitude toward spirits and afterlife. The *Book of Historical Documents* records that when the Zhou founders were rising against the Shang, they had these slogans: "Heaven sees through the eyes of the people, heaven listens through the ears of the people" (*Shu Jing*, 292), "Heaven's good vision and good hearing is derived from our people's good vision and good hearing, heaven's way of showing its dignity is displayed in our people's showing their power" (*Shu Jing*, 74). What appears here to be anthropomorphic is actually the anthropogenic. The will of heaven was no longer considered the will of an anthropomorphic deity that issues orders and gives blessings and sanctions from above, like the previous Shang dynasty notion of *Shang Di* 上帝, "Lord-on-High;" instead, it immanently exhibited itself in popular consensus and in regular patterns of discernible social and natural events, and it could be affected by the moral undertakings of the people.

The significance of this remarkable change can hardly be overstated. Not only did it justify the Zhou revolution in overthrowing the Shang, stabilizing the Zhou government itself, but it also laid the foundation for the Chinese spiritual tradition, which was drastically different from its major Western counterparts. When the Western world showed a general trend of moving from pantheism to monotheism, from worshipping naturalistic spirits to a transcendental Creator and Ruler, the Chinese moved in the opposite direction. The change from Lord-on-High to heaven is a process of depersonification of the ultimate reality and fusion of the secular and the sacred, this world and other worlds, the immanent and the transcendent. The transition is one through which the sacred became secular, and the secular became sacred! Through it the ultimate reality is no longer perceived as a ruler of the world, like a warlord; it is more perceived as the principle behind all that needs to be recognized and respected. Through this transition, rulers began to be considered sacred only so long as they were able to continue to be entrusted with the mandate of heaven (*tian ming* 天命), which is both sacred, like a divine command, and secular, as it is displayed through the will of the people and the order of the natural world.

When Jesuit missionary Matteo Ricci (1552–1610) came to China, he was delighted to find that the Chinese had created the concepts of *Shang Di*, "Lord-on-High," and *tian*, "heaven," all the way since antiquity. This, to him, was evidence that God's revelation was universal. Ricci might have deliberately oversimplified the matter as a hermeneutic strategy for preaching his own religion, but he was cautious enough to have adopted another term,

Tian Zhu 天主, "Heaven's Lord," as the official Chinese term for the Catholic "God." While the term seems to be a combination of *tian* and *Shang Di*, it does maintain a distance from both.

There are important and obvious differences between the Judeo-Christian notion of God and the Shang notion of *Shang Di*. While God is the creator of the universe, *Shang Di* is not. God is a transcendental deity, while *Shang Di* is an anthropomorphic extension of ancestral worship, which should be more appropriately rendered as "supreme ancestral emperor."

"*Tian*" is even further away from the Judeo-Christian notion of a transcendental God. Even though the notion of *tian* found in Zhou literature, such as the *Book of Historical Documents* and in the *Analects*, still carries with it the sense of a reality that governs worldly affairs, it already shows itself in the realm of this world rather than as a transcendent being. In the *Analects*, Confucius is quoted as saying: "Does heaven say anything? Yet the four seasons rotate, and hundreds of things grow" (17.19). In this passage, heaven is a principle according to which natural events take place. Even though the Chinese word *tian* is often used in contrast to the Earth, just like the Judeo-Christian notion of Heaven is in contrast to the earthly life, the word *tian* in this passage is taken to be identical with the immanent world, including the Earth! Indeed, Daoist literature composed during the same period of time shows the same way of using the word. For example, the *Zhuang Zi* says "Horses and oxen have four feet—this is what I mean by the heavenly" (*Zhuang Zi*, 590).

Not only did the founders of the Zhou culture see heaven as immanent in this world, but they also began to see humans as a key part of heaven. During the Shang dynasty, worship of deities was accompanied by the practice of human sacrifice. The idea was simple: If the spirits are conceived to be living in an extension of the human realm and affecting the human world from there, then they would necessarily like to receive food and servants sent to them through sacrificial rituals. Just as a sheep would have more weight in a sacrifice than a chicken, and a cow would have more weight than a sheep, a human sacrifice would have more weight than any animal sacrifice, and a sacrifice of a noble person would have more weight than the sacrifice of a commoner. In one occasion, the Duke of Song even had the ruler of another smaller state killed as a sacrifice to the spirit of the land!

Because humans were not treated as humans but as material goods, the Shang dynasty collapsed like a pile of loose sand. It took the Zhou only a month to defeat the army of 700,000 soldiers and to overthrow the Shang, because wherever they reached, the Shang army would surrender and turn their weapons around, joining the Zhou forces and helping them to attack the Shang. The stunning victory was an alarm to the new rulers. Why did the Shang collapse so quickly? How could we, they asked, avoid having the same tragic ending? The answer was pretty obvious: Humans needed to be seen as the basis of a society, and should be treated humanely!

Due to the rising humanitarian spirit of the Zhou, human sacrifice began to be conceived of as wrong, and wooden and clay figures were used as sub-stitutions for real people. Regarding the case we mentioned earlier about the Duke of Song, who killed another ruler as a sacrifice, a subject named Ziyu 子鱼 remonstrated: "A big sacrifice is not necessary for a small matter, not to mention to use a human sacrifice. The purpose of sacrifice is for humans. The mass people are the very subject of the spirit. If we use human sacrifice, to whom are we offering it?" (*Zuo Zhuan*, Duke Xi, Year 19)

Regarding Confucius, we find that the Master even condemned the use of wooden or clay figures as substitutes simply because they resemble real humans. He exclaimed passionately: "Doesn't the inventor of burial figures in human form have progeny himself?" (*Mencius*, 1A:4)

Mandate and Destiny

The word *ming* 命, a term usually translated as "destiny" or "fate," appears many times in the *Analects*. Since the word also means decree or mandate, it is easy to confuse it with *tian ming* 天命, or "the mandate of heaven." *Ming* is different from the mandate of heaven in that the latter is more of a moral imperative, and the former refers to a definite order or sequence of events. For instance, when a natural event happens that is beyond a person's control, it would be considered *ming* (see, for example, 6.10 and 12.5). Similarly, whether the Way eventually prevails or not, given the human efforts involved, is determined by *ming* (14.36). Yet, since humans are a part of heaven, we can affect our *ming*.

According to the most popular reading of 7.17 of the *Analects*, Confucius said: "If I were given a few more years to study the Yi 易, the *Book of Changes*, at the age of fifty, I should be free from serious errors."[2] The *Book of Changes* is a mysterious ancient work, primarily used for divination. It consists of three parts. The first part is a set of sixty-four hexagrams, formed by different combinations of six lines. Each line is either in a broken shape (*yin* 阴, the negative) or an unbroken shape (*yang* 阳, the positive). These hexagrams are believed to have been developed by King Wen, the founding father of the Zhou dynasty, on the basis of a set of eight trigrams—that is, combinations of three lines of broken and unbroken lines, created by a legendary king of the remote antiquity named Fuxi 伏羲.

The second part is made up of texts corresponding to each of the hexagrams, which explain the meaning of the hexagrams. The basic part of these texts is also said to have been composed by King Wen, and expanded upon by King Wen's son, known as the Duke of Zhou, the man who carried out the regency with wholehearted devotion for his young nephew, King Cheng, after the death of his brother, King Wu. These two parts were both written before Confucius's time. The third part is a set of texts called the *Ten Wings* 十翼, which, although they have been ascribed by the tradition to Confucius, are more likely a post-Confucius work, probably from the hand of the school deriving from Zixia 子夏, a disciple of Confucius. To use the book for divination, one first goes through a procedure of using either randomly scattered yellow-stalks, coins, or heated tortoiseshells in order to determine a certain hexagram. Then one refers to the text associated with that particular hexagram for explanation and instruction.

Confucius allegedly read the book so often that the leather thread that binds the bamboo strips together wore out and broke three times. Was the Master really interested in divination? To what degree did he believe that life is predetermined? A silk manuscript excavated during the early 1970s from a Han tomb in Mawangdui, Changsha, indicates that Confucius was so fond of studying the *Yi* in his old age that "at home he kept the book on his mat, and when traveling he kept the book in his bag." His disciple Zigong was curious and asked him: "My Master, you used to teach us that 'Those who lack *de* 德 [excellence, virtue, or virtuosity] would approach gods and spirits, those who are far away from wisdom and knowledge would appeal to divination often.' I thought it was correct and hence practiced accordingly. . . . How come you, Master, become fond of it as you get older?" The Master replied, "I was not primarily looking for using it to predict fortune. I was looking for messages about virtuous power and appropriateness. . . . I am only interested in the moral messages in it. The sorcerers and I start from the same path but end differently" (*Mawangdui Silk Manuscript, Zhou Yi*, chapter "Yao" 要).

Indeed, many of Confucius's ideas can be traced back to the *Book of Changes*. Confucius has quoted it directly from the text of hexagram 32, "*heng* 恒," to show that lacking consistency in virtue will always bring disgrace (13.22). He praises YAN Hui for being able to maintain his heartmind, not deviating from human-heartedness for a long time (6.7 and 6.11). The commentary of hexagram 24, "*fu* 复," says, "Return has success, . . . To and fro goes the way. In the hexagram of Return one sees the mind of heaven and earth" (*I Ching*, 505), and the commentary of hexagram 52, "*gen* 艮," says: "When it is time to stop, then stop. When it is time to advance, then advance. Thus movement and rest do not miss the right time, and their course becomes bright and clear" (Ibid., 653). We see in the *Analects*, "When employed, move forward; when unemployed hold oneself in reserve" (7.11), and "When the Way is in the state, be forthright in speech and conduct. When the Way is lost in the state, be forthright in your conduct, but low key in speech" (14.3).

The explanation of the image of hexagram 35, "*jin* 晋," says "The sun rises over the earth: The image of progress. Thus the superior man himself brightens his bright virtue" (*I Ching*, 561). Thus Confucius says, "To be untroubled when not recognized by others" (1.1), and "Do not be troubled by others' not understanding you; worry that you do not understand others" (1.16). The text of hexagram 1, "*qian* 乾," says "All day long the superior man is creatively active, at nightfall his mind is still beset with cares" (*I Ching*, 374). Thus Confucius says, "Exemplary persons do not, even for the space of a single meal, go against human-heartedness. In moments of haste, they are with it. In times of distress, they are with it" (4.5). At the more-fundamental level, the basic idea of the *Book of Changes*—that is, the idea that everything in the universe is interrelated and constantly changes—became a common root for both Confucianism and Daoism.

This does not mean, however, that Confucius was totally against divination. Overall, he was open to the possibility that there might be something to it. During his desperate moments he presumably also tried it. Even though the method of divination appears to be unintelligible or even silly to a modern scientifically minded person, there is something profound in it. It entails the view that everything in the universe is an expression or indicator of the same momentary situation. This principle of "synchronicity" is, says C. G. Jung, "diametrically opposed to that of causality." While the modern notion of causality is about a linear, temporally sequential relation of events, the Chinese view describes the universe in terms of the synchronic correlations between everything. The former explains an event by pointing to another event that regularly occurs prior to it, and the latter explains an event by pointing to its synchronic concurrence or "meaningful coincidence," as Jung puts it (see Jung, xxiv–xxv).

According to the modern notion of causation, the particular pattern coins make when they land on a table is the result of the throw, and the throw is the result of the motion of one's arm, and so forth. Based on the observation of regularity, one shall be able to predict the probability of the pattern of the next position of the coins when they land. According to the synchronic correlation view, the particular pattern that the coins will make on the table as they land must coincide with the other events happening at the time, and bear features similar to them, because they are all exponents of one and the same momentary situation. Based on the observation of the pattern of the coins, one can therefore acquire knowledge of the tendency of other events in the environment. It is on this foundation that traditional Chinese medicine developed a sophisticated theory of correlation between human organs, moods, and seasons, using the system as the basis for diagnosis and treatment. The belief in omens, inserted into Confucianism by DONG Zhongshu during the Han dynasty, is also rooted in the same principle of synchronicity.

Confucius may not have been aware of the difference between this theory of causation and synchronicity, but the principle of synchronicity was surely in his mind, albeit implicitly. Some ancient Chinese might have believed that the universal correlation is *shen* 神, "spirit-like," and perhaps they took it to be the work of a mysterious agent. But it is far from being irrational to believe in such a correlation, for this spirit could also be taken as the very marvelousness of the universe itself, just like a modern believer of causality takes the uniformity of nature (i.e., that the regularity we find in the past will continue to hold true in the future) as a wonderful feature of nature itself rather than evidence of God's plan. It does not necessarily involve the view that some sort of mysterious spirit is controlling the destiny of everything.

Contrary to fatalism (the belief that everything is predestined to happen or not to happen, regardless of what one does), the philosophy entailed in the *Book of Changes* is that human activities *can* make a difference. The divination and the text do not simply tell people what will definitely happen, as if all were predetermined. After explaining the momentary situation, the text typically offers instructions as to what would be the most appropriate thing to do in the given situation. In turn, what one does will affect the entire correlation, and bring some differences, whether small or large.

Just as the *Book of Changes* does not imply fatalism, Confucius fully recognizes the fact that, even though humans do not have full control of everything, we can still greatly affect our own lives. What he was looking for from the *Book of Changes* is most likely the "virtuous power and appropriateness" through which we can affect our destiny. As Mencius puts it, "He who understands *ming* does not stand under a wall on the verge of collapse" (*Mencius*, 7A:2). While it is *ming* that the wall is going to collapse, it is in our power to not stand underneath the wall, or to repair the wall. One can actively change one's *ming* by avoiding potential dangers, by altering situations, or even by changing one's own attitude toward life.

For example, the *Analects* says that when Confucius's disciple SIMA Niu lamented, "Everyone has brothers except me," another disciple, Zixia, said to him: "Life and death are a matter of *ming* [destiny]; wealth and honor depend upon heaven. Exemplary persons are reverent and not careless, and they treat others with respect and observe ritual propriety. All within the four seas are their brothers. Why does an exemplary person have to worry about having no brothers?" (12.5) Zixia showed SIMA Niu how he could gain control of his *ming* by becoming an exemplary person and redefining what it means to have brothers, or how to *ming* (order) his *ming* (destiny)! The dual meanings of *ming*, as both to order or to mandate, and as a definite order of nature or destiny, are thereby connected together seamlessly.

This feature of Confucian spirituality naturally goes along with a strong sense of anxiety and responsibility, which comes from realizing the close connection between one's own conduct and its consequences, whether pertaining to one's own life or to the lives of others that one affects. Since our power to affect the world around us varies from person to person, the more power one has, therefore, the more one is accountable. As contemporary Confucian scholar XU Fuguan 徐复观 says, in other religions piety "is a state of the mind when one dissolves one's own subjectivity and throws oneself entirely in front of God," yet in Confucian spirituality, human subjectivity becomes highly concentrated as the embodiment of heaven, and piety becomes sincerely accepting one's own responsibility (Xu, 22). The *Analects* expresses this sense of responsibility through these statements:

> Yao [an ancient sage King], said to his successor Shun: "Oh! you Shun! The line of succession conferred by heaven rests on your person. Hold fast devotedly to the center of it. If all within the four seas suffer hardship and poverty, heaven's blessings shall come to a perpetual end."

In just this manner, Shun in due course also ceded his throne to Yu.

> [King Tang, the founder of the Shang dynasty] said [in a sacrificial ceremony], ". . . If I do wrong, let not the people of the ten-thousand regions be implicated. If the people of the ten-thousand regions do wrong, the blame is on me." (20.1)

Confucius says: "At the age of fifty, I knew the mandate of heaven" (2.4). He did not explain specifically how he came to know it, but he shows a strong confidence that heaven has bestowed virtue/virtuosity in him. The Master said, "Heaven has embedded virtue in me. What can Huantui do to me?" (7.23). "With King Wen being gone, is civilization not lodged here? If heaven were to let the civilization perish, we latecomers would not have gotten such a relation to that civilization. If heaven does not let the civilization perish, what can the people of Kuang do to me?" (9.5)

Reading these remarks, one may get an impression as if the Master believes that, because he embodies the mandate of heaven, no one can harm him. But then we read in the *Mencius* that when Huantui in the state of Song attempted to kill him, he traveled in disguise to escape the state (see *Mencius*, 5A:8). If he truly believed he was bulletproof, why would he bother to disguise himself? Here, if you think the Master is self-contradictory, you are misreading his statements as descriptive. When Confucius made these remarks, he and his disciples were in life-threatening danger. Given the context, his statements were more likely "speech acts" intended to *declare* his willingness and determination to be the carrier of the mandate of heaven. They *encourage* his disciples not to be afraid. In other words, the Master was using his words to *do* things or to *affect* his audience, rather than *describing* his beliefs. Such a reading would not only resolve the apparent contradiction between his words and actions—demystifying the Master's bragging about being the chosen one, which is so uncharacteristic of him—but it would also make these passages more consistent with his skeptical attitude toward anything transcendental. It shows that the religiosity of Confucius is more a spirituality derived from within the human heart-mind than a system of faith that can be reduced to a set of beliefs about some mystical reality. Even though otherwise heaven often appeared to be at odds with him, the Master believed that "It is humans who can broaden the Way, not the Way that can broaden humans" (15.29). Humans no longer passively receive mandates from above and without; rather, heaven shows up from within!

This statement also sheds light on the notion of "the Way" (*dao* 道), because it suggests that the Way is more a trajectory, a mode of acting or road building, than a metaphysical entity that is purely objective and external to human conducts. To take the Way as an entity will lead one to miss the basic feature of Confucianism entirely, for it is more about guiding human life than about gaining knowledge of the ultimate reality.

This subjectivity is not subjectivism. Subjectivism is an epistemological position about the nature of beliefs (as in "Truth is in the eyes of the beholder"), whereas the subjectivity in Confucianism is, so to speak, "Waymaking." This sense of subjectivity is well displayed in the famous passage by the Song dynasty Confucian ZHANG Zai 张载:

> To establish heart-mind for heaven and earth,
> To shape destiny (*ming* 命) for the common people;
> To revive the lost scholarship for ancient sages,
> To generate peace for ten-thousand generations to come.

In this statement, there is a clear sense of human subjectivity, standing resolutely not only together with heaven and earth as a co-creator of the universe, but also as the meaning-maker for heaven and earth! Heaven gives humans our *xing* 性, "natural tendencies," and *de*, "virtue/virtuosity." It is reliant on humans to make the most of their own *xing* and *de*, and indeed, the *xing* and *de* of other fellow human beings and things, to participate with heaven and earth in the transformation of the universe as a creative force in this triad (*Zhongyong*, Chapter 22). As this is to fully develop or to consummate our heavenly given human potential, it is therefore also the mandate of heaven.

The highest aim of both Confucianism and Daoism is often characterized by the expression *tianren heyi* 天人合一, "the unity between heaven and human." For Daoists, this means being in harmony with nature, blending in with the environment while retaining one's own natural tendencies and individuality. For the Confucians, this means achieving harmony in the universe by playing an active role in creating it. It comes with a strong sense of mission, a sense of enormous responsibility, and a vision that is "anthropocosmic" rather than anthropocentric, as Tu Weiming puts it. While being anthropocentric is to put humans at the center of dominance over all others, being anthropocosmic is to place humans at the center of responsibility toward the entire cosmos.

Through the teachings and examples of the sages, the Confucian way was laid out. With the establishment of Confucianism as an authority, as the standard of rights and wrongs, it actually stood in the place of a national religion in China. Obviously, this Confucian ideal of unity between heaven and human as the consummation of human *xing* and *de* is not easy for ordinary individuals. Even though as we quoted before, "Heaven sees through the eyes of the people; heaven listens through the ears of the people," and by the same logic, heaven's will is exhibited through people's will, humans are not by default in full unity with heaven. While full unity still has to be achieved through effort, the practice of it is right within every person's reach, even in the most ordinary life.

Immortality and the Meaning of Life

For Confucius, just as heaven is immanent in humans, immortality and the meaning of life also exist right within the human realm.

In reference to the custom of preserving a three-year mourning period for one's own parents, Confucius stated a basic fact about human life as a reason why one should preserve the tradition: "It takes three years before an infant is able to leave the arms of its parents" (17.21). Whether or not this reason is adequate for the specific mourning custom, the recognition of this fact is itself very significant to Confucianism.

Unlike most animals, humans are much more dependent on parental care during an extensive period of their early life. As a result, both caregivers (parents) and care-receivers (children) will normally experience a bond that impacts their own existence to such a degree that they would find the meaning of their existence, and even an extension of their own existence, in each other's lives. Being a parent is a primary way of finding meaning in one's own life. It is not uncommon that the mere existence of a child would give a person in a dire situation the courage and determination to continue to live. The fact that someone is entirely dependent on you and loves you makes you feel significant. Seeing one's own children grow up and live well also gives one a sense of fulfillment that would allow a person to die peacefully. This sense of the extended existence of oneself in the lives of one's children is not something unique to Chinese culture. In Christianity the sacrifice of Abraham's only son is taken to be a special test of his faith in God. Similarly, God's sacrifice of his only son, Jesus, also means much more than any other sacrifice. Only because parental love is a most fundamental love of human beings, the sacrifice of one's own children can become an uttermost way of showing commitment.

We also commonly observe that little children develop a special affection toward their own parents, or whoever happens to be their primary caregiver. This is obvious to anyone who has seen how little children's eyes light up when they see their parents coming to pick them up from day care. Children from a very early age have already developed their sense of identity in part through their relationship with their parents. We find that in different cultures, bringing in a person's parents, especially the mother, in name-calling is commonly used as a most vicious way of insulting a person (e.g., "The son of a bitch!"). This shows that people universally consider their parents an essential part of who they themselves are.[3]

Confucius used different words for parents' love toward their children and children's love toward their parents, as these two are different. For the former he used ci 慈, "kindness" or "caring," and for the latter, he used xiao 孝, "filial piety." Usually there is no need to preach to parents about loving their children, for they naturally will. Children's love toward their parents, on the other hand, is not as strong and biologically bonding. After they have grown up and start to look for independence, they tend to care more about themselves and their own children than they would care for their parents. The seed of filial piety exhibited in little children's affection toward their parents can wither away if it is not nurtured by education and cultivation. From a purely biological evolutionary point of view, filial piety is even unnecessary for the continuation of the human species.

To Confucius, the mere fact that we are brought into the world and tended by our parents before we are able to stand on our own feet means that we owe our parents an obligation to acknowledge the favor, and to return the favor in some way. Not only do elderly people rely on the younger generation to provide care for them during the later stages of their life, but also, even after they pass away, the perpetuity of their existence and the fulfillment of the meaning of their lives, and hence, their immortality, depend on their offspring. This is what gives filial piety its religious significance, which has led to the long-lasting tradition of ancestral worship in China. The idea of bringing honor to one's family and ancestors is also rooted in this.

With this understanding of the meaning of life and immortality, perpetuation of one's family line became the main reason for marriage. It was taken as the way through which one could achieve one's own continuous existence, as well as one's ancestors' immortality. This is why Mencius says that, among the things that are considered bad to do to one's parents, the worst is to have no heir (*Mencius*, 4A:26). Up until today, the large majority of Chinese people still take having an heir as a matter of tremendous importance. It was carried so far that men would take it as the reason for having more than one wife, especially when the first wife failed to give birth to a son. It also became a big obstacle for China's population control, for people did not want to stop until they had a boy to carry on the family name. Consequently, the imbalance between male and female in the population became a social problem.

Being filial to one's parents also extends to the realm of continuing their cause, or their way of life. Confucius says, a person who "for three years refrains from reforming the way of his late father can be called a filial son" (1.11, 4.20). Even though some commentators have convincingly argued that Confucius did not intend this to mean one should foolishly stick to whatever the late father did, and that the word *way* in this context means only the *good* way (see, e.g., Yang, 8, and Cheng, 43), this saying still contributed enormously to the conservative tendency of traditional Chinese culture. The mere fact that "it has been the way of our forefathers" was often taken as adequate justification for the continuation of a tradition.

The reason that the idea of filial piety has been able to grow deeply in Chinese culture—whether in the form of continuation of a family line, or in the form of retaining the way of one's forefathers—is because filial piety does not have to be preached merely as a moral imperative. Not only is it based on one's natural affection and an intuitive sense of obligation of returning a favor, but more importantly, it is also one's own way of acquiring meaning of life and immortality. Having heirs not only fulfills an obligation to one's ancestors, but it also allows a person to become a parent and grandparent, and thus to have one's existence enter into the lives of children and grandchildren. Continuing one's forefathers' way of life is itself setting an example for the children so that they will continue your way of life. With the assurance of having offspring who are carrying on the forefathers' way of life, including the way of your own, one can die with contentment and with no fear of death.

Interestingly, under this idea of immortality, even taking care of oneself becomes a sacred duty to one's ancestors! As *Xiao Jing* (the *Book of Filial Piety* or the *Classic of Family Reverence*) says, "Your physical person with its hair and skin are received from your parents. Vigilance in not allowing anything to do injury to your person is where family reverence (*xiao* 孝, filial piety) begins" (*Xiao Jing*, 105). The fact that it is both caring for oneself and an imperative for preserving the life of the ancestors shows that there is no separation between self-interest and one's filial duty.

Confucius emphasizes filial piety as the fountain of all good conduct. One is supposed to extend one's love beyond the immediate family to the kin formed through marriage, to the village community in which one was born and brought up, to the teachers who gave one a cultural life, to the friends who helped promote one's human-heartedness (12.24), and all the way to the multitude broadly (1.6). Compared to other human relationships, family relationship has a deep-rooted primacy, and there is arguably no better soil in which to develop moral compassion and spiritual meaning for life than starting from familial love. As You Zi says, in the *Analects*,

> There are few who, being filial (*xiao* 孝) and fraternal (*di* 弟), are fond of offending against their superiors. There has been none, who, not liking to offend against their superiors, has been fond of stirring up chaos. Exemplary persons cultivate the root, for having the root established, the Way will grow. Filial piety and fraternal love—they are the root of human-heartedness (*ren* 仁), are they not? (1.2)

The practice of creating meaning for life and achieving immortality starts from filial piety, but is not limited to it. To articulate this we can look at a conversation that took place when Confucius was only five years old. In the spring of 546 BCE, an officer of Confucius's home state of Lu named MU SHU 穆叔 went to the state of Jin, where he met a man named FAN Xuanzi 范宣子. Knowing that Lu was a state of great cultural heritage, FAN Xuanzi asked MU Shu, "The ancients had the saying 'Dead but immortal.' What does it mean?"

Before Mu Shu replied, Fan Xuanzi went on to say, "The ancestors of our Fan family can be traced all the way back to the time of Emperor Shun [third millennium BCE] and earlier, when they were the Princes of Tao and Tang. Afterwards, in the time of Xia, they were the lords of Yu Long. In the time of Shang, they were the lords of Shi Wei. And in the time of the beginning of Zhou, they were the lords of Tang and Du. Now Jin has achieved control of the great alliance of the states and we become the lords of Fan. Is this [unbroken heritage] what is meant by immortality?"

Mu Shu said,

> According to what I have heard, this is called hereditary rank and emolument, not immortality. There was a former great officer of Lu by the name of Zang Wenzhong. After his death his words remain established. This is what the ancient saying means. I have heard that the best course is to establish virtue, the next best is to establish achievement, and still the next best is to establish words. When these are not abandoned with time, it may be called immortality. As to the preservation of the family name and bestowment of membership in the clan branch in order to preserve ancestral sacrifices uninterrupted from age to age, no state is without these practices. But even those with great emolument cannot be said to be immortal. (*Zuo Zhuan*, Duke Xiang, Year 24. See Chan, 13)

The notion of immortality stated by Mu Shu in this conversation, later known as *san buxiu* 三不朽, "three immortalities," is particularly significant because it shows that according to this tradition, the mere continuation of the family line or inheritance of a rank is still not good enough to be called true immortality. True immortality has to extend beyond one's family line to the broader world. By establishing virtue for other people to emulate, achievements for other people to benefit from, and words for other people to follow, one can continue to "exist" infinitely, without boundary!

Although there is no evidence that Confucius was aware of Mu Shu's particular remarks, the fact that the sayings came from his home state of Lu is an indication that he may very well have inherited the same general concept. Confucius's endorsement of this idea is indicated in the *Analects*, where he says, "Exemplary persons dislike having their names not properly established at the end of their life" (15.20). In the context of his overall teachings, one's "name" clearly refers to the three establishments mentioned above, particularly the highest one of the three: the establishment of virtue/virtuosity. Another passage suggests the same: "Duke Jing of Qi had a thousand teams of horses, but on the day of his death, he did not have any virtuous legacies for people to praise him for. Boyi and Shuqi died from hunger at the foot of

Shouyang Mountain, and the people, down to the present time, praise them. Is this what it is all about?" (16.12)

This traditional Chinese notion of immortality is well exemplified in the numerous temples in China that honor those who have achieved one or more of the three establishments. The best example is YUE Fei Temple. YUE Fei 岳飞 (1103–1142) was a Southern Song dynasty general who defended his country heroically against a Jin invasion from the north. But the emperor was not on his side; instead, the emperor was on the side of those around him who would rather let go of the northern territories. He and his pacifist ministers were afraid of losing their positions, because the victory over the Jin would mean that the previous emperor, who was taken hostage by the Jin, would be restored to his ruling position. They ordered YUE Fei to withdraw immediately, despite the fact that Yue's army was well on the way to defeating the Jin army. Shortly after he came back to the capital, he was put in prison for allegedly plotting treason, and then poisoned to death by prime minister QIN Hui 秦桧. His son YUE Yun 岳云 was also prosecuted and put to death in public by being cut in half at the waist. The fate of YUE Fei and his son triggered enormous anger from the people. Twenty years later, the subsequent emperor restored their innocence.

Remarkably, YUE Fei was known for his exemplary Confucian virtues: He was filial as a son, authoritative as a father, courageous and tactful as a general, caring as a superior, learned and talented as a scholar, frugal and self-disciplined as a person, and he was even accomplished as a calligrapher. His tragic ending eventually made him truly immortal. People built numerous temples to honor him. Interestingly, one of the temples, built initially in 1221 in Hangzhou, the capital of the Southern Song, also provides and ensures his murderers a sort of immortality. The statues of QIN Hui and others who plotted YUE Fei's murder were cast in black iron in a kneeling position, forever on display as a way of condemnation. While the punishment for evil deeds in some other religions is eternal condemnation to hell, in Confucianism it is eternal condemnation from the people, a method which completely corresponds with the Confucian view of immortality. This example shows that Confucians replaced religious judgment with historical judgment and the judgment of the people: The reward for good and the punishment for evil is achieved through placing both good and evil deeds into the historical record or public display for people to praise or condemn.

Here we can readily observe three important and mutually related features of Confucian religiosity: For Confucianism, there are no inherent dichotomies between the secular and the sacred, between self-interest and altruism, and between real-life experience and moral ideal.

First, according to this Confucian understanding, both the meaning of life and immortality can be found and achieved in this world, and not in an unknown realm beyond the human society. The sacred is located within the secular, and one's salvation is dependent on oneself and one's offspring and other associates in this human world, but not on the mercy of any deity.

Second, in the Confucian religiosity the meaning of one's life and immortality are both achieved through interpersonal relations, and not from personal survival of death. Whether it is the continuation of family line, or the preservation of the forefathers' way, or the "three immortalities" we mentioned above, they are all achieved relationally through the manifestation of one's efficacy in the larger community and in the ever-enduring history. This is quite different from the notion of immortality familiar to the Greco-Roman and Judeo-Christian traditions in the West. According to the Confucian conception, a life is not limited by its narrow, biological span, nor does one have to survive personal death in order to continue to exist. A life can continue to exist through its causal, processional relation with other lives without the survival of a disembodied, imperishable substance called a "soul." One exists and becomes fully alive through one's causal relationship with others. The fulfillment of one's own life in this Confucian way is intrinsically related to the fulfillment of the lives of others.

Third, this understanding of the meaning of life and immortality is rooted in the most basic human life experience—familial love—and not in any abstract principle. The persons in parent-child relationships are not abstract "everybody" or "anybody," but very concrete family members. The affection among family members is not an abstract principle preached by an authority figure. Once it became a tradition, it turned into a way that people conceive of themselves. It is well known, for example, that Chinese people typically expect their children to bring honor to their family and community, and they take the way others look at them very seriously. For the same reason, the mentality of the nobles in China meant they were not afraid of the judgment of the gods, but rather, afraid of the judgment of history and the public.

While the Confucian way of creating a meaningful life and achieving immortality provides a secular spirituality, it means little to those who are radically individualistic and hedonistic. It provides no adequate ground for prohibiting these people from doing harmful things. In comparison, some other religions are much more effective in this regard. Buddhism, for example, has the concepts of reincarnation and the law of karma, according to which bad deeds will lead to bad future lives, and hence generates much stronger deterrence.

Interreligiosity

Even though there were no radical religious conflicts during Confucius's lifetime, Confucius encountered people with different ideas concerning the proper Way (*dao* 道). In the *Analects*, for instance, we find a few occasions in which the Master came across the Daoists. Once when they were on a journey, Confucius sent Zilu to ask directions from two men who were plowing a field. One of them, named Changju, said, "Who is that man holding the reins of your carriage?"

"It is Kong Qiu," replied Zilu.

"The Kong Qiu of Lu?"

"Indeed."

Upon hearing this, Changju responded with an obvious tone of sarcasm, "Then he should already know the way."

Seeing that there was no hope for getting anything from Changju, Zilu turned toward the other one, named Jieni.

"Who are you?" asked Jieni.

"I am Zilu."

"A disciple of Kong Qiu of Lu?"

"Yes."

"Turbulent floodwater is surging everywhere under heaven. Who is able to change this? Besides, rather than following a man who avoids some people here and there, would it not be better to follow those who avoid the world altogether?" As he spoke, he continued to turn the earth over the seeds.

Zilu came back to the Master and told him about the conversation. The Master said, "One cannot be in the same herd with birds and beasts. If I am not with my fellow humans, with whom shall I associate? If the world had the Way, I would not be involved in changing it" (18.6).

The tone of the Master is not one of accusation. He was stating his position and his reason. Of course, there is a bit of sorrow in it, for he realizes that "Those who pursue different ways cannot consult each other" (15.40).

Another time, Zilu was accompanying the Master but fell behind. He came across an old man using his staff to tote his baskets on his shoulder.

"Have you seen my Master?" asked Zilu.

The old man replied, "If one does not keep his four limbs busy, he would not be able to distinguish the five kinds of grain. Who is your Master?" Then he stuck his staff in the ground and went on weeding.

Hearing this, Zilu did not say a word. He simply stood by the old man with his hands cupped respectfully in a salute. The old man invited Zilu to spend the night at his house. He killed a chicken and prepared some special millet for the occasion, and he presented his two sons to his guest.

On the following day, Zilu left the old man and caught up with Confucius. Upon hearing the story from Zilu, the Master said, "He must be a recluse," and sent Zilu back to see him again. However, on Zilu's arrival, the old man had already departed (see 18.7).

In another encounter, Confucius got down from his carriage, wanting to speak with a recluse, but the person disappeared quickly (18.5).

The willingness of the Master to engage in conversation with people who hold other beliefs and even to learn from them is ironically displayed in a story most likely created by Daoists to make their master look superior to Confucius. According to the story, Confucius went to the capital of Zhou to study the early Zhou culture of ritual propriety, and he went to see Lao Zi, who was there serving as an imperial archive librarian.

Lao Zi said to Confucius, "What you are asking about is long dead and rotten to the bones. Only the words are still heard. An exemplary person would go forward if the time is right, and would cover his head and leave if it is not. I heard that a good businessperson would hide his possessions as if he has none; an exemplary person would be full of virtuosity but appears like a fool. Reduce your self-pride, desires, attitudes, and ambitions, as none of them are good for your person. This is all I can tell you."

When Confucius came back from the meeting, he reportedly told his disciples, "I know that birds can fly, I know fish can swim, and I know beasts can walk. A net can capture those that walk, a fishing line can catch those that swim, and an arrow can shoot those that fly. As for the dragon, I don't know how it can ride the wind and cloud and fly to heaven. I saw Lao Zi today. Perhaps he is more like a dragon?" (SIMA Qian, "The Biography of Lao Zi")

The Confucians did not seem to be bothered by the story. After all, Confucius is a man fond of learning, and, though his philosophy is vastly different from that of Lao Zi, the two are not entirely opposite to each other. Furthermore, Confucius is not entirely against the idea of "taking to the high sea on a raft" (leaving the world behind) were it that the Way could not prevail (see 5.7), even though he himself would be the last one to do so. In his praise for ancient sages, he did not exclude Boyi 伯夷 and Shuqi 叔齐, who chose to live their lives on a mountain and eventually starved to death because "they did not want to compromise their purposes or bring disgrace to their own persons" by living under a ruler who overthrew his own lord. Nor did Confucius disapprove of Yuzhong 虞仲 and Yiyi 夷逸, who "lived in seclusion and said whatever came to their mind." He "does not have presuppositions as to what may or may not be done" (see 18.8). But he said he himself is different from these people.

This flexibility, however, is methodological; it does not constitute a lack of firmness on principle. This is illustrated in an interesting episode recorded in the *Analects*: Zilu spent the night at the Stone Gate. The morning gate-keeper asked him, "Where are you from?" "From the residence of Confucius," replied Zilu. "Isn't he the one who keeps trying although he knows that it is in vain?" asked the gatekeeper (14.38).

After Confucianism was established as an official ideology in the Han, especially with Dong Zhongshu's policy of "denouncing all other schools and upholding Confucianism only," which is a radical departure from Confucius's own attitude toward other belief systems, there were numerous large-scale re-ligious suppressions in the long history of China. Among them, several were targeted toward Buddhism, some were aimed at Christianity and Islam, and still others were suppressions of sects of religious Daoism, or various kinds of cults. While each of these had complicated sociopolitical reasons (for ex-ample, often a religion or cult was used to launch organized rebellion), none of them were really initiated by a conflict between religious belief systems. Overall, the three major religions in traditional China, namely Confucian-ism, Daoism, and Buddhism, coexisted rather peacefully, and the general population in China never perceived them as mutually exclusive. A Chinese intellectual could well be a Confucian when young, ambitious in pursuing a sociopolitical career, a Daoist when on vacation or when hopelessly set back by obstacles, and a Buddhist when hit by tragedy or when facing death. The three are perceived to be like three different medicines for different health problems, each with its own usefulness.

There is certainly something about these traditions that allowed them to coexist peacefully. Confucius's openness to the possibility of unknown realms of reality, and his willingness to constantly learn from others in order to improve himself, determined the non-exclusivist nature of Confucianism. There is nothing oxymoronic about Confucian Christianity, or Confucian Islam. Yet at the same time, the Master's determination to devote himself to humanity through creative reinterpretation of the Zhou tradition makes his spirituality distinctive. Confucianism not only has not lost itself in maintain-ing its openness, but it also has displayed an astonishing ability to maintain peace with other religions even while transforming them.

One such example is the Great Mosque of Xian, first built during the reign of Emperor Xuanzong (685–762) of the Tang dynasty. Not only was the mosque designed in the style of a typical Chinese temple, but there are even many obvious signs of Confucianism in it. On a stone tablet that explains

Islam and the reason for building the temple, the language is utterly Confucian. In the script, for instance, Mohammad is described as *xifang shengren* 西方圣人, "a sage in the West." The basic teaching of the religion is called *dao*, "the Way." "Allah" is first translated as *shangdi*, or Lord-on-High, and then rendered equivalent to the Confucian *tian* by quoting Confucius's saying that "There is nowhere to pray if one offends against heaven" (3.13). The practice of Islam is explained in terms of Confucian self-cultivation. The basic theme of the script is simply that even though there are differences between Islam and Confucianism, the *dao* and the *xin* 心, "heart-mind," are the same. Reading the script, it is hard to tell whether it is making Confucianism Islamic or making Islam Confucian.

Of course this does not mean that Confucianism only seeks harmony and never tries to defend its own position. A good example of this is the encounter between the pioneer Jesuit missionary in China, Matteo Ricci 利玛窦 and his Chinese Confucian critics. When Ricci came to China, he first called himself *xi seng* 僧, a "monk from the West," but soon he began to address himself as *xi ru* 儒, a "Confucian from the West." This was perhaps partly due to the realization that, in order for the Catholic religion to be accepted in China, it was more important to gain support from the Confucians than from the Buddhists. But it was also because he felt that Confucianism (more so in its classic form than in the Song-Ming School of Principle version) could more easily accommodate his own faith than could Buddhism and Daoism.

In his work *Tian-zhu Shi-yi* 天主实义, *The True Meaning of the Lord of Heaven*, he took pains to filter through Confucian classics, trying to equate *Shang Di* (Lord-on-High) and *tian* (heaven) with God, eliminating anything that indicated ancestral worship, and importing Christian proofs of the existence of God. Interestingly, in a book entitled *Shengchao Poxie Ji* 圣朝破邪集 (*Collected Writings against Heresy during the Current Dynasty*), Chinese critics of Ricci did not focus on challenging the arguments for the existence of God, nor did they try to prove the existence of *tian* or *tian dao* as something different from God. Their attention was mostly focused on what kind of practical orientations the two belief systems lead to (see ZHANG Xiaolin, 260–66). For instance, they argued that the Christian attitude toward their God is *mei* 媚, which means "to fawn on," "to beg for mercy," whereas the Confucian attitude toward *tian* is *jing* 敬, which means "to be in awe." The difference will affect how people conceive of human subjectivity in practical life. The Christian attitude would lead people to cringe and expect salvation from an external and elusive transcendental deity, while the Confucian attitude would lead people to respect the greatness of heaven even as they are aware of their own duty as a co-creator of the universe.

The critics also took issue with another difference: The Jesuits' way of preaching is through the use of crafts and techniques, whereas Confucians aim at transforming people's heart-mind. The subtle difference here is that to the Christian, the most important issue is "what to believe as true," but to the Confucian critics, it is "how to live one's life in this world."

Since Confucianism had been the official ideology for a long time, the Confucians at Ricci's time in the late Ming dynasty had a great deal of self-righteousness to shake off. This attitude was significantly weakened later, especially in the earlier part of the twentieth century, during which the New Culture Movement (mid 1910s and 1920s) and the Cultural Revolution (1966–1976) both made Confucianism a major target for criticism.

Despite the fact that Confucius was deified to some degree and was deemed the highest authority over right and wrong, there is nothing internal to Confucianism that allows for blind faith in it. To the contrary, there are abundant resources in the teachings of the Master that demonstrate its willingness and ability to be self-critical. As Tu Weiming 杜维明 points out, within the Confucian tradition, Confucius is neither considered the creator of Confucianism nor the symbol of the highest level of perfection (See Tu et al., 108). A Confucian can readily criticize even Confucius himself. "Do I possess knowledge?" asks Confucius. "No, I do not," he says. "Once a common fellow asked me a question and I felt empty-like, I queried both ends of the issue to reach the bottom of it" (9.8).

Being a model learner, Confucius tells his students that one must not hesitate in correcting oneself when in error (1.8). When the Master was told that he had misjudged someone, he said, "I am fortunate. If I make a mistake, others are sure to inform me" (7.31). "When you err and yet do not correct yourself, that is to err indeed" (15.30). All of these teachings show that Confucius never presented himself as an infallible speaker for *tian* or as a perfect being. The spirit of constant self-critique and self-improvement exemplified by Confucius, rarely seen among major representatives of other religions, is understood within the Confucian tradition not as self-negation, but, to the contrary, as the very practice of self-perfection.

In his reflection about Confucianism after a yearlong visit to China in 1920–1921, British philosopher Bertrand Russell echoed the critics of Confucianism in attributing China's backwardness to Confucian ethics, yet at the same time he said,

> Confucius must be reckoned, as regards his social influence, with the founders of religions. His effect on institutions and on men's thoughts has been of the same kind of magnitude as that of Buddha, Christ, or Mohammed, but curi-

ously different in its nature. Unlike Buddha and Christ, he is a completely historical character, about whose life a great deal is known, and with whom legend and myth have been less busy than with most men of his kind. What most distinguishes him from other founders is that he inculcated a strict code of ethics, which has been respected ever since, but associated it with very little religious dogma, which gave place to complete theological skepticism in the countless generations of Chinese literati who revered his memory and administered the empire. (Russell, 34–5)

Notes

1. The practice of lavish burial with valuable goods and even human sacrifices was rooted in the idea that the deceased would continue to live in another world and would hence need goods and servants. It was so popular that it motivated many people to earn their living by robbing graves.

2. Typical to classic Chinese texts, there were no punctuation marks given in the text, and depending on how one punctuates the original passage, there can be very different readings of it. Another difficulty in getting a definite reading of classic Chinese texts is that they were hand-copied, and hence more liable to errors. Sometimes a word that was pronounced similarly to another may have been used by mistake for the other. In this particular passage, the word yi 易, "change," appears in some other copies as yi 亦, "then," "after all."

3. See ZHANG Xianglong, 2008, chapter 8, for more elaboration on these points.

~

CHAPTER III

Confucius as a Philosopher

Confucius could not have considered himself a philosopher, because there was no such concept in China at the time. The term "philosophy" originated from the Greek words *philos* (love) and *sophia* (wisdom), and the Chinese did not come to know of it until the late nineteenth century, when it was introduced to China through Japan.

The word *sophia* primarily refers to intellectual wisdom. From quite early on, Western philosophy became preoccupied with gaining intellectual and propositional knowledge.[1] Confucius's thought, however, always focuses on how to live a better life and how to become a better person. His teachings are mostly instructions about *how* rather than descriptions about *what*. While descriptions and discourses of propositional knowledge are evaluated as convincing or unconvincing, true or false, instructions are evaluated as good or bad, effective or ineffective. Propositional views about reality are typically presented with recourse to reasoning. Instructional statements, on the other hand, are typically presented authoritatively, as their power lies not in persuading people to accept conclusions, but in the practical experience and results they generate. As we mentioned in the preface, this orientation is best captured by *gongfu*, a term Song-Ming neo-Confucians used frequently in their articulation of Confucianism as an art of living, which requires embodiment and manifestation of excellent abilities.

This means that the Confucian tradition should be considered philosophical in the broader sense of the term: the pursuit of wisdom. The particular Confucian *gongfu* orientation not only introduces important philosophical issues and concepts that have been neglected by mainstream Western philosophy, but also includes rich implications about metaphysics, epistemology, ethics, and even the nature of language—topics that are central to even the narrowest sense of "philosophy."

One Cannot Be Fully a Human in Solitude

Central to Confucius's philosophy, the word *ren* 仁 appears 105 times in the *Analects*, and 58 of the 499 sections in the book are devoted to discussing it. No other term has such a prominent place in the *Analects*. Yet nowhere in the book can one find a precise definition of it, nor have translators been able to reach an agreement on any satisfying English translation. As far as whether to take it as "benevolence," "human-heartedness," "authoritative person/conduct," "altruism," "humanity," or "goodness," there always seems to be something left out, or something that does not fit perfectly with its full meaning. *Ren* seems to be an ideal that even the Master himself claimed never to have fully reached (7.34), and yet everyone is so close to achieving it that the Master says, "Is *ren* far away? No sooner do I seek it than it has arrived" (7.30).

Our explanation of the term can start from looking at a peculiar way in which the term is used. In Confucian texts, *ren* is sometimes used interchangeably with a word that is pronounced exactly the same, *ren* 人, but means "human" or "person" (see *Mencius*, 1B:15 and *Zhongyong*, 20). An obvious explanation for this is that the term signifies what it means to be a human. In Chinese and in other languages, we find the need to give two meanings to the term "human," so that we can meaningfully say "A human should be like a human," or "A human should be treated like a human." We do not treat these statements as simple tautologies because, in these expressions, the first occurrence of "human" is used in a biological sense, whereas the second is used in a moral or cultural sense. This means there is commonly a moral expectation for being human. It is quite reasonable to say that for Confucius, *ren* 仁 must have meant a quality that makes a person an authentic human being, which every biological human should strive toward.

An etymological analysis of the Chinese word for *ren* 仁 can also reveal important information about its meaning. Chinese written words, called "characters," are pictographic and ideographic in origin; that is, they are not alphabetical signs for pronunciations, but pictures that signify the meanings directly. The character *ren* 仁 consists of two parts: The left side is the radical, which means "person 人," and the right side has two horizontal lines, signifying the number two 二. This etymological analysis, says Roger Ames and Henry Rosemont Jr., "underscores the Confucian assumption that one cannot become a person by oneself—we are, from our inchoate beginnings, irreducibly social" (Ames & Rosemont, 48).

Indeed, many descriptions of *ren* in the *Analects* are about interpersonal relationships. *Ren* is to "love people" (12.22), says the Master, and the method to be *ren* is *shu* 恕—comparing one's own heart with other hearts, with compassion (6.30). The interrelatedness of a person is so important to Confucius that, as Rosemont puts it, for Confucius, one does not *play* the roles of a father, a friend, a teacher, and so forth; rather, one *is* these roles (see Rosemont 1991, 72). *Ren* is essentially relational, and the *ren* person defers to his or her relationships and interactions with others for the completion of oneself. No one can become fully human in isolation, nor can anyone say that what happens to others has nothing to do with one's self.

The notion of the contextual human being is well exemplified in the Confucian notion of immortality, as we have explained in the preceding chapter. It is also traditionally reflected in how Chinese people conceive of their own identity. The fact that Chinese always put their family names first and their given names last indicates that they consider themselves first of all as members of their families, and then, only secondarily, as individuals. Even the given names of siblings often show contiguity or relatedness. It is common for a Chinese to be addressed as "so-and-so's father" or "so-and-so's mother." The way Chinese write their mailing address also indicates their way of identifying individuals first and foremost through the community to which they belong. When filling out a mailing address, they begin with the largest jurisdiction and then move down to the more and more specific information. So, in sending a letter abroad, a Chinese writes the country first, then the province or state, then the city, the street and number, and finally, the name of the individual receiver.

The fact that Chinese people traditionally consider others' opinions of them seriously can also be traced back to the idea of the contextual human being. It is well known that Chinese people expect their children to bring honor to the family and community, and they consider making one's parents ashamed to be one of the worst things anyone can do to their parents. These facts clearly indicate that, in the Chinese tradition, each person's own existence and identity extend into the lives of others.

This relational notion of self serves as an essential and distinctive philosophical foundation for Confucianism, and it is also a key to understanding the meaning of *ren*. However, it should not be taken to mean that in Confucianism there is a lack of subjectivity. It is tempting to take the Confucian notion of self as the exact opposite of the popular Western notion of self.

When a European or an American refers to an "authentic human being," they tend to think of someone who is "true to oneself," meaning that the person does not conceal or sacrifice him- or herself for the sake of others' opinions. As French philosopher Jean-Paul Sartre argues, human beings are "condemned to be free," meaning that the only thing we are not free to choose is not to be free. He also says that "Man is nothing but what he makes of himself." To think that our identity is dependent on our relationships with others is therefore taken as a self-deception or "bad faith" by Sartre.

Out of this view, morality becomes essentially a personal choice. Yet to Confucius, to be an authentic person (a *ren* person) seems like just the opposite. For Confucius, humans are irreducibly social. Only through recognizing one's interrelatedness and by living accordingly can one transform oneself from merely a biological human into a genuine member of a civilized society. But the Confucian relational self does not mean that one will simply surrender oneself to public opinions. While others' opinions may be an indication of one's identity, they do not constitute one's identity. Confucius made it clear that "to be untroubled when not recognized by others, is this not being an exemplary person?" (1.1) The purpose of study is for improving oneself, and not for impressing others (14.24). The real difference between the popular Western and the Confucian notion of self is that while the popular Western conception of self focuses on individual choice and considers subjectivity in opposition to the other, the Confucian view requires human subjectivity to emerge through one's interrelatedness with others rather than standing against or withdrawing from it. The kind of subjectivity that merely insists on being true to oneself as a choice-maker is not enough to make the subjectivity distinctively human, or *ren*. It is interpersonal love and compassion that display real human subjectivity. In this regard, even Sartre's view is not entirely the opposite of Confucius's, for Sartre also acknowledges that when one chooses his or her own action, he or she is making the choice for all mankind, and hence should take responsibility for it.

Extending beyond personal interest and into interpersonal caring, love is a characteristic of *ren*. This is why one of the four things that the Master abstains from is self-absorption (9.4).[2] Whether in daily life or in governmental affairs, a *ren* person is always considerate and has others' interests in mind. In running a government, the *ren* ruler "is frugal in his expenditures and loves his subordinates, and puts the common people to work only at the proper season of year" (1.5). Above these minimum requirements, if a ruler were able to "be broadly generous with the people and is able to benefit the multitude," the ruler would be even better than *ren*, and should be considered a sage (6.30).

In daily life, an exemplary person "loves the multitude broadly" (1.6). He "does not exploit others' fondness of him, nor does he exhaust others' kindness to him" (*Li Ji*, chapter 1). He "does not intimidate others by showing off his own talents, nor belittle others by revealing their shortcomings" (*Li Ji*, chapter 32). Indeed, the statement that all men "should act toward one another in a spirit of brotherhood" in the United Nations' *Declaration of Human Rights* is derived from the Confucian saying that "all within the four seas are brothers" (12.5). This text was added upon the recommendation of P. C. Chang, an outstanding Confucian scholar.

Love by itself does not guarantee that what it dictates is always appropriate. Confucius thought that love should be distributed differentially according to one's relationships and circumstances. One should first and foremost love one's immediate family, and then extend that love outwardly. The abstract idea of loving everyone equally never came into Confucius's mind; for him, that insinuated putting forth one's love without distinction. He says, "Sacrificing to ancestral spirits other than one's own is being obsequious" (2.24).

In comparison to loving animals, one's love toward fellow human beings should take precedence. "When his stables caught fire, the Master hurried back from court and asked, 'Was anyone hurt?' He did not inquire after the horses" (10.17). Confucius also differentiates love according to circumstances. When Confucius's disciple Zihua was serving in the state of Qi, RAN Qiu asked to supply Zihua's mother with some grain. Confucius said, "Give her a full measure of grain." RAN Qiu asked to give her more. The Master said, "Then give her a double measure." RAN Qiu, however, took the liberty of giving her ten measures of grain. The Master said, "In traveling to Qi, Zihua was driving well-fed horses and was wearing fine furs. I have heard it said, 'Exemplary persons would rather help out the needy than make the rich richer' " (6.4).

Shortly after Confucius, however, Mo Zi put forth and advocated the principle of universal and undifferentiated love. Although Mo Zi's idea sounds attractive, Mencius rejected it vehemently in defending Confucian love. Mencius argues that love without distinction implies treating one's own father no different than you would treat a stranger, and the denial of one's own father is to be no different from beasts (*Mencius*, 3B:9). Confucians believe we owe our parents for giving us life, to say the least, if not also for the loving care they provided us when we were young.[3] A human being should be enormously grateful to his parents, giving them the love and care they deserve in return. Here the Confucians are holding the principle that "unmerited generosity should yield to gratitude," which is, says Scottish philosopher Thomas Reid, one of the self-evident principles in morality (see Reid, 639).

But the Confucian perspective is not merely about honoring a moral principle for its own sake (i.e., "because the principle is right in itself"); it is also about the practical consequences of the principle. Their primary concern is that, when a parent is loved no more than any stranger, the very basis of family relationship collapses, and consequently, the order that is vital to social harmony will no longer exist.

Confucius would never have anticipated that his teaching about differentiated love would later become the soil for nepotism, and be blamed for China's lack of public spirit and the idea of fairness. It must be stressed that Confucians are not saying that one should not love broadly; rather, as Mencius puts it, one should "treat the aged of your own family in a manner befitting their venerable age and extend this treatment to the aged of other families; treat your own young in a manner befitting their tender age and extend this to the young of other families" (*Mencius*, 1A:7).

Born to Become a Human

If *ren* is a caring disposition toward others that has to be developed and fully embodied before a biological person can become an authentic human being, then to be *ren* amounts to becoming fully human. For Confucius, becoming human is more an achievement than simply a gift of nature.

"By nature (*xing* 性), humans are similar; through habitual conduct, they diverge widely," says Confucius (17.2). The Master, however, did not say what it is that is similar about the nature of different humans. From Zigong, we learn that the Master may have deliberately withheld from talking about this issue. Zigong said, "We can hear about the Master's cultural refinements, but do not hear his discourse on subjects such as our nature and the Way of heaven (*tiandao* 天道)" (5.13).

In this regard, Confucius is different from his famous followers, Mencius and Xun Zi, who developed elaborate theories about human nature. Commentators have speculated about why Confucius did not want to talk about human nature and the Way of heaven. Some believed that the Master did not talk about these topics because they are by nature transcendental and ineffable, and therefore could only be understood "silently" or intuitively. Some believed that these things require a high level of understanding, and that the general assembly of his students were not yet ready to hear about them. And some felt that abstract metaphysical ideas tend to mislead people and cause them to turn away from the actual phenomenal world in their search for the Way (see Ivanhoe, 2002).

But the most reasonable explanation is probably quite simple: They are both open possibilities! Human nature is similar in that we all possess the capacity to become a genuine human, and the Way of heaven is to be actualized in its own unfolding. Seen from this perspective, human nature and the Way of heaven are not objects of intellectual knowledge (knowledge of *what is there*), but rather indefinite potentials of *gongfu* (embodied abilities), to be developed and lived.

With regard to human nature, actually, when we look at Mencius's theory of human nature from the *gongfu* perspective, we find that it is more a recommendation about how to look at one's self than a pure description of human nature. Like a mother who says to her child, "You're a good child," the real intention behind Mencius's view that "Humans are by nature good" is not to make a judgment, but instead, to give encouragement![4] In this regard, Mencius's theory is not in conflict with Xun Zi's view that humans are by nature bad, because by warning people in this way, Xun Zi is reminding everyone of the necessity of self-overcoming, as the process of actualizing the potentiality of becoming fully human must also be a process of transforming oneself. The aim of both Mencius and Xun Zi is the same: Both thinkers tried to help people become genuine humans. They are just recommending different methods, each of which may suit different groups of people.

With regard to the Way of heaven, for Confucius there is no predetermined, fixed *telos* (aim) intended for humans to actualize. Just as there is no single fixed way of being a sage (18.8) or an artist, everyone should create one's own unique way of becoming a human, because a person's life has to unfold in one's own particular environment and through one's own particular relationships. "It is humans who can broaden the Way, not the Way that can broaden humans," says the Master (15.29). This means that the Way is not a ready-made road for people to travel on. It is a road created by walking. In making the Way great in one's own particular manner, one is also creating oneself, consummating one's own life.

Often *ren* is considered as a Confucian virtue, and due to its central position in Confucius's thought, Confucianism is widely taken as a version of virtue ethics, comparable to Greek philosopher Aristotle's ethics. Indeed, both Confucius and Aristotle focus on building the moral agent rather than on formulating rules of conduct. Both Aristotle's *areté* (virtue) and the Confucian *de* 德 (virtue/virtuosity) are dispositions or abilities required for living an excellent life, and both need to be embodied through constant practice so that they become one's second nature. Confucius and Aristotle both agree that the virtuous person's ability to discern particularities in individual situations can-not be simply formulated as rules of conduct. However, there are important differences between the two. While Aristotelian virtue is based on teleological metaphysics, and therefore is a matter of moral obligation for people to develop simply for the sake of fulfilling the preestablished *telos* (aim) of a human being, the Confucian *de* is more a power or an art that enables one to develop one's human potential creatively as an author of one's own life. We may characterize this key difference between the two as the difference between ethical virtue and virtuosity. If we consider ethical virtue to be a character or ability that conforms to a predetermined moral standard or moral excellence, virtuosity is the embodiment of characteristics and skills, the value of which is only in reference to the excellence it is able to create.

Another important difference between Aristotle and Confucius is that, due to his teleological metaphysics, Aristotle places intellectual virtue at the center of his theory, making rationality a defining feature of a human being, and thus contemplation the most distinctive human activity. The Confucian *de*, on the other hand, centers on the affective aspect of caring and loving; Confucius considers the cultivation and manifestation of proper emotions and attitudes to be more important than the use of the intellect—of course, important in the sense of creating an excellent human life rather than in the sense of fulfilling a predetermined *telos*.

Since practice is the determining factor for becoming a human, Confu-cius's descriptions about *ren* are often given in terms of what will lead one to be a *ren* person. Twice in describing *ren*, the Master says, "Do not impose on others what you yourself do not desire" (15.24, 12.2). This is known as a negative version of the "Golden Rule." It is "golden" because it seems to cap-ture what is moral at a substantial level, and can be considered a general rule of conduct to which other rules would follow. Indeed, various versions of it are found in all the major religions of the world. This is a "negative" version because unlike the popular version of the Golden Rule, which says "Do unto others as you would have them do unto you," it tells people what *not* to do.

But the main difference between the Confucian characterization of *ren* and the popular version of the Golden Rule lies not in their positive or nega-tive forms. Actually, Confucius also offered a positive version, for he says: "If you want to establish yourself, establish others. If you want to unblock yourself, unblock others" (6.30). The main difference is that Confucius never took it as a rule, much less as golden. He states clearly that a morally exem-plary person, *junzi* 君子, "is never for or against anything invariably. He is always on the side of the appropriate" (4.10). Confucius rejects inflexibility and rigidity (9.4, see also 15.37). He himself was characterized as a sage who acted according to circumstances rather than rules (*Mencius*, 5B:1).

The Master deems the art of flexibility so important that he says finding a partner good enough in the exercise of *quan* 权 (discretion) is more difficult than finding a partner good enough in taking a stand or in the pursuit of the Way (9.30). The word *quan* originally meant "scale," and thus, the action of "weighing" or "using discretion" as well. According to the *Gongyang* version of the *Spring and Autumn Annals* 公羊传, dated probably in the Warring States period (ca. 476–221 BCE), "*quan* means moral goodness resulting from transgressing well-established classics" (Duke Huan, Year 11).

Indeed, to take Confucius's above-quoted statements as the "Golden Rule" would result in making them subject to the problems known to the Golden Rule for centuries. For instance, for a person who likes to be bribed, the Golden Rule would not only permit him to bribe others, but it would also obligate him to do so. For a judge who does not like to be put in jail, the Golden Rule would allow the criminal sentenced to jail time to be justified in disputing the punishment. The root of these problems is that the Golden Rule bases rights and wrongs on personal unqualified likes and dislikes, and personal likes and dislikes can be moral or immoral. Confucius is not at all uncritical about one's likes and dislikes. In fact, one of Confucius's major descriptions of *ren* is "to restrain the self" (12.1). For Confucius, cultivating one's heart-mind is a lifelong journey. He says that he himself did not reach the state where he could follow his heart's desire without overstepping the line until he reached the age of seventy (2.4).

How should we take the Confucian "Golden Rule," if it is not meant to be a rule at all? Let us look at the contexts in which Confucius's "Golden Rule" statements are found. When a disciple asked, "Is there one expression that can be acted upon throughout one's entire life?" the Master replied, "There is *shu* 恕. Do not impose on others what you yourself do not want" (15.24). In another passage, right after stating his positive version of the "Golden Rule," the Master says: "Taking an analogy near at hand is the method of becoming *ren*" (6.30). The word *shu* consists of two parts; the upper part, *ru* 如, means "like," "as if," "resemble"; and the lower part, *xin* 心, means "heart-mind." This etymological analysis helps us to understand that for Confucius, the application of the Golden Rule is to take one's own heart as an analogy near at hand, and to extend one's considerations to the wants and needs of others empathically.

According to such a reading, statements regarding the "Golden Rule" in the *Analects* should be read as no different from *shu*, a *method* to be *ren*. A rule is evaluated as either *right* or *wrong*, but a method is evaluated as *effective* or *ineffective*. Even though there is no guarantee that the method will lead to right actions all the time, it helps a person to become more sensitive to the interests of others. Unlike a rule, which allows no exceptions and is typically *imposed upon* the agent as an obligation that serves to *prohibit* the agent from doing certain things, a method is *mastered* by the agent, *enables* the agent to perform the right action, and is certainly not to be used when its application is unwarranted.

Ren is more associated with one's heart and one's whole bodily disposition than with rational knowledge or decisions. It must be embodied, and not merely understood and followed as a universal principle or imperative. For this reason, it is a matter of cultivation rather than gaining propositional knowledge or knowing what rules to follow.

In Confucius's mind, *ren* is also what makes a person worthy of respect, and the basis for respecting others. Unlike German philosopher Immanuel Kant's view that humans are ends in themselves because, as rational beings, humans can make free choices and hence are the source of all values, or the Christian view that humans have dignity because we are made in the image of God, for Confucians, human dignity is more of an achievement than a natural quality given by nature or by God. For Confucius, one earns reverence from others by being respectful in oneself. "If one is respectful, one will not suffer insult" (17.6, 1.13). Confucius says, "The exemplary person does not speak more than what he can accomplish, and does not behave across the line of proper conduct; people revere him without being forced to" (*Li Ji*, chapter 27). The respect one deserves is therefore in proportion to one's level of cultivation.

This does not mean that no one will insult a well-cultivated person, but rather that the insult will display only the insulter's own lack of humanity. When someone spoke disparagingly of Confucius, Zigong made the following remarks:

> This is in vain. Confucius would not be hurt. The worthiness of other people is like a mount or a hill which can still be stepped over, but Confucius is like the sun and the moon which no one can climb beyond. Although a person may wish to shut himself off [from their radiance], what harm will it do to the sun or the moon? It would only demonstrate that such people do not know their own limits. (19.24)

Because Confucius took human dignity as an achievement, he has been blamed for China's lack of respect for the universal human dignity (*Menschenwürde*) that is supposed to belong to everyone equally. Since universal human dignity serves as the foundation for human rights, Confucius, again, is taken to be responsible for China's poor record on human rights. But the issue is far from being as simple as this, for if "being human" is defined through certain attributes, such as the ability to make choices, to reason, or even being created in the image of God, one is still vulnerable to discrimination due to any lack of these abilities, or to insufficiently resembling the image of God (e.g., does being white and male mean you resemble God more than others?).

To be fair to Confucius, his teaching aims at reminding everyone to cultivate oneself and to not disrespect others, including those who are not well cultivated. Repeatedly Confucius reminds his students to set strict standards for themselves and to be lenient to others (see 15.15, 4.14, 14.30, 15.19, and 15.21). From this perspective, one's respect for others is more of a requirement for achieving one's own humanity than a moral act based on judging whether or not others possess certain attributes.

What Makes a Vessel Sacred?

While *ren* is the internal quality or disposition that makes a person an authentic human, one also needs the guidance of *li* 礼, ritual propriety, to provide an external structure of acceptable conduct. The word *li* originally meant holy ritual or sacrificial ceremony, and it is used by Confucius more broadly to mean behavioral patterns established and accepted as appropriate by a community, including what we call manners, etiquette, ceremonies, customs, rules of propriety, etc. The place of *li* in the Confucian tradition is so prominent that often Confucianism is said to be *li jiao* 礼教, a religion of *li*. If we say that in the West the word *barbarian* was used to mean "pagans," in the Confucian tradition, it means those who do not know *li*.

When YAN Hui inquired about *ren*, the Master replied, "To restrain oneself and return to ritual propriety is to be *ren*. A day when restraining oneself and returning to ritual propriety is practiced, all under heaven will bend toward *ren*. To be *ren* is dependent on oneself. How can it be dependent on others?"

YAN Hui said, "May I ask for more detailed explications?"

The Master replied, "Look not if it is contrary to ritual propriety; listen not if it is contrary to ritual propriety; speak not if it is contrary to ritual propriety; act not if it is contrary to ritual propriety."

"Though I am not quick-witted," said YAN Hui, "allow me to follow these instructions" (12.1).

YAN Hui is probably the most diligent disciple of Confucius. He does seem a bit too obedient to the Master, though he is not at all stupid (see 2.9). Zigong, however, is not so obedient. Among Confucius's disciples he is the most economic-minded, and he is quick in his wit and speech. Once he wanted to dispense with the sacrifice of a live sheep at the Declaration of the New Moon ceremony. The Master said: "Zigong! You grudge the cost of the sheep, but I, the disappearance of the ritual propriety" (3.17).

Why is Confucius so keen on ritual propriety? Indeed, putting aside the moral issue about animal rights, why should Confucius insist on having elaborate ceremonies, which seem to be only a matter of formality? In Sigmund Freud's view, rituals are at best fantasies that provide escape or distraction from the immediate urges of human desires, and at worst they are constraints set up by external authorities that lead to neurosis and guilt. Modern critics of Confucianism also charged traditional Confucian ritual propriety with being an invisible rope that strangles human freedom.

Just as we tend to take air for granted, even though it is vital for human life, in the same way ritual propriety is indispensable in human society, but it takes penetrating insights to see its vital importance. First of all, ritual propriety is the carrier of *ren*, or human-heartedness. Let us begin with another story related to Zigong. When Zigong asked the Master, "What do you think of me?" the Master made a puzzling remark: "You are a vessel." Zigong was confused, and asked, "What kind of vessel?" Confucius replied, "A sacrificial vessel" (5.4). As Herbert Fingarette points out, this passage reveals the profound significance of ritual propriety, for the vessel's sacredness does not reside in the preciousness of its beauty; rather, it is sacred "because it is a constitutive element in the ceremony. . . . By analogy, Confucius may be taken to imply that the individual human being, too, has ultimate dignity, sacred dignity by virtue of his role in rite, in ceremony, in *li*" (Fingarette, 75). Outside of a certain ritual setting, a vessel would have no sacredness, no matter how beautiful or expensive it is.

Of course, the analogy should not be taken so far as to mean that one can be sacred merely by being in a ritual setting, without personal cultivation and active participation in the ritual. But the analogy shows clearly the importance of a ritual setting in which a person is positioned. The metaphor of holy ritual serves as a reminder that most ordinary activities in our lives can also be ritualistic or ceremonial, which sets human activities apart from animal activities. A handshake, for instance, is ritualistic, for it is not a mere physical touching of hands, and two hands coming together is not necessarily a handshake. Only in a ritual setting does a physical touching of hands become a handshake. Through a handshake, people can respectfully exchange recognition of one another. Far from being an empty formality, it is through this kind of ritual that we encounter each other on a civilized, humane level.

Similarly, we stand up to greet our guests and walk them to the door as they leave. These are rituals that could be spared if we were merely concerned with efficiency. We say "Excuse me" as a way of getting someone's attention, though, practically, "Hey, you!" could be much more effective. We even look at each other according to some implicit rituals, as at a young age we start to know that it is impolite to stare at people, especially at certain parts of their body. When a disciple asked about filial conduct, the Master replied: "Those who are called filial today are considered so because they are able to provide for their parents. But even dogs and horses are given that much care. If you do not respect your parents, what is the difference?" (2.7) By serving and dining with respect and appreciation in a proper setting, mere physical nourishment becomes a ceremony, and a dinner becomes a uniquely human event.

If to be *ren* is to cultivate oneself toward becoming a loving and caring person, then learning ritual propriety is to learn how to behave in a loving and caring way. "Without ritual propriety, in being respectful, one will be arduous; in being careful, one will be timid; in being brave, one will be unruly; in being straightforward, one will be rude" (8.2). The relationship between *ren* and ritual propriety is like the relationship between an energy source and the medium through which the energy is conveyed. Without the medium, the energy cannot be put to proper use, whereas without the energy source, the medium is empty and meaningless, or even worse, as it may become a constraint for new constructions.

As a repository of ancient wisdom and insight about what is appropriate (*yi* 义), ritual proprieties are guidelines for ensuring proper behavior. Just as any craft or art needs both *zhi* 质, the material or basic stuff from which it is made, and *wen* 文, the refined form, shape, or pattern, a good human activity consists of a well-balanced admixture of both. "An exemplary person takes appropriateness as the *zhi*, and carries it out in the *wen* of ritual propriety" (15.18). "When there is a preponderance of *zhi* over *wen*, the result will be churlishness; when there is a preponderance of *wen* over *zhi*, the result will be pedantry. It is only when one's *zhi* and *wen* are in appropriate balance that you have the exemplary person" (6.18).

Speaking about the relationship between *wen* and *zhi*, Zigong made an insightful remark. When someone asked, "Exemplary persons should focus on the substance [*zhi*]; what do they need refined form [*wen*] for?" Zigong replied, "Refined form is no different from substance; substance is no different from refined form. The skin of a tiger or a leopard, shorn of hair, is no different from that of a dog or a sheep" (12.8). Whereas it looks as though Zigong's remark is inconsistent with Confucius's idea, mentioned above, the two differ only in emphasis. Zigong's remark points out the fact that the form and the substance of an action are so closely connected to each other that not only *should* they match each other, they are actually inseparable! Appropriate conduct must have a refined form; otherwise, it would not be appropriate; and a form cannot be considered refined unless it is appropriate. Confucius's remark cautions people: In their cultivation, people should pay attention to both *wen* and *zhi*, as a preponderance of one over the other results in hurting both.

To better appreciate the philosophical significance of this oneness of substance and form, we may again follow Fingarette's idea, to relate it to a class of linguistic actions called "performative utterances," the discovery of which is associated mainly with the work of British philosopher J. L. Austin, *How to Do Things with Words*, published in the early 1960s. Unlike the common assumption that words are used to describe something, Austin shows that there are many other ways of using words. For example, when I utter the words "I promise" in an appropriate context, I am not describing something; instead, I am *performing* the act of promising.

The "appropriate context" in the above example is exactly a ritual setting. As Herbert Fingarette says, the lesson of Austin's work is not so much about language as it is about ceremony, for all performative acts of language are dependent on ceremonial or ritual context; without such a context they are nothing. "No purely physical motion is a promise; no word alone, independent of ceremonial context, circumstances and roles can be a promise." "In short, the peculiarly moral yet binding power of ceremonial gesture and word cannot be abstracted from or used in isolation from ceremony. It is not a distinctive power we happen to use in ceremony; it is the power *of* ceremony" (Fingarette, 12, 14).

In the example of making a promise, the utterance "I promise" (*wen*, the form) and the act of promising (*zhi*, the substance) are one and the same. If Peter says these words without the intention of keeping the promise, we do not say that Peter used a wrong form for conducting the act. We simply say that Peter made a false promise—false, but still a promise! Since it is false, it is a corrupted promise; yet since it is still a promise, we can hold Peter responsible for it. In this sense we can say that rituals are not merely extrinsic forms of action. They *are* actions. In light of this, Confucius's advice to have a well-balanced admixture of form and substance is in fact no other than advice to choose proper actions.

Second, ritual propriety is an effective means of education. Confucius believes that humans are like raw materials, and they need to be "carved, chiseled, grounded, and polished" (1.15). Learning ritual propriety is such a process. Studies in moral psychology and our experience both tell us that before a person makes an ethical choice, the person's upbringing has pretty much already shaped the overall direction in which the person will go. No one makes choices as a pure rational being without a previously instilled sense of what is a real live option and what is unthinkable to the person. Personal character plays such a strong role in our lives that sometimes even when we intellectually know that a certain attitude is inappropriate, it is difficult to change it, and it is usually more so for people at an older age than a younger one. Confucius says, "When a person at forty still provokes dislikes, it is hopeless" (17.26). By learning ritual propriety at a young age, a person not only learns outward forms of behavior, but is also transformed and established (8.8). One cannot practice ritual propriety well without being affected as a person. In teaching children proper manners, we are building their character, making them not only respectful themselves but also appreciative and caring persons. In this sense learning rituals is no other than learning to be human.

To Confucius, the educational function of ritual propriety is no less aesthetic than it is moral. He often puts the word *li*, ritual propriety, together with *yue* 乐, a word that means aesthetic activities such as music, dance, poetry, and, when pronounced as *le*, it means happiness or joy (see 11.1, 16.2, 16.5, 17.11). Ritual ceremonies are traditionally composed of dance, song, and music. The beauty of these rituals reinforces their ethical and social meaning by giving them an aura of sacredness. At the same time, persons who are refined by rituals also become artistic. They have grace that profoundly enhances the natural beauty of one's body. To the contrary, lacking proper manners, the natural beauty of a person will diminish dramatically, and, in extreme cases, will become nothing but what is of the flesh. An unsightly behavior is always opposed to ritual propriety, and a conduct in accord with ritual propriety is always elegant and aesthetically pleasing.

Furthermore, *li* is also the fabric of social order. "Let a ruler be a ruler, a minister be a minister, a father be a father, and a son be a son" (12.11), says the Master. All roles carry certain expectations about how people in these roles should behave and how they should be treated in return. Ritual proprieties pertaining to the roles give people specific guidance on how to carry out these expectations. The role of a father, for example, requires the person to love, nurture, educate, and take care of his children. Reciprocally, the children must treat the father with due respect and filial piety (*xiao*). The etiquette of the parent-child relationship gives the father and his children concrete guidance in carrying out their reciprocal responsibilities. No society can function on the basis of legal or administrative rules alone. Where legal and administrative rules cannot reach, it is usually ritual propriety that provides the guidance for people's relationships, not to mention that quite often, legal and administrative rules are themselves about rituals.

The *Analects* offer many detailed descriptions of how Confucius acted toward different people with different rituals. "At court, when speaking with lower officials, he was congenial, and when speaking with higher officials, straightforward yet respectful. In the presence of his lord, he was reverent though composed (10.2). . . . When drinking wine at a village function, he would wait for those with canes to depart before taking his leave" (10.13).

Once a blind master musician named Mian came to see Confucius. When he was about to reach the steps, Confucius said, "Here are the steps." When he was approaching the mat, Confucius said, "Here is the mat." When they had all sat down, Confucius informed him of who was present: "So-and-so is here, and so-and-so is here." After the master musician had left, Confucius's disciple Zizhang 子张 asked, "Is this the way that one should speak with a blind master?" Confucius replied, "Indeed, this has been the traditional way of assisting a blind master" (15.42).

Later Confucians summarized human relationships into five kinds, or *wulun* 五伦: the relationships between ruler and subject, father and son, husband and wife, elder and young, and between friends. Each pair is ordered with the superordinate before the subordinate, except for the last one, which is equal unless some other differences become relevant. Those who are in superordinate positions enjoy more authority while bearing more responsibility, and those who are in subordinate positions enjoy more protection and less responsibility, but are expected to reciprocate the former with virtues appropriate for each particular relationship, such as *zhong* 忠, which means "doing one's best in service," in the case of a subjects-to-ruler relationship; *xiao* 孝, "filial piety," in the case of a child-to-parents relationship; and so forth.

Correspondingly, there are more elaborate rituals pertaining to each of these relationships to ensure proper manifestation of the virtues. While Confucius rejected abstract equality and recognized differentiated reciprocal relations, his late followers placed an emphasis on the asymmetry, and turned the theory of five relationships into the basis of what is known as the "Confucian hierarchical society," in which the powers of ruler over the subject, father over the son, and men over women were absolutized.

While the abovementioned five relationships may be among the most basic ones, real-life relationships are much more manifold in the various types. Not only does a person change his roles when dealing with different people, but sometimes one can bear multiple roles in relation to one and the same person. For instance, a person may be a subject to his ruler and, at the same time, be the ruler's teacher. At court, the person should perform the ritual of being a subject to his ruler, whereas in giving instruction as a teacher, the ruler becomes a student and therefore should perform the ritual required for a student to his teacher. Rituals in honor of teachers are therefore important measures to keep rulers in check.

It is expected that social relationships regulated by ritual propriety will be harmonious. When engaging in ritual propriety, humans correspond and interact with each other artistically, like performers in a well-trained orchestra, in which the artistic performance of each is aesthetically dependent on and enhanced by one's cooperation and coordination within the whole. Once rituals become a cultural heritage in the form of social habit, saturated in a given society, they generate a cohesiveness that no administrative legislation is able to achieve. This cohesiveness reaches the very bottom of society, and makes it more stable than if it were ruled by administrative force alone. This is probably one reason why the traditional Confucian society was able to last for thousands of years despite dynastic changes.

However, along with the recognition of Confucianism as a state-sanctioned ideology, traditional rituals were increasingly accepted as rules of proper conduct and less as an effective means of a human-hearted way of life. The Master's teachings about ritual propriety were dogmatized into a rigid system of rules and used by the ruling class to limit the freedom of the common people. For example, the convention that once a woman marries a man, she should remain his wife for her entire life, even after he dies, was attributed to Confucian ritual propriety, even though Confucius never indicated that this should be the case. Widows who refused to remarry were praised as *jiefu* 节妇, "women with integrity," whereas those who remarried were looked down upon.

Exactly because ritual propriety is saturated in social tradition, it has the potential to become an invisible boundary and a restriction that is almost impossible for any individual to defy. Unfortunately, rigid adherence to ritual forms can lead to tragedy and suffocate social reform and creativity. It was this kind of practice that enraged Lu Xun, and led to his labeling the tradition a form of "cannibalism."

For Confucius, ritual proprieties are actually meant to serve as a method to enable a person to be an effective father, an effective son, and so on, and not as externally imposed rules to limit freedom and creativity. Not only were many of the rituals enforced later on in the name of Confucianism unheard of by the Master himself, but Confucius's perception of ritual propriety was much less rigid than most people thought. Though he valued traditional ritual proprieties, nowhere did he say that they must be inflex-ible. For example, the Master said,

> The use of a linen cap was prescribed by the rituals, but now a silk one is used instead. It is economical, and I follow the common practice. Bowing before ascending the hall was prescribed by the ritual, but now the practice is to bow only after ascending it. This is arrogant. I continue to bow below the hall, though it is contrary to the common practice. (9.3)

Clearly the Master did not blindly accept whatever was prescribed by tradi-tion. When asked about the root of observing ritual propriety, the Master re-plied, "What an important question! In observing ritual propriety, it is better to be modest than extravagant; in mourning, it is better to express real grief than to be particular on tedious formalities" (3.4). The principle behind this is that the formality (*wen*) should serve the purpose of the substance (*zhi*), the humanitarian spirit (see also 11.1), and the right rituals to adhere to should be the ones that will promote social harmony (see 1.12).

Rituals are supposed to be entirely situation-sensitive. When Confucius was at home, or when he was at leisure, he was relaxed (7.4). When he was with his close friends, he was straightforward. As Confucius had warned, in emphasizing ritual propriety, there is the danger of a preponderance of *wen* over *zhi*. In a close relationship and an informal setting, overuse of rituals conveys a coldness that distances people from one another.

Once when Yuanrang 原壤, an old friend whom Confucius grew up with, was sitting on the floor with his legs stretched out, waiting for Confucius, Confucius scolded him directly, saying, "In one's youth to be neither mod-est nor respectful to one's elders, to grow up without having accomplished anything at all to pass on, and on growing old, not to have the courtesy to die—such a person is a thief." He then rapped Yuanrang on the shin with his cane (14.43). Given Confucius's particular relationship with Yuanrang, and given Yuanrang's own disrespectful gesture, we see that only by being direct is the Master treating Yuanrang properly. It would have been insincere, and hence improper, for Confucius to speak politely to Yuanrang. In this case, Confucius's apparent lack of a refined form in treating Yuanrang is in fact a proper refinement, considering the person he was dealing with.

Naming Means Illuminating

For Confucius, most, if not all, of our utterances are performative: They are actions through which things are done, or from which results and consequences will follow. Since their meaning goes beyond describing facts, the evaluation of this type of utterance should not be in terms of truth or falsity, but instead should be assessed in terms of appropriateness or inappropriateness, acceptability or unacceptability.

Given that ritual propriety is dependent on the clarification of roles, Confucius takes *zhengming* 正名, ordering or rectifying names, seriously (13.3). Almost any linguistic expression can have ritual content. Ritual expressions are usually vague enough that they defy any clear definition, yet they are concrete enough to carry rich practical implications. When the Master says, "Let a ruler be a ruler, a minister be a minister, a father be a father, and a son be a son" (12.11), he is far from uttering simple tautologies. These expressions are reminding people of the expectations associated with each of the "names," so that everyone will know what is expected of him or her in a given web of particular relationships. Not only "A ruler must rule, a minister must minister . . . ," but also "A ruler should be treated as a ruler, a minister as a minister . . ."

Henry Rosemont Jr. and Roger Ames characterize Confucian ethics as "role ethics," based primarily on consciousness of roles as defined by "names" and the expectations attached to them. A couple of interesting stories will help to illuminate this. It is said that once when Zeng Zi was working in his vegetable garden, he accidentally cut the root of some melon plants. His father Zeng Xi 曾皙 was so angry that he hit him on the back with a big rod, rendering him unconscious for a while. After Zeng Zi woke up, he approached his father with no ill feelings, saying, "I offended you, Father, and you disciplined me hard. Did you injure yourself?" When he returned to his own room, he took out his lute and sang, so that his father could be assured that he was fine. Upon hearing about this, Confucius was furious. He told other disciples, "If Zeng Zi comes, do not let him in!" Zeng Zi was puzzled. He sent someone else to ask the Master what he did wrong. The Master said,

> Didn't you know that when Shun [ancient sage king] was serving his father, he would always be available when the father needed his help, but he could not be found when his father wanted to kill him? A mild spank is fine for misconduct, but one should run away when facing a big rod. In this way Shun's father could not find a chance to commit the crime of becoming a cruel father and Shun did not become an un-filial son. The way Zeng Zi served his father today was to wait there for his father to burst his anger, as if he would not run away even when facing death! Had he really died, he would have led his father into a terrible crime. What could be more un-filial than this?

Hearing this, Zeng Zi deeply regretted his actions, and came to Confucius to apologize (see *Kong Zi Jiayu*, 4.15).

In another story, we are told that when Zilu was serving as the governor of a county called Pu, he led the people to construct an irrigation system. Seeing that the people worked hard, he offered each person some food and drink, which he paid for from his own money. When Confucius heard about it, he sent Zigong to stop Zilu from continuing the conduct. Zilu was really upset. He went to see Confucius and said,

> I was leading the people to construct the irrigation system to prevent floods, as the storm season is coming. Since the people were hungry and exhausted, I gave them food and drinks. Now you sent Zigong to stop me. That is to stop me from practicing *ren* [human-heartedness]. You teach us to be human-hearted and yet prohibit us from practicing it. I cannot accept your order!

Confucius replied,

> If the people were in shortage of food, why didn't you report to the lord and open the state food reserve to relieve the famine? Using your own money to feed them is to show off your own moral virtue by making the lord look uncaring. You have to stop doing this immediately. Otherwise you will surely be accused! (*Kong Zi Jiayu*, 2.8)

These stories reveal that for Confucius, knowing one's role means to be fully aware of the reciprocal responsibilities. One cannot be a good son without at the same time trying one's best to make one's father a good father; and one cannot be a good subject without at the same time trying one's best to make the ruler a good ruler. This mutuality is a crucial part of Confucian human-heartedness.

Indeed, Chinese have from the very beginning looked at naming as a way of illuminating, thereby positioning both the person as well as everything else in the context of practical life. *Shuo Wen* 说文, a dictionary dated in the Han dynasty by XU Shen 许慎, says, "To name is to announce oneself. The word 'naming 名' has as its components the characters for mouth 口 and for evening 夕. Evening implies darkness. In darkness people do not see each other, and hence the need to use one's mouth to announce oneself." Another Han dynasty scholar, LIU Xi 刘熙, also says in his work *Shi Wen* 释文 (*Explanation of Words*), "To name is to illuminate." In other words, naming is the act of making announcements and recognition, rather than simply referring to people or things.

Out of this tradition, Chinese people have developed an elaborate system of naming. It is interesting to observe that the system makes clear distinctions—so clear that separate terms are used for younger brothers, elder brothers, younger sisters, elder sisters, uncles and aunts on one's mother's side, uncles and aunts on one's father's side, and so forth. Proper application of these terms implies knowing proper rituals and the reciprocal responsibilities associated with them. By calling a government officer by his official title, "minister" or "chief," a subordinate is simultaneously affirming the person's authority and reminding the person of one's official responsibility.

Making a general contrast between this Chinese Confucian approach to language and the predominant Western approach to language, Chad Hansen says,

> Western philosophy discourses about language in a realistic, Platonic way, focusing on metaphysics and epistemology. We conceive of our philosophical activity as the study of how to represent reality in our minds. In contrast, Chinese philosophers discourse about language in a pragmatic, Confucian way, focusing on social-psychological techniques for shaping inclinations and feelings that direct behavior in accord with a moral way. (Hansen, 495)

According to Hansen, the Chinese use language not to try to get to the truth understood in the sense of correspondence to reality, and not to invoke proof, knowledge, or beliefs. Instead, they try to ensure the acceptability of names. While in the West, "sentential belief statements represent a relation between a person and a sentence believed, [the Chinese] term-belief statements characterize a person as having a disposition to use a certain term of some object. Term-belief, in Chinese, represents a way of responding rather than a propositional content" (Hansen, 501).

The *Analects* has a story that illustrates the power of rectifying names. When SIMA Niu lamented, "Everyone has brothers except for me," Zixia said to him,

> I have heard it said, "Life and death are a matter of one's destiny; wealth and honor lie with heaven." Since exemplary persons are respectful and not careless in their own conduct, and they are deferential to others and observe ritual propriety, everyone in the world is their brother. Why would exemplary persons worry over having no brothers?" (12.5)

Interestingly, SIMA Niu had four brothers. One of them is SIMA Huantui, who tried to kill Confucius in the state of Song (see 7.23). Taken referentially,

SIMA Niu's lament was simply false. However, when seen from the perspective of rectification of names, his brothers' behavior had apparently disappointed SIMA Niu so much that he refused to acknowledge them as his brothers, as the reality no longer matched the expectations carried by the name of "SIMA Niu's brother." While SIMA Niu's rectification of names excluded his brothers as true brothers, Zixia's remark, which is also an act of rectifying a name, stretched "brother" beyond its narrow meaning of male sibling. This technique reshapes SIMA Niu's feelings and directs his disposition to an inclusive and loving attitude toward a broad multitude.

Out of this Confucian tradition, Chinese people constantly and deliberately stretch the meaning of terms. As a way of extending one's family, a good friend of mine would call me "brother," and my daughter would call him "uncle." As a way of showing respect and friendliness, a stranger could be called "auntie" or "big uncle," and a person who has some specialized knowledge may be addressed as "teacher," or "*shifu* 师傅" (master). By using names in this way, Chinese people actively make their mutual relations closer.

Furthermore, this Confucian understanding of naming and roles can help us to understand why Chinese people are overall more concerned with the practical implications of their words rather than with their truth-value (i.e., being true or false). People from other parts of the world often feel uncomfortable with Chinese rituals and their indirect way of communication. For instance, when someone asks a Chinese person, "Would you like to have a drink?" the person may say, "No, thank you," even though he really would like to have one. The real meaning is not that "No, I wouldn't like to have a drink," but "No, I don't want to bother you." When they host a dinner for a guest, after presenting a full table of wonderful dishes, they may say, "Sorry to let you have just an everyday meal." The real message is not "This is what I ordinarily eat," but rather, "You are such a distinguished guest that you deserve a better meal." When a foreigner requests something that a Chinese person cannot grant, a typical response from the Chinese person would be something like, "Let us talk about it later," or perhaps "It is not convenient now," with an expectation that the person would understand this is really a polite "No," rather than literally meaning it will be considered later.

Even though Westerners can get frustrated with this kind of indirect communication,[5] the sophisticated use of *wen*, the refined form, in which language is used as a way of doing something rather than describing something, is not totally absent in Western culture. For this we only need to look at an example not uncommon in the West: When a lady asks a man, "How do I look?" unless the man is in a close relationship with the lady, no one with any civility would say "You look terrible," even if that were indeed the case.

Hit the Mark Constantly

As paradoxical as it may sound, Confucius is a philosopher who is not interested in forming a philosophical theory. This is not because he was not aware that his instructive teachings had philosophical implications at the same time. It is because of the fact that his philosophy aims at something quite beyond having a philosophy!

Confucius says, "No excellence (*de* 德) is more supreme than *zhongyong* 中庸. It has been rare among the common people for a long time" (6.29). *Zhong* means "centrality" or "not to be one-sided." *Yong* has three meanings: "ordinary" or "commonality," "practicality" (用), and "constancy." When *zhong* and *yong* are used together as one term, its rich meaning can be put as: to constantly practice in one's everyday life so that one achieves the ability to always hit the proper mark, like a good archer is able to do.

There is considerable overlap between the Confucian notion of *zhong* and the Aristotelian Golden Mean. Both signify the embodied disposition (virtue/virtuosity) of avoiding the extremes of deficiency and excess. To stay at *zhong* requires one to be in a state between excess and deficiency. *Zhong*, for instance, is the state between rashness and timidness, rigidity and spinelessness, conformity and antagonism, total attachment and complete indifference, or callousness and fervidness. When Zigong inquired, "Who is of superior character, Zizhang or Zixia?" the Master replied, "Zizhang oversteps the mark, and Zixia falls short of it." "Does this make Zizhang better?" asked Zigong. "Excess is as bad as deficiency," replied Confucius (11.16). Confucius's method of teaching was in tune with this aim. When Zilu and RAN You asked the same question, "On learning something, should one act upon it?" the Master gave opposite directions. With Zilu, he held him back, and yet with RAN You, he urged him to go ahead. Another disciple was puzzled, and asked the Master why. The Master replied, "RAN You is diffident, and so I urged him on. But Zilu has the energy of two, and so I sought to rein him in" (11.22). Clearly these instructions are not aiming at describing truth, but at helping the particular disciples.

But the "middle way" should not be understood as staying between extremes regardless, as taking no position in controversies or trying to reconcile everything, or as staying mediocre. Taking either the Confucian *Zhongyong* or Aristotle's doctrine of the Golden Mean in this way misses the point entirely. The advice is to stay between two vices, not between excellence and vices. "Never stop before reaching the highest excellence" is in the very first sentence of the *Great Learning*. The excellence of the mean is itself the supreme excellence of hitting the right target, of staying where it is appropriate among the ever-changing situations and variations of conditions. The word *zhong* is therefore appropriateness in a more general sense than *yi* 义 (often translated as "appropriateness"). While *yi* is the appropriateness in moral matters, *zhong* applies to everything. However, in regard to what is appropriate, *zhong* requires the utmost, which means never being content with merely "not so bad," and never feeling that one has done well enough. It requires one to take a clear stand on what is most appropriate and to be able to respond to the changing situation accordingly.

The reason that *zhongyong* is difficult is because, unlike hitting the target just once by chance, being able to hit the target all the time in various conditions requires a lot of practice and cultivation. This is why *zhong* has to be associated with *yong*, constant practice of *zhong* in everyday life. First, the ability to hit the target is more a matter of having embodied abilities or dispositions than following abstract universal principles. A person who merely knows that he should hit the mark is far from being good enough to actually hit it. Everyday life situations are dynamic, and hence, there is no rigid rule to follow. Those who really know how to respond to changing situations are not the ones who merely have theoretical knowledge, but the ones who have practiced so well that their skills and sensibilities have internalized into their second nature. This means that a cultivated person can simply respond to these situations spontaneously. In fact, the need to have self-control is itself an indication of imperfection. Real possession of *gongfu* is to no longer have the need for self-control; it is manifest in one's ability to allow appropriate actions to flow out as a form of self-expression.

Second, the practice is not limited to some "big moments" in which one needs to make critical choices about right or wrong; it applies to all daily life activities which may even look trivial, such as serving parents, taking care of children, respecting teachers, helping friends, and collaborating with coworkers. Everyone is able to live happily in union with family members and everyone else sometimes, and everyone is able to behave altruistically occasionally. The real strength, or *gongfu*, of the well-cultivated person is the ability to continuously practice *zhong* and hit the mark constantly. The sage is just one who sees the significance of that which is common to us all, and is able to embody it and universalize it fully.

In fact, to have self-control—or better yet, to have no need for self-control—is easier during alarming situations than it is during one's daily routine. The ability to hit the mark at ease in most tiresome matters displays more greatness than heroic deeds in alarming situations, though the person who possesses such greatness still looks ordinary and amiable and does not claim to have found something beyond the possibility of the common people. As the book of *Zhongyong* says, "There is nothing more visible than what is hidden and nothing more manifest than what is subtle" (chapter 1). It is exactly because humanity is hidden right in front of us in our ordinary, common life that it is difficult to see. People tend to think that the profound should be obscure, the great should be beyond easy reach, and the sacred should transcend the secular. They would rather go to a monastery to pray to the invisible than to seek within and nearby for what they really need. The word *yong* is thus not merely a description; it is an instruction as well. It tells us where to look for the *gongfu*.

Being a practical person, Confucius knew that it was unrealistic to require everyone to be perfect. "If one cannot find the company of those who can travel at the mean (*zhong*), one has no choice but to turn to the rash or the timid. The rash will forge ahead in their actions and the timid will at least not do what they think is wrong" (13.21). The aim of hitting the mark constantly is not as much a moral imperative that everyone is obligated to follow as it is a recommendation for achieving excellence in one's life in general. Compared to the aims of ethics set by mainstream Western moral philosophers like Immanuel Kant and John S. Mill, the aim of Confucius's theory is actually higher. Both Kant and Mill construct their theories as if ethics only need to deal with rational decisions or choices, mostly when serious rights and wrongs are at stake. For Confucius, ethics aim at the transformation of the entire person, and its scope covers a person's entire life, not just pivotal moments of moral decisions. Through cultivation, one will increasingly find that wrong actions become unthinkable, choices become unnecessary, and one's style of life becomes both ethically sound and aesthetically enjoyable.

Like other parts of his theory, *zhongyong* has its drawbacks as well. From this theory, it is difficult for an average person to grasp a clearly defined way of judging rights and wrongs. But it is worth considering whether this is a problem with the theory itself, or rather a fact determined by the nature of the very issue that it deals with. In other words, an abstract moral principle that can be universally applied regardless of the particular contexts in actual human life might not exist. Moral matter may in its nature be like the art of archery: In failing to hit the mark, no archer can blame the lack of concrete rules every time he misses a shot.

Notes

1. The tendency was already seen in Socrates' famous statement that "The only good is knowledge and the only evil is ignorance." But as Pierre Hadot points out,

early Greeks overall thought of philosophy as a way of life rather than merely an intellectual discourse (see Hadot, 1995).

2. The other three are sheer speculation, insisting on one's own certainty, and being inflexible.

3. In the case of the ancient sage king, Shun, for instance, he treated his father with all love and care, even though his father wanted to have him killed.

4. Mencius gives a clear clue about the real intention behind his theory of human nature. He says, "It is due to our nature that our mouths desire sweet taste, that our eyes desire beautiful colors, that our ears desire pleasant sounds, . . . But there is also fate (ming 命) [whether these desires are satisfied or not]. The superior man does not say they are man's nature [and insist on satisfying them]. The virtue of humanity in the relationship between father and son, the virtue of righteousness in the relationship between ruler and minister, . . . —these are [endowed in people in various degrees] according to fate. But there is also man's nature The superior man does not [refrain from practicing them and] say they are matters of fate" (Mencius, 7B:24).

5. See, for instance, American missionary Arthur H. Smith's famous book, Chinese Characteristics (first published in China, 1890), chapter 8, in which the author lists many examples of the Chinese "talent for indirection," and expresses his frustration with an obvious tone of sarcasm.

CHAPTER IV

~

Confucius as a Political Reformer

Master Kong was, by all standards, not successful as a political reformer during his lifetime. Though he was more than willing to serve states, and was fully aware of the tactics needed to gain the favor of rulers, he was too firm in his principles and too blunt in his way of presenting ideas. When the Ji family, which was not the head of the state, used the imperial scale of eight rows of eight dancers in their courtyard, the Master said, "If this can be condoned, what cannot be?" (3.1) Upon hearing that the Ji family violated the rites for Mount Tai by performing sacrifices on the Mount, Confucius scolded his disciple RAN Qiu, who was serving the family, for not being able to save them from the impropriety (3.6). When the three powerful families in Lu performed the *yong* ode at the conclusion of their family sacrifices, the Master said, " 'Assisting were the various nobles, and the Emperor stood regal and majestic.' What relevance do these lines of the ode have to the ancestral halls of the Three Families?" (3.2) This kind of attitude did not serve him well politically. Even though there are records of Confucius holding some government positions, such as the governor of Zhongdu and the minister of justice in Lu, with stories of his remarkable ability in handling his duties, the *Analects* mentions only his leaving the state of Lu in disappointment, unable to make the rulers listen to him.

In terms of his vision about social and political reform, however, Confucius is certainly one of the greatest who ever lived, and after more than two millennia, his legacy is still enchanting the world today.

Ideal Society—Harmony and Holism

The Confucian ideal society is well described in this passage of the *Book of Rites*:

> When the great way prevails, a public and common spirit is everywhere under the sky. People of talents and virtue are chosen, trustworthiness advocated, and harmony cultivated. People love not merely their own parents, nor treat as children only their own children. The aged are provided [for] till their death, the able-bodied all have places to utilize their ability, and the young have the means for growing up. Widows, widowers, orphans, childless, disabled, and ill, all sufficiently maintained. Men get their share and women have their homes. People hate to throw goods of value away upon the ground, but see no reason to keep them for their own gratification. People dislike not putting their strengths into use, but see no reason to use them only to their own advantage. Therefore schemings diminish and find no development; robberies, thefts, rebellions, and treason do not happen. Hence the outer doors need not be shut. This is called the Grand Union. (*Li Ji*, "Li Yun 礼运," in Legge trans. vol. 1: 364–66)

Contained in such an ideal is a humanitarian spirit, the spirit of *ren* (human-heartedness) and the extended application of *xiao* 孝, "filial piety." One notices that in this passage there is no mention of political governance structure. Instead, it is the extension of people's love for their own parents and children to others in the community that is playing the role of public administration. From the filial point of view, everyone is exhorted to respect the elders who established their authority through their moral conduct in the family. These people will be in charge of the management of family affairs and the settlement of intra-family disputes, if any. The village chief, usually a most senior and well-respected person in the community, will be the one to settle inter-family disputes amicably and call for meetings when necessary. While the village elders will take the place of the administrator and the judge, the observance of the traditional rituals will also ideally eliminate the need for having any legal provision.

This does not mean that in Confucius's vision, there is no need for a ruler. For Confucius, an ideal ruler should be like a good parent, diligently taking care of the people just as he would treat his own children, and offering all he can to ensure that they live well. Compared to the Legalists, who perceived the interests of the ruler as opposed to the interests of the common people, and who advocated "making the state rich and keeping the people vulnerable" so that the people would be easy to control, Confucius conceives of the interests of the ruler and the common people as reciprocally related. The primary role of a ruler for Confucius is to ensure that the people are living well.

At a time when rulers of China mostly considered the common people nothing but their dispensable possessions, Confucius taught that a good ruler should be like a good parent who extends the love he feels for his own children to other children; he should extend the care for his own people to all the people in the world. It is said that the lord of Chu lost his archery bow when he was traveling in his state. His followers wanted to launch a search for it. The lord stopped them, saying, "The lord of Chu lost his bow and the people of Chu got it. Why should we bother to search for it?" Confucius sighed, and said, "I wish he could be more broad-minded. He should have said, 'A human lost his bow and another human gets it.' Why does it have to be in the hands of a Chu person?" (*Kong Zi Jiayu*, 2.10)

When Confucius traveled to the state of Wei, he remarked, "What a teeming population!" His disciple RAN Qiu asked, "When the people are already so numerous, what more can be done for them?" The Master said, "Make them prosperous." "When the people are already prosperous," asked RAN Qiu, "what more can be done for them?" "Teach them," replied the Master (13.9).

When Zigong asked, "What about the person who gives extensively to the common people and is able to help the multitude—is this what we could call human-hearted (*ren*)?" The Master said, "This is no longer merely human-hearted. A person like this must be called a sage!" As a realistic person, he added, "Even Yao and Shun [ancient sage kings] would find such a task difficult to accomplish. Human-hearted persons establish others if they want to establish themselves, and unblock others if they want to unblock themselves. To be able to draw analogy nearby is the method of becoming human-hearted" (6.30).

The way to lead a state, says the Master, is to "pay reverent attention to state affairs, be trustworthy, be frugal in expenditure, and love the people, putting the populace to work at the proper seasons" (1.5). During the early years of the Zhou dynasty, the common rate for government tax was one-tenth of the people's income. Later, many states increased their taxes. The most outrageous example of this tax increase is Marquis Jing of Qi, who charged his people two-thirds of what they produced and left them with only one-third for their own food and clothing (see *Zuo Zhuan*, Duke Zhao, Year 3. Legge, 589).

In comparison, Duke Ai of Lu was relatively moderate: He taxed his people two-tenths of what they produced. At a time of bad harvest, Duke Ai asked YOU Ruo 有若, a distinguished disciple of Confucius, "The harvest has been bad and there is not enough for the government expenditure. What should I do?" You Ruo replied, "What about taxing the people one part in ten?" The Duke was confused: "With two-tenths, I still find it not sufficient. How could I do with one-tenth?" You Ruo said, "When the people have sufficient, how could you not be sufficient? When the people have insufficient, how can you expect to have sufficient?" (12.9)

Confucius taught his disciples that an exemplary person should be gracious in deporting himself, deferential in serving his superiors, generous in attending to the needs of the common people, and appropriate in employing their services (5.16). When Confucius found out that his disciple RAN Qiu was gathering excessive revenues for the Ji family, which already had more material possessions than the ancient sage, the Duke of Zhou, had great fame, he was so enraged that he said to his other disciples, "This man is no disciple of mine. You students have my permission to sound the charge and attack him!" (11.17)

Loving people requires teaching them, properly informing them, and being reliable in one's own conduct as a ruler. The Master said, "To lead uninstructed people to war is to abandon them" (13.30). "To execute a person who has not first been educated is cruel; to expect a job to be finished without having first given notice is oppressive; to enforce a timetable when slow in giving orders is injurious; to reward people and yet do it in a stingy way is called acting like a clerk" (20.2).

For Confucius, it is important for the government to make the people prosperous in their material lives, since only when the people are prosperous can the government be strong. Somehow many have mistakenly thought that Confucius would have preferred a nation of equally poor to a nation in which there was an uneven distribution of wealth. This misconception comes from a statement in the *Analects* that says, "The head of a state or a family worries not about his people being poor but about inequitable distribution of wealth, not about underpopulation but about instability. If the wealth is equitably distributed, there is no poverty; if the people live harmoniously, the population will not be few in number; if the people are secure, they are not unstable" (16.1).

The word *jun* 均 in this passage, which we rendered as "equitable," does not refer to an absolute even distribution of wealth, but rather that wealth is distributed fairly. The passage we quoted from the *Li Ji* shows partly what Confucius had in mind: The ideal distribution of wealth contains a welfare system in which the needy (such as the elderly and the disabled) are provided for, and the contribution one makes to the society is not merely for one's own profit. This is not a society in which no one is richer than others. The point Confucius makes deals with proper distribution and the right way to gain wealth. "When wealth can be pursued, I will be willing to do it even as a guard holding a whip. But if it is not, I shall follow my own preferences," says the Master (7.12). There is nothing in Confucius's thought that is against wealth itself. In fact, the Master thinks that for a person with a normal ability, it would be a shame to remain poor when the Way prevails, and to be wealthy when the Way does not prevail (8.13), because when the Way prevails, to remain poor must be due to one's own laziness, and when the Way does not prevail, wealth can only be gained through improper means.

The most distinctive feature of the Confucian vision of an ideal society is harmony. Confucius contrasted harmony (*he* 和) with conformity (*tong* 同). He says, "The exemplary person pursues harmony rather than conformity; the petty-minded is the opposite" (13.23). Nowhere is the difference between harmony and conformity explained better than in a story recorded in *Zuo Zhuan*. When the Marquis of Qi returned from his hunt, Yan Zi 晏子 was with him in the tower, and Ziyou 子犹 drove up to it at full speed. The Marquis said, "It is only Ziyou who is in harmony with me!" Yan Zi replied, "Ziyou is only in conformity; how can he be considered in harmony with you?" "Are they different," asked the Marquis, "harmony and conformity?" Yan Zi said, "They are different. Harmony is like broth. One uses water, fire, vinegar, sauce, salt, and plums to cook his fish and meat. It is made to boil by the firewood, and then the cook mixes the ingredients." Yan Zi then pointed out to the Marquis that the relations of ruler and minister are similar:

> When there is in what the ruler approves of anything that is not proper, the minister calls attention to that impropriety, so as to make the approval entirely correct. When there is in what the ruler disapproves of anything that is proper, the minister brings it forward so as to remove occasion for the disapproval. In this way the government is made fair, without infringement, and the people will not go against it. . . . With Ziyou, whatever you say "Yes" to, he also says "Yes." Whatever you say "No" to, he also says "No." If you add water to flavor water, who can eat it? If you keep playing the same note on the lute or zither, who can listen to it? The failing of conformity lies in this. (*Zuo Zhuan*, Duke Zhao, Year 20. Legge, 684)

What Yan Zi says shows clearly that harmony is a state of coexistence and interaction between distinct participants. Without differences, harmony cannot exist. In other words, difference is a prerequisite for harmony. The different parts of a harmonious whole interact with each other, blend in with each other, and enhance each other without sacrificing their uniqueness.

When parts are forced into conformity, however, they are made in agreement with each other at the cost of losing their uniqueness. The parts of a harmonious whole *participate in* the dynamic construction of the whole, whereas the parts of a conformed unity are merely *constituents of* it.

The above conversation took place when Confucius was thirty (521 BCE). Even though there is no direct evidence that suggests Confucius knew about it, his view on harmony is in fact fully in accord with Yan Zi's. Confucius says that, in political matters, if what the ruler says is good and no one takes exception, fine indeed. But if what the ruler says is not good and no one takes exception, it would ruin a state (13.15). "Exemplary persons are conscious of their own merits, but not contentious; they gather together with others, but do not form cliques" (15.22). Duke Ai of Lu asked Confucius, "Isn't the son who obeys whatever his father says a filial son? Isn't a subject who follows whatever order his King issues a loyal subject?" He asked three times and Confucius remained silent. Afterward, Confucius explained to his disciple Zigong:

> When a state has subjects who dare to stand up and appeal to the King, it will not be in danger. When a father has a son who dares to speak up, he will not deviate from ritual propriety. When a person has friends who dare to speak up, he will not take inappropriate action. Hence, how can we say that the son is filial, if he obeys whatever his father says? How can a subject be considered loyal if he follows whatever his King orders? Those who examine what they are expected to follow, that is what filiation and loyalty means. (*Xun Zi*, 29.3)

As the way to serve one's lord properly is to "make no offense when taking a stand against him" (14.22), Confucius gave Duke Ai a silent reservation in the hope that the duke would be able to figure it out himself.

As the harmony of a broth is not only dependent on having multiple ingredients, but also on the condition that no ingredient is sharply at odds with other ingredients, Confucius does search for agreement on the Way. "People who pursue different ways [*dao*] cannot consult each other," says the Master (15.40). But he never states the Way in an abstract universal proposition. The commonality of the Way is a togetherness of an overall direction, an open-ended path toward human flourishing; it is not conformity in propositional beliefs. If we call the search for universal agreement on abstract principles "universalism" and its opposite, the insistence on retaining difference and particularity, "particularism," Confucius's position is actually a third alternative, which is "holism." The main problem with universalism is that it leads to absolutism and exclusion of plurality, like having everyone wear the same uniform. The problem of particularism is that it leads to relativism and disintegration of unity, like animals in a zoo, preserved and protected but having no mutual encounters, depending on the zoo keeper for survival. Holism, however, is the togetherness that retains plurality, like an ecosystem in which different species both compete with and depend on each other.

You Zi says, "Achieving harmony is the most valuable function of observing ritual propriety" (1.12). In contrast with the pursuit of universal agreement on principles stated in the form of propositions, the practice of ritual propriety is ambiguous and leaves maximum space for uniqueness and creativity. A handshake itself does not specify what is agreed upon, and yet certain trust and mutual recognition is established. The meaning carried in a handshake can be richer than any agreement on a principle, and it will not lose mutuality for the sake of having an agreement, nor will it lack emotional content for the sake of retaining rationality. Indeed, not only is the observance of ritual propriety a necessary condition for any healthy dialogue, whether among civilizations, between political parties, or within a troubled family, it is often also the way to generate the best outcome of dialogue: harmony (but not conformity).

Comparing the Confucian ideal society with a society ruled by rational principles, Roger Ames and David Hall point out that the social order brought forth by the Confucian sage is an aesthetic one. In contrast with a logical or rational order, which enforces some external or transcendental rule or principle from without, the aesthetic order emerges as embodied rules and principles through self-cultivation and mutual coordination. In a logical/rational order, there is only consistency and continuity, whereas in an aesthetic order, individuals and communities are able to creatively interpret and reinterpret the rules and principles. In a logical/rational order, everyone is equal, because everyone is conceived abstractly as an agent, and hence they are substitutable with any other agent, whereas in an aesthetic order, individuals are concrete particulars, un-substitutable, and the inequality is a matter of deference to excellence (see Hall and Ames, 131–38).

Sageliness Within and Kingliness Without

When Ji Kangzi asked Confucius about the way of zheng 政 (governing), Confucius replied with its homophonous etymological root, zheng 正, which means "being proper," "straight," "orderly," or, when used as a verb, "to correct," or "to make straight." The Master says, "Governing (zheng 政) requires one to be proper (zheng 正). If you, sir, lead by doing what is proper, who would dare do otherwise?" (12.17) Jı Kangzi asked further, "What if I kill those who do not follow the Way in order to move closer to those who are on it?" Confucius replied, "If you govern effectively, what need is there for killing? Just desire the good yourself and the common people will be good. The virtue of those in high stations is like the wind, and the virtue of the common people is like the grass. The grass will for sure bend when the wind blows across it" (12.19). "Being proper in their own position, what difficulty would the rulers have in governing? But if not able to set themselves proper, how can they set others proper?" (13.13)

For Confucius, being proper means both setting good examples and assuming proper ritual positions. The power of ritual propriety is so extraordinary and amazing that, as Fingarette says, it can be considered "magical" (Fingarette, 1–17). It accomplishes what one intends to do directly and effortlessly, without the use of coercion or any physical force. In public affairs, if those who are in superior positions are fond of ritual propriety, the common people will be easy to command (14.41)—so easy that they will follow without even being commanded to do so (13.6). The Master says, "If there was a ruler who achieved order without taking any action (*wuwei* 无为), it was surely Shun. What did he do? He simply assumed an air of respectfulness and faced due south. That was all" (15.5).[1]

Here emerges the Confucian *wuwei*—"action by nonaction," a notion more well known for its Daoist affiliation. It is nonaction because in doing nothing, the agent does not seem to be making an effort or exerting any force. While the Daoist *wuwei* is to do things naturally and spontaneously, the Confucian *wuwei* is to accomplish intended results by ritual proprieties enlivened by their *de*, virtue/virtuosity. When a person walks toward another and reaches out her hands with a smile, the other will spontaneously turn toward her, return the smile, and raise his hands to shake hers. When a teacher calls a student to lead a class discussion, she is magically empowered by positioning herself solemnly in front of the podium so as to have the authority to conduct the class. Without coercion or command or any tricks, the life of the ritual brings about cooperation (Fingarette, 9).

Confucius explicitly views the use of administrative order and rule by law as inferior to the way of ritual propriety and moral excellence. One obvious reason is that ritual propriety was already there as a tradition, actualized in custom at the bottom of society, whereas administrative orders and laws during that particular historical era could only be arbitrary—power-driven enforcement sanctioned from above. More importantly, as Confucius says, "Lead the people with administrative injunctions and keep them orderly with penal law, and they will avoid punishments but will be without a sense of shame. Lead them with virtue/virtuosity (*de* 德) and keep them orderly through observing ritual propriety, and they will develop a sense of shame, and moreover, will order themselves" (2.3).

Compulsion and punishment can only ensure outward conformity at best. People will avoid causing trouble not because they are ashamed of doing wrong, but because they fear punishment. Confucius never rejected the need to have administrative orders and laws. But even in a modern society, where laws are well established through a democratically elected body of legislature, rule of law is still limited, as it can only set a minimalist bottom line for what is not allowed. At places where legal enforcement cannot reach or where no one else is around to see, people may still do wrong. However, if the social order is secured by virtue/virtuosity and ritual propriety, an internal supervision will develop, which is not only more effective in its penetration into people's lives, but also elevates people to become better citizens. The Master said, "In hearing litigation, I am no different from anyone else. But if you insist on a difference, it is that I try to get people to have no need to resort to litigation in the first place" (12.13).

This also defines the Confucian approach to foreign relations and his view regarding military force. Indicative of Confucius's view is the story about his successful defeat of a plotted attempt to coerce the ruler of Lu in a summit meeting between Qi and Lu. In the summer of the tenth year of Duke Ding of Lu's reign (499 BCE), the rulers of the two states met at a place called Jiagu, with Confucius assisting his duke. Prior to the meeting, Limi, the advisor to the Marquis of Qi, said to his marquis: "Confucius knows rituals, but he lacks martial courage. If you send armed men from Lai to coerce the ruler of Lu, you will certainly get what you want." At the meeting, when the Marquis of Qi brought up the armed men for a war dance in an attempt to threaten the Lu ruler, Confucius had his duke withdraw from the meeting, and said to the Qi side:

> Our two lords have hitherto had good relations. But when armed captives from afar are used to throw the meeting into confusion, this is not the way for the lord of Qi to make good faith with other lords. . . . With respect to the spirits, such conduct is inauspicious. With regard to virtue/virtuosity, it is an offense against appropriateness. With regard to human affairs, it is a deviation from ritual propriety. I am sure your lord would certainly not endorse this.

Upon hearing this, the Marquis of Qi had to abandon his plan. Through his apt reminder of ritual propriety, Confucius single-handedly defeated Qi's plan to enlarge Qi at Lu's expense, shamed the Qi negotiation party, and consequently even restored Lu's lands of Yun, Huan, and Guiyin, previously annexed by Qi (see *Zuo Zhuan*, Duke Ding, Year 10. Legge, 776–77).

Confucius was not simply idealistic and optimistic. Litigation and the use of military force are often needed when things are not going well, but they tend to inflict ill feeling and animosity, a side effect hard to avoid even in the most fair court rulings and just wars. It is worth noting that in 1948, when P. C. Chang 张彭春, the Chinese delegate to the UN, and a distinguished Confucian scholar, recommended adding the Confucian clause that all men "should act towards one another in a spirit of brotherhood" to the *Universal Declaration of Human Rights*, he could not have expected to merely set a law that would guarantee all the "brothers" the basic rights to speak, to be fed, and so forth. The spirit of brotherhood requires a sense of caring, love, and respect, beyond the mere protection of a sibling's legal rights. When a person acts toward his brother in a legal but otherwise unkindly manner, there is nothing a legal authority can do. Confucius's teaching is thus still worth remembering: "Those today are considered filial because they are able to provide for their parents. But even dogs and horses are given that much care. If you do not respect your parents, what is the difference?" (2.7) The spirit of brotherhood cannot be enforced by any rule. It has to be inculcated by a moral force, which serves as a principled authority that demands deference rather than passive submission.

Confucius did not come up with the idea of democracy. His way of government is often called a *meritocracy*, meaning that the qualification of government officials is based on their merits, not on being elected by the people. At a time when nothing but inherited aristocracy was accepted, Confucius's saying that his disciple Yong 雍, who apparently had no royal family background, "could as ruler take his place facing south" (6.1), was a radical departure from the accepted norm. It virtually declares that everyone is equal, and that a ruler should be chosen according to his merits rather than his family lineage.

As meritocracy works on the basis of the merits of government officials rather than well-established procedures, the effectiveness of the government is largely built on the common people's confidence in the government. When Zigong asked the Master about governing, the Master says, "To have sufficient food, sufficient arms, and have the confidence (*xin* 信) of the common people." Zigong pushed further: "If you had to give up one of the three things, which should be given up first?" "Reduce the arms," says the Master. "If you had to give up the remaining two, which should be next?" "Reduce the production of food. Death has been with us from ancient times, but if common people do not have confidence, they will not endure" (12.7).

The idea of a meritocracy did not find an institutionalized way of application until the later Sui 隋 and the early Tang 唐 dynasties (ca. seventh century), when *keju* 科举, an imperial examination system through which able and virtuous men were selected and appointed, was established. During the most flourishing period of the Tang dynasty, the Imperial Academy of Learning, known as *Guozijian* 国子监, took ethics as the most important of all studies, and the total enrollment, including aspirants from Korea and Japan, was as high as eight thousand. Although the *keju* system had its fatal flaws— such as being purely based on literacy of the classics, and allowing little room for originality and creativity—it was better than most other systems that had prevailed previously, such as inheritance, nepotism, bribery, and so forth.

The idea behind the *keju* system, the Confucian idea of electing meritorious people to hold government offices, even served as a source of inspiration for modern democracy. In Europe, the birthplace of modern democracy, numerous Enlightenment philosophers, including Leibniz, Wolff, and Voltaire, used the name of Confucius to advocate for their ideas. They argued that under the influence of Confucianism, China had abandoned inherited aristocracy a long time ago. In America Thomas Jefferson proposed, as one of the cornerstones of the American government, an education system that shows remarkable similarities to the Chinese *keju* system (see Creel, 4–5). The father of the Chinese democracy movement, SUN Zhongshan 孙中山 (SUN Yat-sen), also said that "Confucius and Mencius are advocators of democracy" (SUN Zhongshan, 10).

Of course, a government *for* the people is not necessarily a government *of* the people and *by* the people. Confucianism falls short of coming up with the idea of a democratic system in which people do not have to rely solely on morally good rulers to offer them a good life, but will participate in politics and take up the responsibility of securing a good government for themselves. Critics of Confucianism often refer to a troubling passage in the *Analects*— "The common people can be made to follow a path, but not to know 民可使由之, 不可使知之" (8.9)—to illustrate that Confucianism is elitist and authoritarian in nature, treating people merely as beneficiaries and not as subjects themselves who have the right to know what the government does and to have their opinions heard.

Even though this interpretation makes sense—for, given the historical background, many people of the elite class at that time *did* think in this way—it is inconsistent with Confucius's philosophy of education. According to Confucius, everyone motivated to learn has the right to receive instruction. For this reason, the passage has been interpreted in a number of more sympathetic ways, one of which is to take it as saying that the sages can make the common people follow, as if the sages were a spiritual force that excites and motivates people invisibly. In a well-governed society, the common people should not feel the presence of their rulers when they plow the land to get their food, or when they dig a well to get their water. To let the common people know the presence of their ruler means that the ruler's way is still visible, and hence, not good enough (see Dai, 9).[2]

Many scholars have pointed out that there is nothing inherent in Confucianism that is opposed to democracy and human rights; to the contrary, its humanitarian spirit is fully in accord with them. The Confucian authority is not the authority of a particular ruling class, but the authority of the humanitarian spirit. This is well illustrated in Mencius's teaching that "the common people are of supreme importance; the altars to the gods of earth and grain come next; last comes the ruler" (*Mencius*, 7B:14). Furthermore, the Confucian notion of the embodied, relational, duty-bearing person allows each member of society to have a clear sense of mutual dependence on other people, and to develop a sense of caring for the interest of others.

In this regard, Confucianism is not only compatible with but also has valuable insights to offer the modern spirit of democracy and human rights. As Henry Rosemont Jr. says, the modern Western notion of the autonomous right-bearing individual is fundamentally flawed. "[Ninety-nine percent] of the time I can fully respect your first generation civil and political rights [the rights of speech, of religion, of a fair trial, etc.] simply by ignoring you. You certainly have a right to speak, but no right to make me listen" (Rosemont, 1998, 59). Without a Confucian communitarian notion of self, meaning, the self as a nexus of social relations, the practice of human rights could result in "excessive individualism, competitiveness, and vicious litigiousness" that "is not only endangering the well-being of others but also detrimental to our own wholesomeness" (Tu, 305). With the Confucian relational notion of personhood, we can reconstruct our notions of democracy and human rights as the right and duty of every member of the community to participate in public affairs and to take the public welfare of all the other members as one's own.

To Confucius, governing a state is no different from regulating a family. Families are small societies, and they are the basis on which the larger society is structured. On the other hand, society is an extended family. Confucius was not the first one who had this idea. The *Book of Odes* contains poems that call rulers "parents of the common people." Confucius's contribution is to rationalize the idea and make it a powerful basis for individual and social transformation. In a family, parents take care of their children, and children return the caring with respect for the parents' authority and deference to their sacrifice. A well-regulated society is similar. If one can be a good member of a family, one can be a good member of a larger community. If one can regulate a family well, one can rule a country well. When someone asked Confucius, "Why do you not actively search for a career in governing?" the Master replied, "The *Book of Documents* says, 'It is all in filial conduct (*xiao* 孝)! Just being filial to your parents and befriending your brothers is carrying out the work of government.' In so doing a person is also taking part in government. How can there be any question of my actively taking part in governing?" (2.21)

Clearly for Confucius, the democracy and human rights of a well-functioning society should be like the democracy and rights of a harmonious family, in which the rights of each member is respected, but one does not hear "This is my right!" often, and decisions are made with everyone's input considered, but not with everyone's opinions always counted with equal weight. Deference to moral excellence, reverence for elders (who have gained more rights by having had more life experience and by having contributed more to the family), and respect for reason will all play their roles in negotiating the final outcome. At different stages, the family will be conducted differently. When the children are small, good parents will provide more guidance for them rather than let them make big decisions. When the children grow up, parents will increasingly let them make their own decisions and listen more to their opinions. Finally, the ideal state is that every member of the family is able to live with a feeling of full participation and harmony, without the feeling of governing or being governed, or the feeling that they need to exercise their rights.

Names and Rituals as Political Devices

Once Zilu asked the Master, "Were the Lord of Wei to turn the administration of his state to you, what would be your first priority?"

Confucius replied, "Without question it would be to order names properly."

"Would you be as impractical as that?" responded Zilu, with a blunt manner. "What is it for names to be used properly anyway?"

"How can you be so rude!" replied Confucius. "An exemplary person defers on matters he does not understand. When names are not used properly, what is said will not be effective; when what is said is not effective, things cannot be accomplished" (13.3).

As explained in the last chapter, the Chinese tradition, which Confucius both inherited and shaped, takes naming as "illuminating." Names do not simply stand for their references; they also carry practical expectations, and are often inseparable from ritual propriety. Because the act of using a name is an affirmation of particular expectations, words carry a force that affects reality, and therefore proper use of names has enormous social and political implications.

For instance, a subject is expected to follow the ruler, and yet a student is supposed to follow the teacher, or anyone who is more virtuous. It is therefore politically significant to recognize teachers and those who are virtuous when they are at the same time also subjects. When Mencius was summoned to see King Xuan of Qi, he refused to go. He says,

> There are three things which are widely acknowledged in the world: rank, age, and virtue. At court, rank is supreme; in the village, age; but for assessing the world and ruling over the people it is virtue. How can a person who has one of these treat the other two with condescension? Hence a ruler who is to achieve great things must have subjects he does not summon. If he wants to consult with them, he goes to see them. (*Mencius*, 2B:2. See also 5B:7)

In this statement, Mencius is trying to limit the power of a ruler by emphasizing the "names" of teacher and virtuous person. Similarly, Xun Zi placed teacher together with heaven, earth, ruler, and parents as one of the most venerable beings that humans must honor (see *Xun Zi*, 19.2a). The *Book of Rites* also says that one of the cases in which a ruler does not treat a minister as a minister is when a minister is a teacher. "In the rituals of the Great Academy, even if a teacher is summoned by the Son of Heaven, he would not stand facing north [the position of an inferior]. This was the way in which teachers were honored" (*Li Ji*, Chapter 18, "Record on Learning." Legge, vol. ii, 88).

The Legalists, such as HAN FEI, on the other hand, aim at establishing the absolute superiority of the ruler, and hence downplayed the importance of teachers and worthy persons. In Chinese history, many political battles were fought for the recognition of being called "teacher" and "worthy person." One such example is the relationship between the powerful ruler Kublai Khan and his Tibetan tutor Phagpa during the Yuan dynasty. When Kublai asked Phagpa to serve as his spiritual tutor, Phagpa refused to do it unless the Khan would show deference to his superior religious stature. Kublai initially refused the condition, but eventually relented and agreed to sit on a throne lower than the lama during tutoring sessions, as long as the lama sat lower in all other settings. Phagpa's title of being a spiritual tutor, together with the ritual of being seated even higher than the Khan under the specific condition, consequently gained Tibetans a huge political advantage over the Han Chinese during the period.

It is said that when Confucius was editing the *Spring and Autumn Annals*, he paid special attention to the use of words. For instance, in the book there are different words for "killing." While *sha* 杀 is a neutral, general term for "killing," *shi* 弑 means "wrongful killing" (of a lord or parent), and *zhu* 诛 means "rightful killing." The words for battles are also differentiated into *qin* 侵 and *fan* 犯 for "unjustified invasion and attack," *fa* 伐 for "punitive expedition," and *zhan* 战 for "battle" in a general sense. By positioning the "names" in different places, Confucius imbedded moral judgments into an apparently simple record of history.

Confucius also rectified the terms *junzi* 君子 and *xiaoren* 小人. *Junzi* originally meant "prince," and *xiaoren* meant "ordinary person." Both of these terms were about social status, but Confucius transformed them into moral terms. In his vocabulary, *junzi* means "exemplary person," and *xiaoren* means "petty-minded person." Through this "rectification of names," Confucius practically launched a political reform. If an ordinary person is morally exemplary, this person will become as noble as a prince, and, if petty-minded, a prince can be a *xiaoren*!

Mencius understood and used this technique quite well. When King Xuan of Chi asked Mencius, "Is it true that Tang 汤 banished Jie 桀 and King Wu marched against Zhou 纣?"[3] "It is recorded," answered Mencius. "Is regicide permissible?" "A man who mutilates benevolence is a mutilator, while one who cripples rightness is a crippler. He who is both a mutilator and a crippler is an 'outcast.' I have indeed heard of the punishment of the 'outcast Zhou,' but I have not heard of any regicide" (*Mencius*, 1B:8). Through replacing "ruler" with "outcast," Mencius justified revolution against bad rulers.

Xun Zi summarized this insight well in a chapter entitled "Rectification of Names." He says,

> Now, since the sage kings are no more, the preservation of names is neglected, strange propositions have sprung up, names and their realities have become confused, and the boundary between right and wrong has become unclear. . . . Should a True King appear, he would certainly retain some old names but he would also have to invent new names. That being so, it is indispensable that he investigate the purpose for having names together with what is the basis for distinguishing the similar from the different and the crucial considerations for instituting names. (*Xun Zi*, 22.2a)

The significance of protecting names is a lesson that is also valuable to people today. Imagine what would happen if anyone could use the name of Harvard University on their education programs, or if any company could use a well-established brand name on their own products. Once there is infringement on name rights, the reputation and credibility associated with a name will be damaged. In politics, the name of an office is symbolic of its power. Confusion over a title bewilders the authority and responsibility associated with it. One notable recent example of the political manipulation of names is the "Rectification of Names" movement led by the Democratic Progressive Party in Taiwan, which aimed at replacing the word "China" with "Taiwan" in all the names that contained it. For example, "China Airline" was turned into "Taiwan Airline," "China Postal Service" became "Taiwan Postal Service." The political agenda behind the movement that pushes for the independence of Taiwan is obvious.

The use of names is closely connected to the observance of ritual proprieties, as the latter is dependent on the clarification of roles. In the *Zuo Zhuan* 左传, there is a record about the Lord of Wei granting ritual instruments and ornamental bridles to an outsider as gifts. On hearing of this, Confucius said,

> It is a pity. It would have been better to give him more cities. Ritual vessels and names alone cannot be loaned to others—they are what the ruler controls. Names are used to generate credibility, credibility is used to protect the ritual vessels, ritual vessels are used to embody ritual actions, ritual actions are used to enact appropriateness (*yi* 义), appropriateness is used to produce benefit, and benefit is used to bring peace to the people. These are the important measures for effecting sociopolitical order. To loan them to others is to give them control of the sociopolitical order. And when sociopolitical order is lost, that the state will follow is an inexorable fact. (*Zuo Zhuan*, Duke Cheng, Year 2. Legge, 344)

Though the world order today relies much less on ritual vessels, there are still ritual symbols that have enormous sociopolitical importance. A national flag, for instance, is not an ordinary piece of cloth; it is the symbol of sovereignty to which the dignity and credibility of a nation is attached. No nation would loan the full right of using its national flag to other nations or individuals. A piece of jewelry, once used as a symbol of engagement or marriage, becomes a ritual vessel also, and its value to its owner is no longer determined by its sale price. If we understand "ritual vessels" in a broader sense, many objects have ritual meanings. When Confucius's favorite disciple YAN Hui died, his father YAN Lu 颜路 asked Confucius for his carriage to provide an outer coffin for his son. Confucius replied, "Talented or not, a son is a son. My son, Boyu, also died, and I provided him with an inner coffin, but no outer coffin. I could not go on foot in order to give him one—in my capacity as a retired official, it is not appropriate for me to travel on foot" (11.8). Here in this passage, the carriage is clearly a "ritual vessel." It is not appropriate for Confucius to travel on foot because it would be disrespectful for the culture he represents. Similarly, when receiving a guest, the choice of hotel, restaurant, and seating position can all be ritually meaningful. It is disrespectful to set up a distinguished guest in an indecent hotel, or to put that guest in a seat lower than the host's. In court, the seat for the judge is usually higher than anyone else's, exactly because it signifies the authority of the judge.

Confucius is often portrayed as a conservative who wanted to restore the hierarchic order of antiquity at all cost. Critics often quote Confucius's lament about a ritual vessel, *gu* 觚, as evidence of how ludicrous was his rigid attachment to the tradition: "A *gu* is no longer like a *gu*. Oh, *gu*! Oh, *gu*!"[4] (6.25). Indeed, when a controversy arises within the Confucian tradition, this is what typically happens: Each side of the debate refers to what the ancient sages did or said. Opponents almost invariably are accused of deviating from a path laid down in antiquity. In a family, when a question of right and wrong arises, what the ancestors did also tends to be considered a source of authority or justification for its continuous validity. The tradition—the past—actually becomes the criterion of value. Related to the Confucian idea of immortality, keeping a tradition is more a matter of filial piety than the correctness of the tradition itself. The termination of a tradition implies terminating the "life" of the ancestors. Given that filial piety is the root of humanity (1.2), violating tradition becomes in itself immoral.

This remained largely true until the nineteenth-century invasion of Western powers, when liberation from the past took the form of breaking away from the Confucian authority and embracing Western Enlightenment ideas. However, the dogmatic adherence to whatever was done in the past should be attributed more to later interpretations of Confucianism than to the Master himself. Confucius did not simply admire past traditions and work to protect the existing social status quo. He chose the Zhou humanitarian culture and its tradition of ritual propriety because they are truly, in his view, what is good and right. He himself is innovative in rectifying the names of *junzi* and *xiaoren*, which is comparable to what Martin Luther King Jr. did in 1960s America against racial discrimination. His view—"Let a ruler be a ruler, a minister be a minister, a father be a father, and a son be a son" (12.11)—demands that the reality (the person) matches the name, not that a name should be kept by whoever happens to bear it. To use the words of Xun Zi,

Yet although a man is the descendant of a king, duke, prefect or officer, if he does not observe the rituals (*li*) and appropriateness (*yi*), he must be relegated to the common ranks; although he is the descendant of a commoner, if he has acquired learning, developed a good character, and is able to observe the rituals and appropriateness, then elevate him to be minister, prime minister, officer, or prefect. (*Xun Zi*, 9.1)

It is obvious that, according to Confucius, the best way to glorify one's ancestor is to become an exemplary person oneself, and not by sticking to whatever the ancestors did.

The Freedom of Needing No Choice

Since the authoritarian practices of those who dominated Chinese society and politics throughout China's long history were conducted largely under the name of Confucianism, Confucius has been misunderstood as a symbol of authoritarianism and paternalism, and his views have been thought to be opposed to personal freedom. Ritual propriety, for instance, was criticized as an "invisible rope" that not only limits a person's actions, but also a person's thoughts and feelings.

However, not only is the Master not against freedom, his idea of the freedom of cultivated spontaneity and social coordination can help us get deeper into the subject and appreciate a higher form of freedom.

In his famous autobiographical statement, Confucius says, "At the age of seventy, I could follow my heart's wishes without overstepping the boundaries" (2.4). Like a compressed computer file, this short statement contains a lot to be unpacked in order to fully appreciate what is inside.

Normally we consider freedom as either a state of having no constraints (the so-called "negative freedom," or "freedom from") or the ability to make choices (the freedom of the will, "positive freedom," or "freedom to"). But the above statement by Confucius reveals that, for Confucius, freedom does not mean the lack of any "lines" of conduct that serve to constrain what one can and cannot do, nor does it suggest the freedom to deliberate between alternatives and act freely on what one chooses. Confucian freedom is a cultivated spontaneity that frees one from making choices in the first place, because as a result of cultivation, one naturally knows the proper lines of action and has no inclination to overstep them! From this perspective, the "lines" of proper action mean no more than what "No smoking" signs mean to a non-smoker, or what surveillance cameras in a bank mean to those who have no intention of robbing the bank. Just as any decent human does not deliberate over whether or not to kick a child for fun, a well-cultivated person will have no need for deliberation in most cases (see Kupperman, 102–14).

This kind of freedom is not "freedom of indifference" (having no inclination toward anything), either. The so-called "freedom of indifference" is in fact not only impossible, since we are never totally free from inclinations, but even undesirable if it were possible. One who is totally indifferent to alternatives would be like Buridan's fully rational ass, which starved to death between two equally good piles of hay because it could not find a reason to go to one pile and not the other, or like a novice chess player who does not know what to do when faced with many available alternatives.

Of course, the freedom of cultivated spontaneity is not a natural state that people are simply born into and can enjoy without having to earn it, nor is it merely a matter of knowing all the relevant facts of a situation and making deliberate choices. One has to develop proper inclinations or dispositions, like learning *gongfu*, the acquiring and embodying of skills and dispositions. The fundamental Confucian *gongfu* for freedom is *ren* and ritual propriety. "Those who know are not perplexed," says Confucius. But that is not all. Confucius also says that one must be *ren* to be free from worries and courageous to be free from fear (9.29).

Though Confucius does not think that one should submit to whatever is imposed from the outside, he also does not believe that one should simply take for granted that one is entitled to making demands on external conditions as an autonomous choice maker. He says, "If one sets strict standards for oneself and makes allowances for others when making demands on them, one will stay clear of ill will" (15.15; see also 1.16, 4.17, 15.21 and 20.1). Confucius even describes *ren*, the central quality of an exemplary person, in part as the ability "to restrain oneself" (12.1).

When one is not cultivated to a certain level of maturity, the availability of alternatives could even pose a danger or threat. Certainly one can choose to walk with eyes closed, or choose to not follow traffic laws while driving, but by doing so, does one really achieve what might be called the freedom to walk or to drive? Does it not instead just get one injured or killed, making it impossible for one to ever walk or drive again? In general, before one can know and understand what is really good, the availability of some bad options can do no good for the person except to provide an opportunity to learn some painful lessons. Prior to reaching the stage of cultivated spontaneity, one needs to be constrained by "the line," and the line is a necessary guide for one to reach that stage.

For Confucius, freedom is also a sociopolitical matter, and not merely an issue about learning *gongfu*. In this regard, Confucianism also differs from modern Western Enlightenment ideas. For Confucius, the proper sociopolitical environment for personal freedom does not simply leave people alone to do whatever they like. Instead, it is an environment that provides community support. Just as water is a necessary condition for swimming, and proper adjustments of one's bodily movements in water increases one's freedom in it, adjusting one's relationships with others is a necessary condition for an individual to be free within a given social environment. For instance, those who have friends will have more help than those without, and in this sense, they are freer.

A person is so inseparable from others that one's domain of alternatives for choice is itself defined and transformed by her interaction with others. We can illustrate this point by comparing two stories. In French philosopher Jean-Paul Sartre's famous story about a student who came to him for advice, the student was in despair. He wanted to join the Resistance to fight against the Nazis, but he also had to take care of his mother, who was suffering from the half-treason of her husband and the death of her older son. Sartre tells us that nothing could help the student to make his decision. Ethical theories could not help, because he had to choose which theory to follow and how to interpret a theory in the given situation. Instincts or feelings could not help, because it was his decision and his final action that would give a feeling value, not the other way around. Other people could not help, because before others could offer him advice, he had to choose whom he should go to for advice; in that case, he already knew, more or less, what advice he was going to get. Sartre's answer to the student was: "You are free, choose, that is, invent" (see Sartre, 24–28). By using this example, Sartre wants to show the "forlornness" of a free individual, and to show that forlornness will inevitably be accompanied by feelings of anguish and despair.

Interestingly, there is a well-known Chinese story that parallels the Sartre story, yet the Chinese story leads to an opposite conclusion. Song dynasty Chinese general YUE Fei, whom we mentioned before, had a dilemma similar to Sartre's student's: He had to choose between either leading his army to fight against invaders, or staying at home to take care of his aged mother. The solution, however, was not his "invention." It came to him from his mother, who urged him so strongly to defend his country that she even tattooed four Chinese characters, *jinzhong baoguo* 精忠报国 ("to exert absolute loyalty and repay your country"), on his back. Her action dismissed YUE Fei's dilemma because, given her action, if he still chose to stay with her, he would be going against her will, and that would not be a way of caring for her.

The difference between the two stories is not that YUE Fei was simply lucky and the young man in Sartre's story unlucky, or that Chinese society and French society were fundamentally different. Neither YUE Fei nor Sartre's student was an isolated individual. Confucius would say that Sartre's response to his student was actually an action of *making* the student feel lonely and helpless. In both cases, the domain of alternatives for choice was affected by others. In YUE Fei's case, the dilemma disappeared when his mother intervened. But in Sartre's student's case, the dilemma was intensified when Sartre virtually pushed the student away.

It is with this understanding that Confucians take the selection of one's own residence and friends as a matter of vital importance, because both selecting a community in which to live and selecting people to befriend affect one's freedom, as well as one's self-cultivation. Confucius says, "In taking up one's residence, it is the presence of human-hearted (*ren*) persons in the neighborhood that is the greatest attraction" (see 4.1). Similarly, Confucius cautions people: "Do not seek friends from those who are not as good as you" (1.8, see also 9.25). One can tell a lot about a person by the crowd that the person spends time with. If you are around someone long enough, the person will affect the way you behave. This influence can be seen in subtle mannerisms and even in one's accent. By choosing those who are better than oneself as friends, one increases one's own chance of better-ing oneself. The point is not to be taken to mean that you should not *accept* a friend who is not as good as you, for if so, it would lead to the paradoxical conclusion that no one would ever befriend a person who is not deemed to be as good as oneself, and consequently, only those who are equally good could be friends. The point is rather that one should not actively *seek* those who are not as good as oneself to befriend.

Uprightness and Justice

Unlike Hammurabi's "eye for an eye and tooth for a tooth," or Jesus Christ's exhortation to turn the other cheek, Confucius repays ill will with *zhi* 直, "uprightness" or "straightforwardness," or, when taken as a verb, "to straighten," "to correct," or "to help grow." "If you repay ill will with kind-ness," says the Master, "then how would you repay kindness?" (14.34) In responding to Duke Ai of Lu's question about how to gain the allegiance of the people, Confucius said, "Raise up the upright (*zhi*) and place them over the crooked, and the allegiance of the people will be yours; raise up the crooked and place them over the upright, and the people will not be yours" (2.19). This proactive attitude of helping the wrongdoer to correct the wrong provides us with a thought-provoking alternative to retribution at the one extreme, and to "loving your enemy" by letting them continue to do harm at the other extreme.

Though the Confucian concept of *zhi* has a certain affinity with the no-tion of "being just," it cannot be directly translated as such. In fact, the way in which Confucius interprets *zhi* has triggered criticism that he lacks a sense of justice. In a conversation with Confucius, the governor of She said, "In my state there is a man called 'Upright (*zhi*) Body.' When his father stole a sheep, he bore witness against him." Confucius said, "In my state the upright men act differently. Fathers cover up for their sons and sons cover up for their fathers. Uprightness (*zhi*) is to be found in such behavior" (13.18). This story has led to a heated debate recently. There is no question that in the conversation, Confucius endorsed the mutual concealment of both father and son's wrongdoing. Does this mean that Confucius lacks an understanding of the concept of justice? Is he, like his critics say, holding consanguineous affection as the supreme principle, higher than anything else, including social justice?

One might say that in Western countries, it is also widely accepted that one should have the right to remain silent when facing a charge against oneself, or to refuse to offer evidence against the interest of one's own family members. But the practice in the West is based on the respect of individual rights and the careful demarcation between the public and the private, whereas the Confucian motivation for mutual concealment is for protecting filial piety, which is considered the root of *ren* (see 1.2). When asked about why Mo Zi's "love without discrimination" is not taken as *ren*, Ming dynasty Confucian WANG Yangming responds with this root metaphor:

> Take an example of a tree. Sprouting is where the tree starts to develop. Once it has a sprout, it begins to develop a stem, and then branches and leaves, one after another. If there were no sprout, how could it have stem, branches, and leaves? Having a sprout means that there is a root underneath. With the root, the tree can live; without it, the tree dies. . . . The love between father and son and between brothers is the place where the productivity of the human heart begins, just like the tree's beginning from a sprout. From there the love of humanity and the care for everything develops, like the tree's having branches and leaves. Mo Zi's love without discrimination treats one's own parents and brothers like treating strangers, and therefore its starting point is missing. Since there is no sprout, we know that it does not have a root, and hence will not be generative. (WANG Yangming, 27)

Here WANG Yangming does not say that Mo Zi's aim of universal love is morally bad in itself. He is saying that this kind of teaching lacks a *ben* 本, or root, for its growth. Confucian filial piety is the very sprouting of *ren*, or extended love. Since a society is an extended family, filial piety is the source of social justice rather than its rival principle. If one can be filial at home, seldom would one be disorderly in society (1.2).

Indeed, exploring homophones with the word *zhi*, we find characters that carry the meanings of "sowing" seed (*zhi* 植), "clay" (*zhi* 埴), "growing" or "cultivating" (*zhi* 殖), "planting" (*zhi* 植), "placing" or "setting up" (*zhi* 置), and so forth. Examination of these characters reveals that this family of words has an intimate relationship with establishing foundations, rooting, growth, and even potency. This observation provides another indication that, in of-fering his statement of mutual concealment, Confucius is taking filial piety as a way of rooting, laying a foundation, and developing the potency to grow.[5]

In other words, filial piety is fundamental and has priority in Confucian cultivation with regard to practical development of the person and the com-munal environment, and not in the sense of supremacy in a system of univer-sal moral principles or rules of conduct, or putting particular family affection above the universal principles of justice and honesty. It shows the Confu-cian practical wisdom of keeping the "root" of humanity at the cost of some "branches." The logic of "either/or" is not appropriate here, because accord-ing to Confucians, they are not upholding one and abandoning the other. The two sides of the dilemma are not conflicting universal principles, but practical difficulties in achieving ideal results in concrete action. Sacrificing some immediate objectives for securing the same objectives in the long run is very different from a simple choice of wanting one rather than the other. Confucius's endorsement of his fellow villagers' way of dealing with their own family members' misconduct by mutual concealment becomes a defense of injustice if we take it to be an ethical principle, but it becomes sacrific-ing a branch for the sake of saving the root when we treat it as a method of becoming *ren* and extending our love as broadly as possible.

The method of concealment for the benefit of one's own immediate family was accepted by rulers and served as the foundation of law in imperial China since the Han dynasty. But the followers of Confucius understood that there are limitations to the method. For instance, the Yonghui Code 永徽律 of the Tang dynasty stipulated that whoever reported to the authority the crimes committed by their own parents or grandparents would be hanged, except when the reported crime was treason or conspiracy against the empire (see Cao, 793). Obviously, it would be unwise to keep every bit of the root intact at the cost of endangering the entire tree.

Another limitation of the method is that when a family member is at the same time a government official, the duality of roles may require the person to act differently in different roles. A story in the *Zuo Zhuan* illustrates the point well: Lord Xing of Jin and Yongzi had a dispute about some lands of Chu, which remained unsettled after a long period of time. HAN Xuanzi ordered Shuyu to settle this old litigation. Yongzi was in the wrong, but he presented his daughter as a gift to Shuyu, who thereupon decided that Lord Xing was in the wrong. Enraged, Lord Xing killed both Shuyu and Yongzi. HAN Xuanzi consulted another official, Shuxiang, who happened to be Shuyu's brother. Shuxiang said, "The three were all equally guilty. . . . Yongzi knew that he was wrong, and gave a bribe to buy a verdict in his favor; Shuyu sold his judgment in the dispute by accepting bribery; and Lord Xing took it on him to kill them. Their crimes were equally heinous." Based on a historical record of the Xia dynasty, these crimes all deserve capital punishment. Shuxiang suggested that the one who is alive should be prosecuted, and the two that were dead should have their bodies disgraced by being exposed in the marketplace.

Upon hearing this, Confucius said, "The uprightness (*zhi*) of Shuxiang was that which was transmitted from antiquity. In the government of the state and determining the punishment, he concealed nothing in the case of his own relative. . . . He put his own brother to death and thereby increased what is glorious. Isn't this what appropriateness means?" (*Zuo Zhuan*, Duke Zhao, Year 14. Legge, 656)

The main difference between this case and the previous one, in which the son conceals his father's wrongdoing, is that, in the previous case, stealing a sheep is only a minor infraction, and the son is merely acting as a son, who has no official duty to bear witness against his father, whereas in the latter case, it is a matter of public administration, and Shuxiang was giving advice as a government official. Though it is hard to separate the roles when they are played by one and the same person, these cases at least give a clear indication that responsibilities are associated with specific roles rather than with abstract principles.

Regarding the difference between responsibilities and the power to exercise one's rights, Confucius clearly emphasizes the former, and grounds one's rights in one's responsibilities. According to *Xun Zi*, Confucius was once the minister of justice of Lu. During his tenure, there was a case of a father suing his son. Confucius detained the son but did not issue a verdict for three months. When the father requested to stop the proceedings, Confucius released the son. Upon hearing this, the head of the Ji family, Ji Sun, was displeased. He said, "This old man has deceived me! He told me that one must uphold filial piety to govern a state, and yet when he had the opportunity to prosecute a single man to deter unfilial conduct, he would not do it!" When Confucius's disciple RAN Qiu related this to Confucius, the Master sighed deeply and exclaimed, "Alas! Can you prosecute the subordinate if it were the superior's fault? To punish the common people who have not been educated is to kill the innocent. . . . Not having instructed the people, yet to require from them completion of allotted tasks, constitutes cruelty" (*Xun Zi*, 28.3).

Uprightness is a disposition of human agents displayed through their behavior. It is an art that needs to be cultivated and mastered rather than a principle that can be captured by rational formulation and simply remembered and applied. Sometimes simple uprightness may be in conflict with what is ritually appropriate and may lead to harmful results. In these cases it requires both creativity and sensitivity to the particularities of each situation. One example of such creativity is revealed in this story: Prince Kuaikui, the son of Duke Ling of Wei, fled to Jin after an unsuccessful attempt on the life of Nanzi 南子, the wife of his father, who was notorious for having multiple affairs with other men, including her husband's brother. When Kuaikui's son succeeded his grandfather, Prince Kuaikui, backed by the Jin army, installed himself in a border city, awaiting an opportunity to oust his son. Facing the situation of a father-son battle for power, Confucius's disciples were curious as to which side their Master would choose to support. Because they were visitors to the state, it was not fitting for them to discuss Wei's politics in a straightforward way, so Zigong, who was known for being a skillful speaker, asked the Master indirectly: "What sort of persons were Boyi and Shuqi?" The Master replied, "They were persons of good character from bygone days." "Did they harbor any ill will?" Zigong continued. "Seeking humanity in their conduct and having achieved it, why should they have any ill will?" Coming out from the interview, Zigong said, "The Master is not on the side of the son" (7.15). In the conversation, not a single word was spoken about Wei, and yet both sides knew what they were talking about. Boyi and Shuqi were sons of the Lord of Guzhu. When their father died, neither was willing to deprive the other of the succession to their father's position. By endorsing these two ancients, Confucius implicitly denounced the son who was fighting for the throne against his own father.

In this case, both Zigong and Confucius were upright; that is, they did not try to evade taking a stand on the issue, and yet they managed to display their uprightness in an artistic way that avoided harmful side effects. For Westerners, this kind of indirectness may seem to be the very opposite of being upright, because in their common understanding, being upright is simply being truthful. In his book *Chinese Characteristics*, Arthur Smith devoted a whole chapter to ridiculing the Chinese "talent for indirection." In Confucius's mind, however, being truthful without employing creativity and sensitivity to the particularities of the situation indicates a lack of civility and ability. As French sinologist François Jullien points out (see Jullien, 1995, chapter 1), the root of Smith's failure in appreciating the Chinese talent of indirection is that he does not understand the fact that when the Chinese use words, they are more concerned about how to deal with practical issues than merely trying to describe the truth. They use words to mobilize energies, to adjust relationships, or, to put it in general terms, to *do* things. In criticizing someone, for instance, indirectness—such as quoting history or poems—will make the criticism more acceptable, and thus more effective. This is why in Confucius's mind, a good politician must be conversant in history and poems, because even though they may not be straightforward presentations of reality, they are often the ideal way to convey important messages that affect reality.

Notes

1. Shun was an ancient sage king that Confucius revered greatly. "Facing due south" is a ritual position, as, according to ancient Chinese tradition, south is the direction in which the superior's seat should face.

2. Another interpretation, offered by KANG Youwei 康有为, stretches further. By using different punctuation in the sentence and taking the word *ke* 可 (can) to mean "capable," he renders the meaning to be "If the common people are fine [able to guide their own actions], then let them follow their own initiatives. If not, then educate them; help them to know what is right."

3. Tang and King Wu are founders of the Shang and Zhou dynasties, respectively, and Jie and Zhou are the tyrants that they overthrew. It happens that the name of the last tyrant king of the Shang dynasty and the name of the Zhou dynasty came out in identical romanization, though in Chinese, they are two different characters.

4. *Gu* 觚 is a horn-shaped drinking vessel with four vertical ridges distributed evenly around (usually at the lower part), used in ritual ceremonies. Its shape likely reflects the ancient Chinese belief that heaven is round and the earth is square, and hence the vessel could be symbolic to the connection between heaven (the round top) and earth (the four-ridged lower part). The ridges may also signify *dao* 道 (the Way), regulation, and integrity. The Master's lament is not just about a particular kind of vessel; it is about the widespread fact that traditional ritual proprieties were no longer preserved. Just like the name *gu* entails its shape and its specific role within a ritual, the names of social positions (such as ruler, subject, father, and son) imply their expectations. When realities do not match their names, the order that the names imply disappears.

5. I owe this point to Eric Colwell, a former graduate student of mine at the University of Hawaii.

CHAPTER V

~

Confucius as an Educator

In China, Confucius has been awarded the honorable title of "Supreme Sage Teacher." His birthday (September 28) was designated, quite appropriately, as "Teachers' Day." After all, it was due to Confucius's initiation, along with the efforts of his followers, that education became highly esteemed by the Chinese in the first place. Ironically, even though the Master has been honored as China's "Foremost Teacher," some of his basic ideas regarding education were neglected; his teachings were dogmatized, taken out of context, and turned into instruments for rigid control of young minds. During the early twentieth century, "Confucian education" even became a term substitutable for "outdated impractical indoctrination," and the term "Confucian" was considered somewhat synonymous with "bookworm." But this image is largely due to later followers' preoccupation with literacy in the Confucian classics, especially in the imperial examination system. Confucius's own way of education is quite different from the stereotypical connotations that were associated with it. It is significant that China is now setting up hundreds of "Confucius Institutions" around the world, indicating a renewed appreciation of the "Foremost Teacher"!

As a teacher, Confucius's influence on his students was certainly profound and far-reaching. The admiration and devotion of his students, which can only be matched by that felt for other great spiritual leaders of the world, such as Jesus Christ and Siddhartha Gautama the Buddha, is well displayed in Zigong's remarks about the Master. Once a man named Shushun Wushu said to other ministers at court that Zigong was better than Confucius. Upon hearing this, Zigong replied,

> To use the palace wall as an analogy: My wall is as high as shoulders over which one can peep at the attraction of the houses and homes. The Master's wall is many times higher. Without going through the gate, one cannot see the beauty of the ancestral temple or the splendor of the rich array of official buildings. However, only few can gain entry. Was not the remark of the Master [SHUSUN Wushu] no surprise? (19.23)

On a different occasion, another disciple of Confucius said to Zigong, "You are only being respectful—how could Confucius be superior in character to you?" Zigong replied,

> Exemplary persons must be ever so careful about what they say. On the strength of a word others can deem them either wise or foolish. The Master cannot be matched just as a ladder cannot be used to climb the sky. Were he to have become a head of state or of a clan, it would have illustrated the saying: He helps someone to stand and the person will stand; he gives someone guidance and the person will go forward; he wants to make peace to someone and the person will turn to him; he sets a person to tasks and the person will work in harmony. In life, he is honored, and in death he is mourned. How could anyone be his match? (19.25)

After the Master died, his disciples mourned him by living next to his grave for three years. After the three-year mourning period had elapsed, "they went in and bowed to Zigong and, facing one another, they wept until they lost their voices before setting out for home. Zigong went back to build a hut in the burial grounds and remained there on his own for another three years before going home" (*Mencius*, 3A:4). It sounds like a miracle that these men, mostly young and at the active stage of their own career, would spend three or more years of their lives doing nothing but serving at the graveyard, like a living sacrifice, for a man who was not their parent, not a god, and not even a person with a high social stature. But as Creel observes, after the Master died, most of his disciples suddenly disappeared from the historical records in the *Zuo Zhuan* for years. This fact suggests that the miracle did indeed happen (see Creel, 55).

What kind of education did the Master offer that earned him such high esteem from his disciples?

The Kind of Education

Before Confucius, education in China was mainly conducted through private tutoring. Students, usually sons of nobles, were prospective rulers or officials. Since this kind of education was designed mainly for securing social and political powers, teachers were typically themselves government officials. In addition, there were also probably schools for specific training, such as for archery, and apprenticeships for various kinds of crafts.

The education offered by Confucius was different from the education that existed before him. Acting as a private and independent teacher, he accepted students of all social classes. The aim of his education was still practically oriented, but in a different sense. Confucius's form of education focused on transforming people so as to become better persons who could lead good lives and contribute to the making of a better society for all.

The most significant Confucian principle of education is that, "In instruction, there is no classification of people" (15.39). The progressive nature of this principle during his time is all the more remarkable when we contrast it with the fact that even today, the world is still fighting against various kinds of discrimination; the horrendous Holocaust in the last century was led by one of the most developed nations in Europe, and it was just a few decades ago when Martin Luther King Jr. was awarded the Nobel Peace Prize for fighting against racial discrimination, and he was assassinated in the United States for the same cause.

The principle of nondiscrimination was well implemented by the Master himself. Among his students, there were people like Mengyizi 孟懿子, a member of the "Three Families" in Lu, and SIMA Niu, a noble from the state of Song, who was even given a town by the State of Qi as his fief when he went there in exile (See *Zuo Zhuan*, Duke Ai, Year 14). There were also those from *jianmin* 贱民, "the lowest class," like RAN Yong 冉雍 and Zizhang. There were successful businessmen like Zigong, and men like YAN Hui and his father YAN Lu, who were always in dire straits (11.19). There were those from the northern states, like Zixia of Wei, and Zizhang from Chen, and people from the south, like Ziyou 子游, from the state of Wu.

There were also huge age discrepancies among his students, from those who were more than fifty years younger than Confucius, such as SHUZHONG Hui 叔仲会 and GONGSUN Long 公孙龙,[1] to the oldest ones like QIN Shang 秦商, who was only four years younger than the Master, and Zilu, who was nine years younger. There were people in attendance with the Master regularly, among them lifelong followers, such as YAN Hui and RAN Boniu 冉伯牛, and others who would come and go, alternating between studying and taking jobs or doing both at the same time, such as Zixia, Ziyou, Zigong, and RAN Qiu.

There were also those who were not considered the Master's students, but would consult the Master occasionally when they had specific questions. Among the latter were rulers of state, government officials, and even simple peasants (*befu* 鄙夫). When someone asked, "How come the people at your Master's gate are so varied in kind?" Zigong replied, "An exemplary person anticipates others with one's own person rectified. He does not reject those who want to come, nor does he stop those who want to leave. Furthermore, just as there are more sick people at the gate of a good physician, and there is more crooked wood beside the press-frame, this is the reason for having all varieties of people" (*Xun Zi*, 30.6).

Confucius treated students differently according to their need for instruction, but not according to their social status. He was kind to SIMA Niu because his life was not happy, but the Master never gave him special treatment because he was a noble. Confucius appreciated Zigong's talent and wisdom and recommended him to the Ji family, but the Master would not refrain from puncturing his aplomb because of his great success in business (see 14.29). He even openly disowned RAN Qiu as a disciple when RAN Qiu helped the Ji family to collect oppressive taxation, regardless of the high position RAN Qiu held. The Master's favorite disciple was YAN Hui, the most impoverished of them all, who had never held any official position.

The education Confucius provided was not aimed at offering specialized skills to make a living. When FAN Chi 樊迟 came to him, asking for instruction regarding how to grow crops, the Master said, "A farmer would serve you better." When FAN Chi asked to be taught how to grow vegetables, the Master said, "A vegetable grower would serve you better" (13.4). This passage is often quoted by Confucius's critics, accusing him of looking down on the practical knowledge of material production. The point, however, is that Confucius offered what we would call "liberal arts education" rather than "professional training." The aim of liberal arts education is transformation of the person. It seeks to make the person a well-rounded, exemplary human being, able to lead a good life and contribute to the bettering of society. While acquiring practical knowledge and skills of material production has its own value, learning to become a better person overall is considered far more fundamental.

To Confucius, educated persons, *shi* 士, should exemplify some basic form of civility. They should set their purpose on pursuing the Way (*dao*), and not indulging in material comforts (4.9, 8.7, 14.2). Good *shi* should conduct themselves with a sense of shame, able to carry out a mission without disgracing their lord. Their families and fellow villagers would praise them for their filial conduct and for being deferential to their elders (13.20). They are critical and demanding, and yet amicable (13.28). From these descriptions we might say that Confucius did a "rectification of name" on *shi* just like he did for *junzi* (exemplary person) and *xiaoren* (petty-minded person). He turned what was a name of social status to a name of moral quality.

If becoming a *shi* is the minimum accomplishment of getting an education, a higher aim is to become a *junzi*, an exemplary person. A *junzi* is not merely a vessel to be used only for a special purpose (2.12). Farmers, traders, artisans, politicians, and logicians may all possess their own abilities in their special areas of expertise, but they should all primarily aim at becoming a *junzi*. In contrast to a *xiaoren*, petty-minded person, who is motivated by what is profitable, a *junzi* is motivated by what is appropriate (4.16). Confucius said, "Exemplary persons seek for the Way and not for making a living. While tilling the land often leads to hunger, studying would naturally lead to an income. Exemplary persons are concerned about the Way, and not about poverty" (15.32). This is not saying that it is unimportant to make a living, or that the Master does not want to eliminate poverty. The point is rather that becoming an exemplary person is more important, and ultimately, it is also a way to eliminate poverty.

The most important quality of a *junzi* is certainly *ren*, human-heartedness. The Master says, "Wherein do the exemplary persons warrant this name if they forsake *ren*? They do not deviate from *ren* even for the space of a meal" (4.5). Meanwhile, exemplary persons also refine themselves with ritual propriety. Only a well-balanced admixture of human-heartedness as the basic substance and ritual propriety as the refined form will result in exemplary persons (6.18). With these basic qualities, exemplary persons will be calm and unperturbed, but not arrogant, whereas those who are petty-minded will always be agitated, anxious, and conceited (7.37, 13.26).

When looking inside of their heart-mind, exemplary persons will find nothing to be ashamed of, and therefore will not be worried or apprehensive (12.4). They wish to cultivate themselves to such a refined degree that "by maintaining a dignified demeanor, they keep violent and ruthless conduct at a distance; by having a proper facial expression, they keep trust and confidence close; by speaking in proper tones and words, they keep coarseness and impropriety away from them" (8.4). In dealing with others, they seek harmony but not conformity (13.23). They are conscious of their own value but not contentious, and they get along with others but do not form cliques (15.22).

Always making a high demand on themselves but lenient on others, exemplary persons never demand all-around perfection in any single person (15.15, 15.21, 18.10). They "do not promote others because of what they say, nor do they reject what is said because of who says it" (15.23). When they make mistakes, they are not afraid of admitting and correcting themselves. Like the eclipse of the sun and the moon, when exemplary persons stray, everyone sees it, and when they correct their course, everyone looks up to them (1.8, 19.21). They love learning and having their names established through their diligent actions rather than through empty words (2.13, 1.14, 15.20). When others do not acknowledge them, they do not harbor frustration (1.1). They focus on doing what deserves to be acknowledged and on giving proper acknowledgment to others (4.14, 1.16).

Exemplary persons also have things that they detest: "They detest those who enjoy revealing others' problems; they detest those who dwell in low positions but slander those who try to reach high positions; they detest those who are bold but disregard ritual propriety; and they detest those who are unrelenting in getting what they resolve to attain" (17.24). The things they detest are all characteristic of petty-minded persons.

Once, when YAN Hui asked about petty-minded persons, the Master replied that they are those who "take denouncing others' goodness as his eloquence, take deceiving others as his wit, take others' mistakes as a source of his pleasure, look down on learning, and humiliate those who are disabled" (*Kong Zi Jiayu*, 5.18). In contrast to the petty-minded, "in seeing his own lack of ability, an exemplary person respects others, whereas a petty person would distrust others. That is why an exemplary person is able to extend others' merits, whereas a petty person goes above others by belittling them" (*Kong Zi Jiayu*, 5.19).

The difference between the attitudes of *junzi* and *xiaoren* results in entirely different judgments about one's own experience. It is said that Confucius's own nephew KONG Mie 孔篾 and his disciple FU Zijian 宓子贱 were both holding office at the same place. When Confucius passed the place, he asked KONG Mie, "What did you gain and what did you lose since you took the office?" KONG Mie replied, "I gained nothing but lost three things. The official business has been so busy that I had no time for practicing what I studied, hence my learning is not progressing; my income is so low that I had no extra for benefiting my relatives, hence my relatives are distancing themselves from me; and the official business is always so pressing that I had to miss funerals and was not able to visit the ill, hence I lost friends."

Confucius was upset. He went to ask FU Zijian the same question. FU Zijian replied, "I lost nothing but gained three things since I took the office. I have been able to practice what I read before, hence my learning is progressing; I am able to use my income to help my relatives, hence my relationship with them is closer; though I had official business to take care of, yet I was still able to attend funerals and pay visits to the ill, and hence I have more solid friendships." Confucius sighed, "This is what an exemplary person is like!" (*Kong Zi Jiayu*, 5.19)

While everyone should strive to become *junzi*, the highest perfection of learning is to become a *shengren* 圣人, or sage. Confucius himself humbly said that he dared not rank himself as a sage (7.34), and lamented that he had never seen one (7.26). The Master seems to have viewed "sage" as a stage of perfection that only very few have ever reached, such as Yao, Shun, Yu, King Wen, King Wu, and the Duke of Zhou. They are the founders of the culture that Confucius inherited and determined to manifest. It was Mencius and other later Confucians who honored Confucius as The Supreme Sage who encompassed all the virtues of the ancient sages.

While each sage may have his own personal style, what makes a sage greater than a *junzi* are these basic characteristics: First, as Mencius characterized, a sage is one who is "great and transformative" (*Mencius*, 7B:25). The greatness of a sage is notably in the manifestation of virtues/virtuosities and in consequently transforming others and society. This is what a *junzi* should strive for. Secondly, as Zixia said, a sage is one who "walks the path every step from start to finish" (19.12). The determination of a sage may sound like the relentlessness of a *xiaoren*, but a sage's determination is the persistence to cultivate oneself along with consistently manifesting exemplary conduct, rather than relentlessly trying to get whatever one wants for oneself, and it is made possible by flexibility and caring for others. Finally, a sage is one who can "follow his heart's will without overstepping the lines" (2.4). A sage has the ability to see the significance of common life, and to be appropriate and yet at ease all the time in dealing with everything from the most daily routines to matters of vital importance.

From aiming at becoming a qualified *shi* to becoming a *junzi*, and then to becoming a sage, the purpose of Confucian education is to transform the person. The Master said, "People of antiquity studied to improve themselves; people today study to impress others" (14.24). The saying makes it clear that Confucian learning is not merely about trying to make people altruistic; it is fundamentally designed to benefit the learners themselves. It is said that once Duke Ai of Lu asked Confucius, "I heard that the most forgetful person in the world was the one who, in moving to a new residence, forgot to bring his wife with him. Is that so?" Confucius said:

This is not the most forgetful yet. The most forgetful person even forgot himself. In the past Jie was so high in status that he was the King of Xia dynasty, and was so rich that all within the Four Seas was his. However, he forgot the way of his sage ancestors, corrupted their regulations, abandoned traditional ceremonies, indulged himself in lust and pleasure, intoxicated himself in alcohol, allowed his mind [to] be manipulated by bad subjects, and yet those who were truly loyal to the kingdom were afraid of speaking up and had to flee to avoid prosecution. Consequently the whole world rose up to have him killed and took over his kingdom. This is the extreme case of forgetfulness. (*Kong Zi Jiayu*, 3.13)

To use contemporary European philosopher Jacques Derrida's word, *différance*, a word that plays on the fact that the French word *différer* means both "to defer" and "to differ," the Confucian understanding of a person is that one is different from others, and yet one's own well-being is dependent on and defers to one's way of relating to others. In consummating oneself, one consummates others; and it is only in consummating others that one can truly consummate oneself.

Though becoming a sage is a lofty ideal, both Mencius and Xun Zi said that everyone could become a sage. The whole process of cultivating oneself toward this goal is supposed to begin in early childhood and never end until one dies.

The Six Arts

There have been different descriptions about the subjects that Confucius taught. One is that his education program consists of the Six Arts: ritual propriety, music, archery, charioteering, writing, and arithmetic. Another description is that he taught six classics: the *Book of Odes*, the *Book of Historical Documents*, the *Book of Rites*, the *Book of Changes*, the *Spring and Autumn Annals*, and the *Book of Music*. Since neither of these two lists is mentioned in the *Analects*, we have reason to believe that they were later constructions in order to make the Master's curriculum look systematic. However, these two accounts at least give us a rough sense of the main subject matters that Confucius taught.

Looking at the lists today, what impresses people the most is probably the prominent place of ritual propriety and music. Ritual propriety hardly has any place in today's education, and it is often considered a matter of trivial formality, whereas music is basically taken as a matter of art, merely for the sake of entertainment. But for Confucius, they are of vital importance to both personal cultivation and social harmony. The Master says, "In referring time and again to ritual propriety, how could I just be talking about the presence of jade and silk? And in referring time and again to music, how could I

just be talking about bells and drums?" (17.11) Humans are like raw materials—they need to be carved, chiseled, ground, and polished (1.15), and ritual
propriety and music are two main ways of accomplishing such a process.

By practicing ritual propriety, a person can be transformed and established
(8.8). Most people learn basic moral lessons at a young age, but not by studying abstract moral theories, like Kantian formulations of categorical imperative or utilitarian calculations. One learns basic morals by being taught to use
rituals, such as saying "Thank you" when receiving a gift, and saying "I am
sorry" when someone is hurt. These practices increase one's sense of appreciation for others' kindness, and they make people more sensitive to others'
pain. Through the process of learning to use rituals, one not only learns *what*
is expressive of humanity, but also *becomes* a better person.

By acquiring a disposition to behave appropriately in various situations,
from basic mannerisms such as the way to stand, sit, walk, and eat, to skills of
rather complicated ceremonies and intricate interpersonal dealings, a person
displays a lifestyle that is at ease, with physical grace—a style that is both
aesthetically pleasing and morally commanding. As Joel Kupperman points
out, mainstream Western ethical theories have long neglected this important
dimension until Nietzsche brought it back to people's attention (see Kupperman, 26–35). A person who makes all the right ethical decisions may nevertheless still live a miserable life if the person's choices only come from the
dictation of moral reason, and not naturally from ingrained self-cultivation.
Furthermore, style is not merely a matter of decision-making. Take playing
basketball, for example: If one has not had training and does not regularly
practice, conscious decisions from the brain alone will not make one a great
basketball player. Similarly, merely knowing that one should treat others
kindly does not imply that the person knows how. Only from this perspective can we understand and appreciate the passages in the *Analects* that give
detailed accounts of how the Master greeted his guests, dressed himself, ate,
sat, and so forth. The subtlety and complexity of coordinated ritual acts are
certainly beyond what can be encapsulated in any abstract principles.

If ritual propriety sets standards for human behavior and disciplines the
body, good music promotes harmony within and between human beings
(see *Li Ji*, chapter 19). The Chinese word 乐 has two basic meanings. When
pronounced as *yue*, it stands for music, dance, songs, and even painting,
sculpture, architecture, and so forth (see Guo Moluo, 5–6), and when pronounced as *le* or *luo*, it means joy. There is no question that "*Yue* is *luo*" (*Xun
Zi*, 20.1), but music is understood by Confucius far beyond merely a means of
entertainment. For Confucius it is no less than a means of building civilized
persons and harmonious social relations.

The Master's taste in music was entirely in accord with his vision of appropriateness and what would be best for the nourishment of the human person and a harmonious society. His comment on the song "The Cry of the Osprey," for instance, was that it was "pleasing without being excessive, mournful without being injurious" (3.20). The Master advised the people to "cast off the songs of Zheng," for "the songs of Zheng are licentious" (15.11). While good music purifies one's heart-mind and harmonizes relationships, bad music corrupts the soul. Thus, a well-cultivated person has good taste in music.

In Chinese, the word for "sage," *sheng* 圣, has a part that means ear, related to its cognate *ting* 听, to hear, or to listen to. The radical for ear further associates *sheng* with *cong* 聪, "keenness of hearing." Hall and Ames note, the fact "that 'sage' was perceived as acutely aural is an inescapable consequence of its etymology" (Hall & Ames, 257). Interestingly, as they also mention, the traditional Chinese representation of the sage was a person with large, pendant ears. Confucius also put "having my ear attuned" (2.4) as an important landmark in his lifelong cultivation. "Throughout the classics, the sage is portrayed as the premier musicologist: one who can listen to music and discern in it the original details and quality of an age and its culture" (Hall and Ames, 258).

The *Guodian Bamboo Script* (excavated in 1993), a work dated to at least around 300 BCE, summarizes the Confucian view of the importance of music for personal cultivation:

> If one is not keen in hearing, one is not clear-minded; if one is not sagely, one does not have wisdom. If one does not have wisdom, one cannot be *ren* (human-hearted); if one is not *ren*, one's mind will not be peaceful; if one's heart-mind is not peaceful, one will not have joy, and if one does not have joy, one does not have excellence (*de*). (Chapter "Wu Xing," Wei, 17)

In other words, hearing, clarity of the mind, sageliness, wisdom, human-heartedness, a peaceful heart-mind, true enjoyment, and excellence are all conditionally related.

Not only can good music help personal cultivation, but it can also bring about social harmony. When YAN Hui asked about a viable state, one of the things the Master mentioned was the music of *Shao* 韶 and *Wu* 武 (15.11). His comment on *Shao* and *Wu* is that the former was both superbly beautiful and superbly good, and the latter was superbly beautiful, but not equally good (3.25). The difference was that *Shao* praised the ancient sage kings, Yao and Shun, who ruled the kingdom by their moral excellence, while

Wu praised King Wu's accomplishment of using military force to conquer a corrupted regime; although the king's cause was just, the means for achieving it was violent.

> The music of a well governed society is peaceful and pleasant, with it the state is harmonious; the music of a chaotic society is resentful and angry, with it the state is troublesome; the music of a declining society is gloomy and yearning, with it the people are frustrated. The way of music is connected with the way of government. (*Li Ji*, chapter 19. See Legge 1964, vol. II, 93–94)

It is strange that in modern culture, where music has reached a very sophisticated level of complexity, little attention is given to its deep moral and social implications. The confusion between one's political right to hold different opinions and the goodness of an opinion itself seems to have affected people's attitude toward music, as if criticizing a certain kind of music is the same as violating someone's political right to play the music. The obvious fact that music affects the emotions and thoughts of people is largely ignored, except for a small number of psychiatrists who experiment with the use of music as a treatment for mental illness. The tradition of using music as a way of cultivation and meditation to reach a high level of spirituality and social harmony is lost in most "developed" parts of the world.

The art of writing, *shu* 书, entails learning the art of calligraphy—the art of writing Chinese words (called "characters")—as well as the composition of statements and articles. The *Analects* does not contain any record of instructions related to these subjects, except that in composition of verbal expressions, Confucius appreciates accuracy and hates glib talk (15.41, 1.3). It is evident that for the Master, eloquence should be carried by uprightness and appropriateness, not by flowery words.

While little needs to be said about how elementary it is to learn Chinese characters and to be able to compose written statements, some explanation is necessary in order to understand the inclusion of calligraphy in the Six Arts. Just as how the way one stands, sits, and moves around will display a person's manner and personality, calligraphy will also indicate a person's level of cultivation. How one writes sometimes speaks as much about the person as what one writes about. Along with choice of words, sentence construction, and organization of ideas, brushstrokes, the structure of written characters, and the way blank space is distributed in one's handwriting all contribute to the overall meaning of the written work.

A good example of calligraphy with Confucian characteristics is found in the work of Tang dynasty calligrapher YAN Zhenqing 颜真卿 (709–785).

His strokes are always confident and full of energy. When they are thick, they look strong but not swollen, and when they are slim, they look elegant but not weak. Looking at the characters, one can detect that the motion of the brush is rhythmic. Moving fast, it does not appear slick; moving slowly, it does not become static. The structures of the characters are usually stable and solid. They may look a little off the proper balance individually, but as a whole they relate to each other in harmony without losing their dynamics. Through his work one can almost see YAN Zhenqing in action. Entailed in every movement of the brush is subtle and yet clear demonstration of his person. Modeling his calligraphy is just like imitating him; in the process, one not only learns *about* the person, but is also influenced—perhaps even directly transformed—by the model. This is why Chinese people traditionally took the practice of calligraphy seriously, and cautiously selected which model to follow. It also explains why it was a norm rather than an exception that Confucian literati throughout Chinese history have been accomplished calligraphy artists as well.

The arts of archery and charioteering are more like sports, yet they are not without moral implications. An archer is supposed to ascend with proper greeting to others and descend gracefully, and whether having hit the target or not, drinking a salute to those who did. "Even in contesting, they are exemplary persons" (3.7). "A person of *ren* is like an archer," says Mencius. "One first rectifies oneself before he shoots, and if he fails to hit the mark, he does not hold it against his victor. He simply seeks the cause within himself" (*Mencius*, 2A:7). The *Book of Rites* tells us that in ancient times, kings even selected people to fill official positions through archery competitions (*Li Ji*, chapter 46). Similarly, in addition to physical skills of coordination and instantaneous reaction to changing road conditions, charioteering also requires a proper manner of driving as well. An educated person should not fight against others for a better road (see *Li Ji*, chapter 41).

Of the Six Arts, arithmetic has the least to do with morality and character building, but through training in quickness and precision, it also refines the person. Furthermore, if we consider the possibility that the word we rendered as "arithmetic" here, *shu* 数, may refer to all the arts related to numbers in general, including astronomical study, divination, and calendar making, then it becomes a matter of attuning human life according to the cosmic rhythm, which is certainly a vital part of Confucian cultivation, as well as its social order.[2]

Among the Six Classics, the one mentioned most frequently by the Master is the *Odes*. The Master says to his students:

My young friends, why don't you study the *Odes*? The *Odes* can stimulate imagination, strengthen your powers of observation, enhance your ability to get on with others, and give expression to your aversion. Close at hand it enables you to serve your father, and away at court it enables you to serve your lord. It instills in you a broad vocabulary of the names of birds, beasts, plants, and trees. (17.9)

Once when the Master was standing alone in the courtyard, his son, Boyu, tried to pass by quickly but was stopped by his father. "Have you been studying the *Odes*?" Boyu replied, "Not yet." "If you do not study the *Odes*, you will be at a loss as to what to say," said his father (16.13).

The point is quite clear that studying the *Odes* increases one's overall literacy, which is of vital importance to a well-educated person. But being literate is much more than simply knowing some words or expressions. It also involves the ability to be sensitive in observation. For instance, Zixia asked the Master, "What does it [the song in the *Odes*] mean when it says:

> Her smiling cheeks—so radiant,
> Her dazzling eyes—so sharp and clear,
> It is the unadorned that enhances color?

The Master replied: "The application of color is to the unadorned." "Does this mean that ritual propriety comes after?" asked Zixia. The Master replied: "Zixia, you elaborated my thoughts. It is only with the likes of you that one can discuss the *Odes*" (3.8).

Here the *Odes* is used as a source of inspiration: Just as colors must be applied to what is unadorned, in turn bringing out the beauty inherent in the unadorned, ritual propriety is based on human-heartedness (*ren*) and appropriateness (*yi*), in turn, actualizing them and making their beauty and value apparent. By learning the *Odes*, one learns how to draw lessons everywhere.

Furthermore, the *Odes* is also a rich resource of proper expressions. If one recalls our previous discussion about uprightness, one should remember the point that for Confucius, maintaining uprightness often requires exactly the "indirectness" that can mobilize the "energy" of words to get the message through smoothly, in ways that are more appropriate and effective. In this regard, the *Odes* is truly exemplary. For instance, the most well-known song in the Odes, "*Guanjü* 关雎," manages to use some simple imagery to express feelings that are "pleasing without being excessive, mournful without being injurious" (3.20). By studying it, one learns not only how to express oneself, but also how to transform one's feelings at the same time.

The difference between the feelings before and after they are transformed by the proper expressions is somewhat akin to the difference between lust and what Plato calls "*eros*": The former is purely physical, animal-like, while the latter is both physical and spiritual, and truly human. The expression affects both oneself and the audience, and creates a resonance that transforms their relationships as well. This is why the Master says to his son that, not having studied the *Odes*, it would be like standing in front of a wall, unable to take a single step forward (17.10). This is also why he gives priority to the importance of studying this classic, ordering a person's progression in learning as follows: "Be stimulated by the *Odes*, established by ritual propriety, and be perfected by music" (8.8).

Because Confucius put the *Odes* in such a prominent place in his education program, frequently quoting the *Odes* to make his points, a tradition of quoting the *Odes* to legitimize a point was firmly established. Indeed, a Chinese idiom for someone who always quotes authorities is a person who always has *ziyue shiyun* 子曰诗云, "The Master said, the *Odes* said," in one's speech. It was through Confucius's editorial work and frequent citation and interpretation of the *Odes* that the book became part of the Confucian canon.

One interesting piece of evidence for this is that the Master famously said, "Although the *Odes* are three hundred in number, they can be covered in one expression: 'Think without deviation' " (2.2). The line "Think without deviation" is a deliberate stretch of meaning from the original song "*Lu Song, Jiong* 鲁颂駉" in the *Odes*, in which the line means actually nothing but "Oh, let [the horses] be safe and sound." Playing with the ambiguity of the original words, this out-of-context stretch of meaning indicates a creative use of the original text to infuse moral significance, which is characteristic of Confucian aesthetics.

Similarly, Confucius's approach to history, which is the subject of two of the Six Classics, the *Book of Historical Documents* and the *Spring and Autumn Annals*, and his appreciation of the *Book of Changes*, is also pragmatic in the sense that they help the transformation of the person and the establishment of a better society. He is less interested in knowing hard historical facts or methods of divination than in learning moral lessons from the history and in imbedding moral judgments in it. Studying the history books is therefore not just memorizing what happened, but, more importantly, to read the moral messages and learn how to properly describe historical events.

An apparent omission in Confucius's education program is the natural sciences. While Confucius felt close to nature, he never displayed any interest in dispassionate, objective analysis of the natural world, as is fundamental to modern science. Among the Six Classics, the one closest to the study of natural science is the *Book of Changes*. The Master had allegedly read the book so many times that the bamboo strips fell apart three times. But as we have explained in chapter 2, his interest in the book was primarily on the messages about virtuous power and appropriateness. The Master's remarks about nature are without exception objectifications of his moral and aesthetic sentiments and virtues. As Xu Fuguan points out, the names of plants and animals in the three hundred *Odes* are expressions of sentiments and virtues of the poets, not botany or zoology. Western science interprets the human being as part of nature; Confucius interprets nature in terms of the human—an interesting contrast that takes us back to what Xu said about the origin of the two cultures, one from a sense of curiosity (and hence, the preoccupation with objective knowledge), and the other from a sense of anxiety (and hence, the preoccupation with ways of life and moral responsibility) (see Xu, 20–22).

Even though the Confucian spirit does not have a distinct scientific dimension, that does not mean it is against science; rather, given the aim of the Confucian tradition, the methodology that it requires is different. Confucius aimed at the cultivation of the human, the manifestation of virtuosity, and the creation of harmonious society. That is why the selection of plum, orchid, bamboo, and chrysanthemum as representatives of the four seasons reflects more moral ideals than features of the natural world: with plum, the endurance in harsh cold weather and the ability to stand alone; with orchid, the elegance and gentleness rather than competing colors; with bamboo, the emptiness of heart (being humble and willing to learn) and integrity (as the Chinese word for integrity *jie* 节 means also "joint"); and with chrysanthemum, the patience of blossoming late.

Although Confucius never really delved into natural sciences, much less taught his disciples on the subject, the holistic and correlative way of thinking that was prevalent in Chinese philosophy, including Confucius's teachings, has led to remarkable achievements and insights about how the universe (including our own body) functions. It is best exemplified in traditional Chinese medicine. Confucius's own observation about the connection between *ren* and longevity (6.23) and his followers' contribution to Chinese medicine and Chinese theories of health are indications that Confucianism may have a more profound understanding of how the natural world functions than modern medical science does, even though the latter is indisputably much more advanced in detailed local areas. The most remarkable feature of the Confucian outlook toward the natural world is that it helps us to understand the inseparableness between the body and the mind, between moral cultivation and the overall wellness of a person, and between the state of an individual and the person's interpersonal relationships (see Ni, 1996 & 1999).

Learning, Thinking, and Embodiment

As any self-transformation starts from the recognition of one's own ignorance and imperfection, Confucius repeatedly stressed the importance of learning. The Master said, "It is best if one is born with knowledge. Next is to gain knowledge through learning. Still next is to learn after bumping into difficulties. Bumping into difficulties and still not learning, such people end up being the lowest" (16.9) . The Master did not really believe that anyone is born with knowledge; he just left the possibility open. He said, "I am not the kind of person who is born with knowledge. Rather, loving antiquity, I am earnest in seeking it out" (7.20). Comparable to Socrates' belief in knowing one's own ignorance to be true knowledge, Confucius said, "To say you know when you know, and to say you do not when you do not. That is knowledge" (2.17).

Knowing one's own inadequacy is the condition necessary for becoming an exemplary person. When Zigong inquired, "Why has KONG Wenzi been given the posthumous title of 'refined (wen文)'?" the Master replied, "He was diligent and fond of learning, and was not ashamed to ask those of a lower status—this is why he has been called 'refined' " (5.15). Confucius himself is a model learner. He says, "Do I possess knowledge? No, I do not. Once a common fellow asked me a question and I felt empty-like; I queried both ends of the issue to reach the bottom of it" (9.8, see also 7.22).

In the pursuit of learning, one must first be motivated, sincere, and humble in attitude. Confucius said, "I never refused to give instructions to anyone who, of his own accord, approaches me with as small a gift as a bundle of dried meat" (7.7). Even though "a bundle of dried meat" was from then on commonly used in China as an expression for "tuition," the real significance of it was that it served as an expression of the pupil's sincere willingness to learn from a teacher. If one were to assume the position that one does not need to learn from others, showing an attitude of already knowing everything there is to know, or assuming to be equal to those who are in fact more knowledgeable, others would not be inclined to teach him. On one occasion someone asked Confucius whether a boy who was carrying messages for the Master was making any progress. Confucius said, "I have seen him sitting in places reserved for his seniors, and have seen him walking side by side with his elders. This is someone intent on getting quick results rather than making progress" (14.44). On entering the Grand Ancestral Hall, Confucius asked questions about everything. Seeing this, someone remarked, "Who said this son of a man from the Zou village knows about ritual propriety? He asks questions about everything in the Grand Ancestral Hall." When Confucius heard of this, he said, "To do so is itself observing ritual propriety" (3.15), as one should always show a willingness to learn and never presume that one already knows, especially in front of experts.

One must also be persistent throughout the course of learning. "There are indeed seedlings that do not flower, and there are flowers that do not fruit" (9.22). "As in piling up earth to erect a mountain, if, only one basketful short of completion, I stop, I have ended up incomplete. As in filling a ditch to level the ground, if, having dumped in only one basketful, I continue, I am progressing" (9.19).

One story about Confucius illustrates his keenness to learn particularly well. It is said in the biography of Confucius by SIMA Qian that when Confucius was young, he used to learn how to play music from a musician named Shixiang 师襄. Once, seeing that Confucius had continually practiced one and the same piece of music for ten days, Shixiang told Confucius that he could switch to a different piece of music now. Confucius replied: "I have practiced the melody, but not its rhythm yet." After another period of time, Shixiang said, "Now you have got the rhythm." Confucius replied: "I have not got the spirit of it yet." After still another period of time, when Shixiang thought he had got the spirit as well, Confucius said, "I have not got its way of life yet." Finally, after a further period of time, Confucius began to appear in a solemn contemplative state, looking far beyond with great ambition as if he were the king of multiple states. Seeing this, Shixiang was in awe and said, "This is what the music is about: King Wen of Zhou!"

Another important feature of a good learner is to never be afraid to admit one's own errors and to correct oneself (1.8). When Confucius was told that he had misjudged someone, the Master said, "I am fortunate. If I make a mistake, others are sure to inform me" (7.31). He said, "When you err and yet do not correct yourself, that is to err indeed" (15.30). Often the problem is that when something goes wrong, people tend to blame others or to blame misfortune, rather than turn inside themselves to search for the answer. Yet the exemplary person is like an archer who first searches for the fault within when he fails to hit the mark (*Zhongyong*, 14).

Learning must be accompanied by *si* 思, thinking or reflection. "Learning without thinking, one will be perplexed." With diverse and conflicting beliefs and ways of life in the world, it is more than likely that without reflective thinking, the more one learns, the more one gets confused. On the other hand, "thinking without learning, one will be in peril" (2.15). The great minds of past eras and the world in general are resources that we cannot afford to ignore. Not paying due respect to the knowledge and wisdom passed on to us from others is foolhardy and dangerous. The Master said, "Once, lost in my thoughts, I went a whole day without eating and a whole night without sleeping. I got nothing out of it. I would have been better off devoting the time to learning" (15.31).

By *si*, Confucius means more than mere intellectual reasoning from premises to conclusions, or generalization from particulars to universal principles, or deliberation between alternatives. For Confucius, *si* involves the *heart* part of the heart-mind. Since the heart is the part of the body that feels, it is engaged in the process of reaching a deeper understanding, of critical evaluation, and of appropriating what is learned so that one is disposed to apply it. As Mencius says, "An exemplary person steeps himself in the Way because he wishes to find it in himself. When he finds it in himself, he will be at ease (*an* 安) in it; when he is at ease in it, he can draw deeply upon it; when he can draw deeply upon it, he finds sources of help wherever he turns" (*Mencius*, 4B:14).

In responding to a disciple's question about whether or not it was necessary to mourn his parents for three years, Confucius asks, "Would you feel at ease if you do not?" (17.21) The question forces the disciple to bring whatever feelings and ideas that he encounters in front of his moral subjectivity and examine whether or not he can accept them with ease. In the same spirit, *shu* 恕, the method of being *ren*, is also a thinking process that involves the heart. In comparing one's own heart-mind with others' in a compassionate and empathic way, one observes whether one would be at ease doing something or not. When another disciple asked Confucius about the exemplary person, the Master said, "The exemplary person is free from worry and apprehension. . . . If there is nothing to be ashamed of upon self-reflection, what can the person be worried about and afraid of?" (12.4)

It is no coincidence that the Chinese language contains lexicons that are illustrative of the bodily characteristic of the Confucian way of thinking and knowing, such as *ti-yan* 体验 ("bodily experience"), *ti-hui* 体会 ("bodily understanding"), *ti-cha* 体察 ("bodily examination"), *ti-zhi* 体知 ("bodily knowing"), and *ti-ren* 体认 ("bodily recognition"). The subject does not passively receive impressions, nor does one merely reason intellectually. One experiences with the engaged body, understands with one's heart in empathy, examines with the sensitivity of the body, and knows with the body disposed to act upon what is known. The entire outlook is quite consistent with the newly developed study called "embodied cognition," which draws insights from research in linguistics, cognitive science, artificial intelligence, robotics, neurobiology, and philosophy. The general idea of embodied cognition is that there is a close link between all aspects of cognition (formation of ideas, thoughts, etc.) and aspects of the human body.[3]

As Francisco Varela puts it, with the Confucian tradition in mind, this type of learning aims at building the kind of person who acts appropriately as a result of one's dispositions rather than as a result of rational deliberation; it is a matter of know-how rather than know-what (see Varela, 4–6). Since the process of learning and reflection involves dispositioning the body and transforming the entire person, it requires practice to perfect. Confucius believes that, biologically, human beings are similar in nature. It is by xi 习 (practice) they diverge (17.2). "Having learned and then repeatedly practicing what you have learned—is this not a source of pleasure?" (1.1) This statement looks exaggerated when it is taken to mean simply reviewing what has been learned intellectually. If what is learned means only the knowledge about what is the case, reviewing the same thing repeatedly will more likely make a person feel bored instead. But for Confucius, learning means not as much acquiring an accumulated stock of propositional knowledge as it is gaining embodied abilities, which Song and Ming dynasty Confucians call *gongfu*. For this kind of learning, the instructor's teaching can only be understood and appreciated through one's own diligent practice. Repeated practice becomes a source of pleasure because through it, one gradually acquires a deeper and deeper awareness of what is learned, thereby gaining the benefits of the instruction.

It is important to stress that Confucian learning is not merely a matter of acquiring motor skills, as "knowing how" is commonly understood. It is more a transformation of the person. I may know how to overcome procrastination, but not in fact be disposed to do it. I may know how to play soccer, but due to an injury, I am unable to kick the ball. "Knowing how" is still too much related to knowing, and not enough to embodying the ability and the disposition facilitated by the relevant knowledge.

An interesting observation is that in this philosophy that aims primarily at prescribing a good way of life and offering instructions for helping people to gain maturity and to live well, the notion of time also seems different. "The Master was standing on the riverbank, and observed, 'Isn't life's passing just like this, never ceasing day or night!'" (9.17) On the surface, this looks like just a lament on how fast time goes. But the Master always draws moral lessons from observations of nature. The other passages succeeding it indicate that he was more likely reminding people that one should be like the river, making constant efforts to improve oneself. Time for a learner does not always pass evenly. The passage we quoted a short while ago reveals a new meaning when we look at it in this context: "As in piling up earth to erect a mountain, if, only one basketful short of completion, I stop, I have stopped. As in filling a ditch to level the ground, if, having dumped in only one basketful, I continue, I am progressing" (9.19). "If there was anyone who was never tired of practicing what he was taught, it was surely YAN Hui" (9.20), for "I only saw his progress; I never saw him stop" (9.21). One might say that, like Einstein's theory of relativity, time is here perceived as relative to the "speed of motion," which is, in this case, the practice. Whether time goes by fast or slow, or even whether time had existed at all, is dependent on the intensity and continuity of the practice.

Method of Education

The Confucius Temple in Qufu has a pavilion on which is inscribed "Apricot Platform." The book of *Zhuang Zi* says, "Confucius . . . sat on the Apricot Platform, relaxed. His disciples would read books, while the Master flicked the strings of his lute and sang songs" (*Zhuang Zi*, 1023). Even though the book of *Zhuang Zi* cannot be taken literally as a source of historical facts, still, the Apricot Platform came to be known as the place where Confucius taught his classes, and the phrase consequently became a synonym of "educational institution."

Zhuang Zi might have infused his own relaxed style into his description of Confucius's way of teaching. However, one thing he surely got right is that Confucius conducted his teaching mostly in informal ways. Actually, Confucius's "school" was more like a study group with no formal curriculum, no scheduled lectures, and no strict requirements for credits or graduation. Most of the time, the Master just engaged in conversations with his students, responded to their questions, and gave them some directions. Here is a typical "class" scene:

> YAN Hui and Zilu were in attendance on Confucius. The Master said to them, "Why don't each of you tell me what you would most like to do?" Zilu said, "I would like to share my horses, carriages, clothing, and furs with my friends, and I would have no regret even if they [damaged] them." YAN Hui said, "I would like to refrain from bragging about my own abilities, and to not exaggerate my own accomplishments." Zilu then asked the Master, "We would like to hear what it is that you, Master, would most like to do." The Master replied, "I would like to bring peace and contentment to the aged, to share relationships of trust and confidence with my friends, and to love and protect the young." (5.26)

Comparing their own aspirations with the Master's, the disciples would realize that the latter is more all-inclusive.

In fact, the Master's teaching was not even confined to that kind of informal setting. More like parents teaching their children, there was no line between what took place in class and out of class, nor was there even a line between instructing and expressing himself. His teaching style often involved "speech acts" that directly affected the disciples. One interesting example is his lament: "I have never seen a person who loved human-heartedness, or one who loathes the contrary to it. . . . Is anyone able, for a single day, to make efforts at human-heartedness?" (4.6) "I have never seen anyone who, on seeing his faults, is ready to accuse himself inwardly" (5.27). Taken literally, these statements contradict his praises for YAN Hui—that he was able to "not . . . deviate from human-heartedness for as long as three months" (6.7), that he would "never make the same mistake twice" (6.3), and that he only saw him advance and never saw him stop (9.21). However, from the *gongfu* perspective, we can see that the statements in 4.6 and 5.27 are obviously challenges to his students. Rather than telling them that they were all hopeless, the Master was using deliberate exaggerations, like a Chinese parent would typically do with their children, to *challenge* his students to prove him wrong by living a life of human-heartedness.

The effectiveness of Confucius's teaching was aided by his attitude toward his students and by setting an example for the students to follow. He had a genuine respect for the young. He said, "The young should be held in high esteem. After all, how do you know that those yet to come will not surpass our contemporaries?" (9.23) Unlike his late followers, who overly exercised a teacher's authority, the Master expected a great deal from his students while never imposing his points on them. He was a good listener, letting students express themselves freely without interruption while he himself contemplated how to affirm their good points and lead them to overcome their weaknesses. This "student-centered teaching" approach not only created a free atmosphere and allowed students to feel close to the Master, like being with a loving and caring father or elder brother; it also allowed the students to take initiative. Confucius knew quite well that students must ultimately accomplish learning by themselves. He said, "I do not enlighten those who are not eager to learn, nor do I inspire those who are not anxious to find a way of expression. To those who have been presented one direction but do not try to figure out the other three directions, I do not repeat my lesson" (7.8).

The *Analects* shows that when the disciples asked about *ren*, Confucius never tried to describe it per se. He talked about what a *ren* person is like and how they act. He gave instructions according to each disciple's particular condition, letting them know the specific area in which they should make effort. In fact, Confucius's teachings were not limited to verbal instructions. The *Analects* contains many passages that simply describe the way the Master behaves. The teaching method is indeed more typical of *gongfu* masters than of philosophy teachers in the common sense of the term. Since to be *ren* is not a matter of having an intellectual understanding of it, he would be misleading the students if he were to merely describe *ren* verbally.

The contrast between a *gongfu* master and a philosophy teacher is itself an interesting and important philosophical question yet to be explored. The teacher-student relationship from the Aristotelian tradition is based on the assumptions that human beings are essentially rational, and that true knowledge is rational knowledge, always describable and capable of being communicated by language. The primary function of a teacher is to train the students to use the reason they already possess. The way of instruction is to use words or other symbols to represent facts, to persuade students through verbal clarification and argumentation. The student is encouraged to ask "why," and to request a reason for everything he or she learns, unless it is seen by reason as self-evident. In the sense of possessing the faculty of reason, the student is not inferior to the teacher.

The *gongfu* master-disciple relationship from the Confucian tradition—and indeed, from other major Eastern philosophical traditions as well—starts from the assumption that true knowledge is much more than what words can convey, and it requires much more than the intellect to perceive, to understand, and to appropriate. One's reason must be aided by cultivated intuition, and by the awareness accessible only through diligent practice. The master, being well-cultivated, is of a higher standing, capable of seeing things that are not yet accessible to the uncultivated disciple. What the master perceives cannot be conveyed to the disciple by words alone. So the disciples are taught in an entirely different way—not mainly by verbal presentation and persuasion, but by more individualized instruction and the master's demonstrations. The disciples are supposed to follow them and practice accordingly. Sometimes the disciples are even discouraged to ask why, because without trying to experience what is to be understood, a verbal answer could easily mislead the student to think that he has already understood the answer from the words.

Since Confucian learning aims at transforming the person, its teaching style involves offering instructions, like road signs or directives that guide people's lives and their actions, enabling them to lead a good life. It is therefore necessary for Confucius to know the students well on a personal level, and to give different instructions according to their different problems. Once when his disciple Zilu asked, "On learning something, should one act upon it immediately?," Confucius said, "While your father and elder brothers are still alive, how could you, on learning something, act upon it immediately?" When another disciple, RAN Qiu, asked the same question, the Master replied, "Yes, one should."

Upon hearing these apparently conflicting answers, still another disciple, Zihua, was puzzled. To a logical mind this is obviously a self-contradiction. Zihua was direct with the Master: "When Zilu asked the question, you told him that he should defer to his father and elder brothers, but when RAN Qiu asked the same question, you told him that one should. I am confused. May I ask why the difference in your answers?" The Master replied, "RAN Qiu is diffident, and so I urged him on. But Zilu has the energy of two, and so I sought to rein him in" (11.22).

Similarly, Confucius responded differently with YAN Hui and Zigong's attitude toward others. For YAN Hui, he said, "YAN Hui is of no help to me, for there is nothing that I say that he does not like" (11.4). However, commenting on Zigong's tendency to criticize others, Confucius said, "Zigong must be really superior! As for me, I don't have the leisure for this" (14.29).

The tones of these two remarks are interestingly different. The one about YAN Hui is direct and sounds harsh, because YAN Hui is always diligent in cultivating himself, and because in this case, Confucius wanted to encourage the student to criticize the Master himself. If it were soft, "nothing that I say that he does not like" may even be perceived as praise. The one about Zigong, on the other hand, appears to be praising Zigong, for the Master seems to be humbly saying that he himself still had to be busy working on improving himself, and hence could not find the time to criticize others. Yet the sarcasm in the remark is not difficult for Zigong to detect. Instead of telling Zigong directly what he needs to do, which would be humiliating to an accomplished man like Zigong, the statement draws Zigong's attention to the Master himself. By taking this detour, the Master gently but clearly reminded Zigong of the need for self-cultivation. It left enough space for Zigong to think about and come up with his own *realization* of what he needed to do, not merely acquiring the *knowledge* about what he needed to do.

These examples show that Confucius's student-centered instruction does not mean to simply let students take charge of what they are learning. Instead, as a teacher, he is very perceptive of every student's particular merits and weaknesses. Too bad that the *Analects* does not offer us more-detailed contexts of these remarks, so that we might learn how the Master caught the right moment when the students were ready to be instructed. The Master says, "To fail to speak with someone who can be engaged is to let that person go to waste; to speak with someone who cannot be engaged is to waste your words. The wise do not let people go to waste, but they do not waste their words either" (15.8).

But nothing works more effectively than setting an example for the students to follow. One detailed description about the Master in the *Analects* says, "The Master fished with a line, but did not use a net; he used an arrow and line, but did not shoot at roosting birds" (7.27). Seeing how the Master treated animals, one also learns how he treated humans. The description contains no mention of *ren*, but the Master's behavior speaks louder than words.

Another story also illustrates the effectiveness of setting an example. It is said that when the Master and his disciples were stranded on their way between Chen and Cai, they ran out of food. Zigong managed to sneak away from the surrounding troops and bring some rice back. When Yan Hui was cooking the rice, some ash fell into the pot. Yan Hui picked up the soiled rice and ate it. Seeing it from a distance, Zigong was upset because he thought Yan Hui was eating the rice behind their backs. He said to Confucius, "Would a human-hearted (*ren*) and honest person discard his integrity in a dire situation?" Confucius said, "How can the person be called human-hearted if he discards his integrity? To be human-hearted one must be honest." Zigong said, "Then how about Yan Hui? Is he a person who would not discard his integrity?" The Master said, "Indeed."

Then Zigong told Confucius about what he had seen. Confucius said, "I have trusted Yan Hui's human-heartedness for a long time, and I would not doubt it even given what you have said. There must be some other reason. You stay here. Let me ask him." He then called for Yan Hui, and said to him, "I had a dream about my ancestors. Perhaps they had something to say to me? You prepare the rice. I want to use it as an offering to the spirits." Yan Hui replied, "The rice could not be used as an offering to the spirits. There was some ash that flew into the rice. Since it would not be clean if I left the ash in it, and yet it would be a waste if I threw the soiled rice away, I picked it up and ate it." The Master said, "Really? Oh, yes, I would have done the same."

After Yan Hui was out of sight, the Master said to the other disciples, "I trusted Yan Hui long before today." The disciples were fully convinced (see *Kong Zi Jiayu*, 5.20). The story did not specify what the disciples were convinced of and what they were convinced by. Clearly, it was not due to reasoning or lecturing, and what they gained was not merely a firm trust in Yan Hui, but also of the Way of the Master.

Notes

1. This is a person different from the logician with the same name who is famous for the paradoxical proposition, "A white horse is not a horse."

2. I owe this point to Huaiyu Wang, who brought it up in a review of the earlier edition of this book (see Wang, 455–56).

3. Of the scholars who contributed to the general idea, the most well-known are twentieth-century European philosophers Maurice Merleau-Ponty (1908–1961) and Michael Polanyi (1891–1976).

CHAPTER VI

~

Confucius as a Person

Confucius is often portrayed in two drastically different ways. At one extreme, Confucius becomes a supreme sage, a man who transcends ordinary humans in his moral perfection. This image becomes the icon of the Confucian ideal person, who spends his entire life working on perfecting himself and carrying out his various responsibilities. At the other extreme, Confucius becomes an elitist, sexist, and dogmatic conservative, a man who wants to restore an old order of authoritative aristocracy and male dominance, but who is utterly impractical when it comes to real life. The latter image also becomes the icon of feudalist China, a bearer of all the oppressive practices associated with the name of Confucianism.

Both images, however, are distorted and twisted. They were created to serve purposes other than to show the real Confucius. Contrary to the conception of the Master as a man of nothing but lofty ideals, rigid principles, and moral perfection, Confucius is actually a man with rich sentiments, human desires, and a good sense of humor—someone who enjoys life. He is also a man liable to errors. Furthermore, contrary to the conception of him as a stubborn old man who looks down on ordinary people and women, and who curries favor with the mighty, he is in fact a man easily approachable by people of all social classes, and who embodies an uprightness that leads him not to ingratiate himself with anyone. Once we remove all the overly glorifying auras put on him, as well as all the unfair charges levied against him, we find Confucius to be a living, flesh-and-blood person, in which both his real greatness and his limitations reside.

The "Zeng Dian Spirit"

In a conversation that allegedly took place between Confucius and Zigong, Zigong said, "I am tired of learning and frustrated in pursuing the Way. I would like to take a break from it by going to serve my lord instead." Confucius quoted the *Odes*, and showed him how hard it is to be a good subject, and how there is no rest in serving one's lord. Zigong said, "All right, then I would like to take a break from it by going to serve my parents instead." Confucius again quoted the *Odes*, showing him how hard it is to be a good son, and how there is no rest in serving one's parents. Zigong said, "All right, then I would like to take a break from it by going to spend time with my wife and children instead." Confucius replied in the same way, saying that taking care of a family is not easy.

After Zigong had exhausted two more ways he could think of for taking a break from learning and pursuing the Way—one, spending time with friends, and another, farming—and still got the same kind of answer, he said, "I have nowhere to take a break then!" "Yes you do," said the Master. "A place that looks high and open, but solid and isolated [meaning a burial place on a hill]. That is where you will have an ultimate rest." Zigong sighed, "How great is death! It is where an exemplary person will take as a resting place, whereas a petty person will take it as being ruined" (*Kong Zi Jiayu*, 5.22).

Although the reliability of the above record is questionable, the *Analects* contains a saying by Zeng Zi, one of the most accomplished disciples of Confucius, that conveys a similar message: "A *shi* 士 (educated person) must be strong and resolute, for his mission is heavy and the journey is long. He takes *ren* as his mission. Is it not heavy? Only with death does the journey come to an end. Is that not long?" (8.7)

Even though the spirit of the Confucian Way of life proposed in these passages is quite admirable, a life without rest does indeed seem hard and heavy. However, Confucius's own life-orientation does not suggest that, for him, life is, or should be nothing but, a long and hard journey. No passage in the *Analects* reveals this more clearly than section 11.26, which records a detailed conversation between Confucius and Zilu, Zeng Dian 曾点 (also known as Zeng Xi 曾皙, Zeng Zi's father), Ran You, and Zihua, four of his close disciples, when they were all sitting in attendance on Confucius.

Obviously intending to create a relaxed atmosphere and to encourage the students to speak up, the Master said, "Just because I am a bit older than you, do not hesitate on my account. You keep saying, 'No one recognizes my worth!,' but if someone did recognize your worth, how would you be of use to them?"

The four students all expressed what they would do if their qualities were fully recognized and they were free to exercise their abilities. "As for me," Zilu hastily replied, "give me a state of a thousand chariots to govern, set me in between powerful neighboring states, harass me with foreign armies, and add to that widespread famine, I could, within three years, give the people courage and a sense of direction."

The Master smiled at him, and said, "Ran You, what would you do?"

"Give me a small territory of sixty or seventy—or even fifty or sixty—*li* square, I could, within three years, make the people thrive. As for observing ritual propriety and music, I would leave that to abler exemplary persons."

"How about you, Zihua?" asked the Master.

"Not to say that I have the ability to do so, but I am willing to learn: On ceremonial occasions in the ancestral temple or in diplomatic gatherings, I would like to assist as a minor official in charge of protocol, properly dressed in my ceremonial cap and robes."

"And what about you, Dian?" asked the Master.

After he plucked a final note on his zither to bring the music to an end, and setting the instrument aside, Zeng Dian rose to his feet. "I would choose to do something different from the rest," he said.

"No harm in that," said the Master. "Each of you can speak your mind."

"In late spring, after the spring clothes have been newly made, I would like, in the company of five or six young men and six or seven children, to cleanse ourselves in the Yi River, to revel in the cool breezes at the Altar for Rain, and then return home singing."

At this point, the reader would expect that the Master would endorse the first three disciples' wishes, for they all expressed moral and political ambitions. However, after hearing all their ambitions, the Master heaved a deep sigh, and said, "I am with Dian!"

The fact that the Master would be with Zeng Dian, whose wish was to do nothing but freely enjoy the environment and those around him, indeed comes as a surprise to those who perceive the Master as a stern moralist. The detailed description of Zeng Dian's relaxed way of expressing his wish is deliberately recorded as part of the message: Rather than anxiously waiting for his turn, Zeng Dian kept playing his music even after the Master had asked him "What about you, Dian?" Instead of responding like a nervous moralist who is always worrying about staying within the moral boundary, Song dynasty Confucians such as the Cheng brothers and Zhu Xi say that Zeng Dian displayed the aesthetic spirit and ideal of ancient sage kings, whose heart-mind is at ease 安, and who is able to enjoy life by spontaneous participation in the revival of everything and celebrate the transformation of heaven and earth.

This story shows that, unlike the common conception of a Confucian sage as a person who disregards and ultimately eliminates all natural human desires, the Confucian ideal is to regulate and transform natural desires to the human level. There is no question that for Confucius, as for all the great thinkers of his time, humans need to regulate their desires. But Confucius never advocated the elimination of human desires. Confucius's "self-discipline" is based on his recognition of basic human desires. He himself is one who likes fine food, not merely whatever can fill the stomach (see 10.8). With regard to sex, he only cautions young people not to overindulge in it (16.7). The *Odes* that he repeatedly quotes and advises his disciples to study are full of love themes. He is also fond of having fame (15.20), though he also says that one should not be frustrated if not recognized by others (1.1). He is very frank in saying that "Wealth and honor are what people want, but if they are the consequence of deviating from the Way, I would have no part in them" (4.5). "When wealth can be pursued, I will be willing to do it even as a guard holding a whip. But if it is not, I shall follow my own preferences" (7.12). The point is "to desire but not to be greedy" (20.2), and to obtain what one desires without deviating from the proper Way.

Not only is the ZENG Dian spirit a form of true enjoyment, it is also an artistic way of life. If we say that today's conventional notion of art associates artwork with studios, galleries, and articles that are displayed for decoration, the Confucian sense of art refers to the artistic way of life itself. While the conventional artist dissolves the opposition between the mind and the "hands," the Confucian sage achieves unity with heaven, and is able to participate with heaven in creation. Aesthetic enjoyment is actually the culmination of Confucian learning.

Reading passage 7.6 of the *Analects* as relating the process of cultivation, we see that Confucius puts "sojourn in the arts" as the highest ideal, above other stages of practice, such as those characterized by "aspiring after the Way (*dao*), holding firm to virtue/virtuosity (*de*), and leaning upon human-heartedness (*ren*)." Similarly, in passage 8.8, Confucius says, "I find inspiration from the *Book of Odes*, I learn where to stand from observing ritual propriety, and I find fulfillment in playing music [or in enjoyment]." The order of the three sentences indicates that an aesthetic way of life is the result and the final consummation of a person's self-cultivation. For Confucius, "knowing that it cannot be done and yet doing it" (a remark someone made when describing Confucius, see 14.38) is at its best when one "takes pleasure" in doing it (6.20).

When the Duke of She asked Zilu about Confucius, and Zilu did not answer, Confucius said: "Why didn't you say that I am a person who forgets his food when engaged in vigorous pursuit of something, is so happy as to forget his worries, and is not aware that old age is coming on?" (7.19) The word *forget* is a strong indication of the pure nonutilitarian aesthetic ideal. These passages suggest that the ideal of Confucian learning does not lie in morality in the Kantian sense, meaning, it is not moral for the sake of moral duty. The ideal for Confucian learning lies in the opposite: Morality is valuable because of its utilitarian function of leading to the aesthetic ideal. Even though the aesthetic ideal is itself nonutilitarian, this does not mean that arts and artistic activities cannot have utilitarian functions. It only means that an aesthetic ideal does not need any utilitarian function for its justification. Once the ideal is achieved, there is no need to worry about morality. One simply follows the will of the heart-mind without overstepping the line and enjoys the freedom, just like "When the Way prevails in the world, the common people do not dispute about state affairs" (16.2).

The Confucian artistic creation is ideally displayed throughout one's entire life, and not merely in the "big moments" people sometimes face—for example, in jumping into a burning building to save a child, or in taking up a dangerous mission to protect one's country. After all, it is more difficult to be consistently aesthetic during one's daily activities, in providing all sorts of social services for others, and in building strong social relationships. This is where the "ZENG Dian spirit" differs from the Daoist and Buddhist ideals, as both Daoism and Buddhism generally advise people to detach from society. A person who makes life artistic in the Confucian sense may not be considered a prominent artist in the conventional sense of the term, yet for Confucius, the person will necessarily be prominent in the sense of gaining popularity (see 12.20), for one cannot become such an artist without turning one's own relatedness with others into what is harmonious and pleasant.

Elitist?

As most of the time Confucius was courteous and conscientious of ritual propriety, he could appear pretentious at times, as evidenced in the following excerpts from the *Analects*:

> When summoned by his lord to receive guests of the state, his countenance would become serious, and his steps would be faster. He would bend his body, with hands cupped, to salute those in attendance with him, from left to right; and his robes would sway along back and forth, rhythmically. Hastening forward, he would move as if gliding with wings. When the guests had retired, he would always come back to report, saying, "The guests have stopped looking back." (10.3)

Entering the duke's court gate, he would bend his body as if the gate were not tall enough to admit him. He would not halt in the middle of the entrance, nor would he step on the threshold. Passing by the vacant throne, his countenance would become serious, his steps would be faster, and he would hold his voice as if he could hardly speak. Lifting up his robe to ascend the hall, he would bend his body and hold his breath as if he had stopped breathing. On coming out and having descended the first set of steps, he would appear relaxed and content. Having reached the bottom of the steps, he would hasten forward, like gliding with wings. On returning to his position, he looked reverent. (10.4)

Putting aside the question raised by some scholars—whether these passages, as well as others in the same section of the *Analects*, are authentic or not—one must keep in mind that showing reverence to certain social positions is not to be confused with showing reverence to particular powerful individuals. A social position associated with a particular title is like an acupuncture point in a person: It represents a knot in a social web that functionally links to other parts of the net in order to mobilize energies. Showing reverence to a higher social position is not merely recognition of its importance, but also a way of affecting it in a positive way. It serves the twofold purpose of reminding the person in power of the importance of that position, and demonstrating how those in particular positions should conduct themselves.

Confucius was conscious of the side effect that may result from being extremely courteous and conscientious of ritual propriety. He said, "You will be looked upon as obsequious by others if you observe every detail of the ritual propriety in serving your lord" (3.18). Taking the ritualistic manner in which Confucius treated his lord together with his uprightness in confronting inappropriate use of social power, it becomes evident that he was not at all obsequious.

Confucius's relationship with Ji Kangzi, the head of the powerful Ji family, which illegitimately took virtual control of the state affairs in Lu, was quite illuminating in this regard. Ji Kangzi would often come to Confucius for advice and sometimes even participate in discussions with other disciples of the Master, but the Master treated him either with a polite distance or a cold directness. When Ji Kangzi sent a present of medicine to him, the Master accepted it, but added, with an obvious reluctance: "Not knowing its effects, I dare not to taste it" (10.16). When Ji Kangzi was troubled by the number of thieves and came to Confucius for advice, the Master rebuked him, saying, "If you yourself were not so greedy, the people would not steal even if you paid them to do so!" (12.18). Obviously the reply was harsh to a man of high social status, and, looking at it in isolation, it could hardly be seen as an adequate practical advice for dealing with crime. However, when considering the fact that the Ji family was taking much of the control of the state of Lu from its duly appointed ruler, and that Ji Kangzi was charging an excessive amount of tax from the people, the reply could not have been more appropriate! Ji Kangzi's feelings toward Confucius must have been very ambivalent. On the one hand, he seemed to have great respect for the Master. On the other hand, he would not have dared to use Confucius for any important position.

Furthermore, the Master's observance of ritual propriety was not merely directed toward his lord. "When drinking with villagers, the Master would wait for those with canes to depart before taking his leave" (10.13). "In asking after the well-being of a friend in another state, he would bow twice before sending the messenger on his way" (10.15). "On encountering those attired in mourning dress, in ceremonial cap and robes, or those who are blind, even where such people might be his juniors, the Master would, on first catching sight of them, invariably rise to his feet, and on passing them, would invariably hasten his step" (9.10, see also 10.25). Obviously these manners were signs of his reverence for ceremony, his respect for elders, the deceased, and their family and friends, and his care for the blind and others with disabilities. These manners do not suggest that Confucius was obsequious.

Though Confucius was poor when he was young and was never rich in his entire life, he was indeed quite particular about eating and clothing.

He did not eat rice that had gone sour or fish and meat that had spoiled. He did not eat food that had gone off color or food that had a bad smell. He did not eat food that was not properly prepared nor did he eat except at the proper times. He did not eat food that had not been properly cut up, nor did he eat unless the proper sauce was available. (10.8)

In the hot season, he wore a single layer of hemp garment, whether coarse or fine texture, but would always put on an outer upper layer before going out. Over lamb's fur, he wore black; over fawn's fur, white; and over fox's fur, yellow. His casual fur robe was long, with short sleeves. He always had a sleeping quilt, which was one and half times the length of his body. (10.6)

These habits might be associated with the fact that, even though his family was poor, it still belonged to the class of the "nobles." But this does not mean that Confucius valued fine food and clothing more than the pursuit of the Way, for otherwise he would not have traveled for years from one state to another under extreme harsh conditions. He said, "To eat coarse food, drink plain water, and pillow oneself on a bent arm—there is pleasure to be found in these things. Wealth and rank attained through inappropriate means have no more meaning to me than passing clouds" (7.16). "Those who set their heart on the Way and yet are ashamed of coarse food and rude clothing are not worth engaging in discussion" (4.9). He commented on his disciple YAN Hui, saying, "How admirable Hui is! Living in a mean dwelling on a bowlful of rice and a ladleful of water is a hardship most men would find intolerable, but it has no effect on his enjoyment. How admirable Hui is!" (6.11) At one point Confucius even considered moving to the remote region of Yi. Someone said to him, "What would you do about the crudeness of the living environment?" The Master replied, "Were an exemplary person to live there, what crudeness will there be?" (9.14)

An elitist is one who usually looks down on people of lower social classes or those who are less advantaged. Elitism is therefore typically associated with the image of a snobbish, self-inflated personality. Yet one finds no trace of this in Confucius. To the contrary, the Master always saw his own imperfections. Confucius said, "The way of an exemplary person has three features, none of which I have succeeded in achieving myself. The human-hearted is not worrisome, the wise is not perplexed, the courageous is not afraid." Upon hearing this, Zigong said, "That is a portrayal of the Master himself" (14.28). Confucius is also said to have declared:

> Of the four requirements of the exemplary person's way, I have not been able to satisfy even one. I have not served my father as I would expect my son to serve me. I have not served my lord as I would expect a subject to serve his lord. I have not served my elder brother as I would expect a younger brother to serve his elder brother. I have not [been] able to treat my friends as I myself would wish them to treat me. (*Zhongyong*, section 13)

The fact that in this passage he mentioned himself only as a son, a subject, and a younger brother, and not as a father, a superior, or an elder brother clearly shows that what he considered most essential was how to make himself a better person, not that he deserved to be treated as a superior.

But the Master was quite aware of his own merits. It is said that once Zixia asked him, "How is YAN Hui as a person?" The Master replied, "YAN Hui is better than me in his trustworthiness." Zixia asked, "How is Zigong as a person?" The Master replied, "Zigong is better than me in his wit." Zixia asked, "How is Zilu as a person?" The Master replied, "Zilu is better than me in his courage." Zixia asked, "How is Zizhang as a person?" The Master replied, "Zizhang is better than me in his dignified composure."

Zixia stood up and asked, "Then why are these four still following you to study?" The Master replied,

> Sit down. Let me tell you. YAN Hui is trustworthy but unable to use discretion; Zigong has quick wit but is unable to hold his tongue; Zilu is courageous but does not know how to use caution; and Zizhang has a dignified composure but is unable to harmonize himself with others. If I were to be offered to exchange what I have with all the characters of the four, I would not do it. That is why they all follow me and have never had a second thought. (*Kong Zi Jiayu*, 4.15)

Again, even though the reliability of this passage is questionable, it seems to have captured the Master's way of looking at himself and others quite well, for it is fully consistent with the Master's saying recorded in the *Analects*: "Walking along with two others, I am certain there is my teacher among them. I select their good qualities to follow, and their bad qualities to rectify" (7.22). Both passages show that, when he considered other people, the Master first identified what he could learn from others, even if the others were his disciples. To paraphrase Socrates' saying, "Knowing one's own ignorance is wisdom," we might say that for Confucianism, seeing one's own shortcomings is greatness. Also analogous to and in contrast with Socrates' role as a gadfly that irritates people by making them aware of their ignorance, Confucius was like a magnet, attracting his disciples by offering himself as a role model to help them realize their own weaknesses, as well as how they could improve themselves.

Sexist?

In the entire *Analects*, there is no mention of Confucius's mother or wife, and the only place he mentions his daughter is with reference to her marrying one of his own disciples. "GONGYE Chang 公冶长 will be a good husband," said the Master. "Even though he has spent time in prison, it was through no fault of his own." He then gave him his daughter in marriage (5.1). In another passage, the *Analects* reveal that the Master gave another student named NAN Rong 南容 his niece for marriage. He commented on NAN Rong: "When the Way prevails in the land, he does not go unemployed, but when it does not prevail, he avoids punishment and execution" (5.2).

From these facts one may already suspect that for Confucius, the role of women was primarily confined to the household. However, no passage in the *Analects* has triggered more criticism for Confucius's discrimination against women than 17.25, where Confucius says, "It is only 女子 [when pronounced as *nü zi*, typically taken to mean 'women'] and petty persons who are difficult to provide for. Drawing them close, they are immodest, and keeping them at a distance, they complain." This passage has often been quoted by later Confucians to justify their gender bias, and therefore has indeed performed the function of being the authoritative ground for practices oppressive to women.

Some scholars sympathetic to Confucius suspect that the term *nü zi* refers to female servants rather than to women in general,[1] but even if that were true, still, why single out female servants? Putting females in the same category with petty persons is not only logically inappropriate—as "female" is a natural category of sex, while "petty persons" is a moral category of evaluation—it is also obviously a discriminatory generalization. Some others have argued that throughout history, people have misread the character "女" in this passage entirely. Instead of reading it as *nü* (female), it should be read as *ru*, as in ancient times, the character "女" was most often used for *ru* 汝, which means "you." According to this reading, the passage would mean instead: "It is only you young boys and petty persons who are difficult to provide for," where "you boys" refers to some of his disciples. This reading is supported by the fact that among the eighteen other occurrences of the word "女" in the *Analects*, seventeen of them are used as *ru* (you). Nevertheless, this reading brings in another puzzle, as it is hard to explain why the Master would classify his disciples together with petty persons.

Whether we take the passage to be talking about women or not, we should not miss the instructive message under the surface. As Qing dynasty Wang Xuan 汪烜 says in his *Sishu Quanyi* 《四书诠义》 with regard to this passage, "This is saying that in cultivation of the person and regulating the family, nothing can be taken lightly or taken for granted. Do not think that servants and concubines are low in social status, and therefore they can be used in any way you like and [you can] treat them carelessly" (see Cheng Shude, 1244). This is what I call "the *gongfu* perspective"—the perspective of reading a passage more as an instruction about how to live one's life rather than as a description of facts. From this perspective, the passage is more a reminder that one should ideally be able to make even those who are most difficult to provide for "pleased, if they are close, and attracted, if they are at a distance" (13.16). Song dynasty scholar Lü Zuqian 吕祖谦 also made this very clear when he wrote:

> Thinking about how to deal with such people [those who are difficult to provide for], the most difficult thing is to be firm and yet not harsh. Usually people cannot be firm without being harsh. In order to be firm, they have to

make a special effort. This is just like the teaching of being "respectful and yet at ease." Ordinary people usually have to constrain themselves in order to appear respectful. If they behave in an unconstrained way they will not be respectful. Only with deep cultivation of one's nature and disposition can a person be naturally firm and respectful at the same time. If what is inside the person is not sufficiently cultivated, the person will have no way but to appeal to artificial efforts. The reference to being "commanding but not ferocious" is quite similar in meaning. (Lü, 14–15)

Here, "respectful and yet at ease" and "commanding but not ferocious" are both from the *Analects*: "The Master was always gracious yet serious, commanding yet not severe, respectful yet at ease" (7.38). This "at ease" says even more than "giving the heart-mind free rein without overstepping the boundaries" (2.4). For not to overstep the boundaries is still about how cultivation affects oneself—that is, how it enables one not to overstep the boundaries—yet the passages we have just quoted (17.25, 7.38, and 13.16) require one to be both naturally firm on discipline and attractive to those who are most difficult to provide for, even in the most tedious daily personal lives, so that they will be pleased if they are close, and attracted if they are at a distance. Reading the passage as a reminder to cultivate oneself rather than as a description of fact, passage 17.25 looks more consistent with the rest of the book and the overall spirit of Confucianism.

There is another puzzling passage in the *Analects* related to the Master's attitude toward women. Commenting on the fact that ancient sage king Shun had only five ministers and the world was properly governed, and that King Wu had remarked that he "had ten capable officials," Confucius said, "How true it is that talent is difficult to find! . . . Apart from the woman among them, there were only nine" (8.20). This was taken in two very different ways: One is that Confucius excluded the woman, showing that in his mind, women do not even count. However, this interpretation seems too extreme, and hardly squares with the Master's overall level of rationality. Why would he disregard one of these ten capable officials simply because the person was a woman? Some scholars take him to be emphasizing how difficult it is to find talent. Usually people at the time would assume that these ten capable officials were all men, but since one of them was a woman, it is ten out of the entire population, men and women. If one were to consider the male talents only, out of the entire population there were even less than ten. In the words of Huang Kan 皇侃 (488–545), when Confucius clearly says that there was a woman among the capable officials, he was "making it clear that the flourishing of the Zhou was not merely due to men's talent; the abilities of the women also assisted in the transformation of their government" (CHENG Shude, 558).

Putting aside the interpretation of these passages, it is reasonable to believe that, great as Confucius was, he still was not totally free of historical limitations. As a man deeply influenced by the Zhou culture, his view about women may well have been affected by the widespread male-dominant customs and by what happened in history. Before the Zhou dynasty, women actually played quite active roles in social and political affairs. The status of women declined in the Zhou dynasty, presumably because the founders of the Zhou believed that the downfall of the Shang dynasty was largely due to women's influence in politics. King Wu of Zhou reportedly said that the last King of Shang "was listening to no one but his women," and "allowed a hen to do the crowing at the break of dawn" (see WANG Hui, 386).

Interestingly, the early Zhou (typically referred to as Western Zhou) were also believed to have been brought down by a woman. It is said that King You 周幽王's (reigned 781–771 BCE) concubine Bao Si 褒姒 manipulated the benighted King so much that she virtually destroyed the capital of Zhou. As one of the *Odes*, "Zhengyue 正月," says,

> The sorrow of my heart
> is as though someone tied it.
> This ruler now—
> how can he be so cruel?
> The flames, as they rise—
> will someone extinguish them?
> The majestic capital of Zhou—
> Bao Si destroyed it.

A probably romanticized story says that Bao Si had the King repeatedly set fires in vain on alarm beacons to summon his vassals just for her own amusement, to see the feudal lords rushing to the rescue where there was in fact no enemy. By the time a real threat came, none of the king's vassals heeded the alarm beacons, and consequently the King was quickly overpowered, marking the beginning of the Spring and Autumn period, during which constant chaos ensued all the way to Confucius's time.

The actual Bao Si may very well have been a depressed, beautiful woman, who did not care for pleasing the King. The corrupt king brought his kingdom down by his own absurd conduct, and yet people demonized Bao Si and claimed that she was responsible for the consequences. Collective memory of these historical events, as reflected in the *Odes*, may have caused Confucius, like most of his male contemporaries, to become biased in his overall view of women, and thus, to become vigilant when dealing with them. However, it is unfair to say that the Master was as much of a male chauvinist as were some of his late followers, such as DONG Zhongshu. Even though Confucius was limited by history, he still could not have considered virtuous women inferior to immoral men, just as he would not have considered an upright minister inferior to a wicked overlord.

Furthermore, the overall spirit of Confucius's teachings about human-heartedness (*ren*) makes it easy to shake off its gender bias, if any. If we compare Confucianism with contemporary feminism, we find more similarities than differences between the two. As Chenyang Li shows, Confucianism and feminism are similar in their basic moral ideals because both are care-oriented, placing emphasis on particular human related-ness, situational judgment, and character-building, rather than right-based moral theories that emphasize individual rights and universal rules (see Li, 23-42). Of course, Confucius would never go as far as some feminists, rejecting all gender differences for the sake of equality. He would say that men and women have some basic differences, and these differences should be the basis of their differentiated but reciprocal, mutually complementary relationships and responsibilities.

Honesty and Sincerity

Confucius sometimes gives people the impression that he is somewhat less than totally honest. As we have mentioned earlier, he considers father-son mutual concealment of misconduct as a form of uprightness. Even though, as we have explained, it is for the sake of preserving filial piety, which is considered the root of *ren*, and therefore justified according to Confucius, it still shows that for the Master, sometimes it is permissible to lie. This is further confirmed by a story in the *Analects*: "Rubei 孺悲 sought to meet with Confucius. Confucius declined to see him, feigning illness. Just as the envoy conveying the message had stepped out of the door, Confucius took his lute and sang, making sure that the messenger heard it" (17.20).

Apparently Confucius disliked Rubei and so did not want to see him. However, Confucius did not refuse to see him directly, presumably because it would have been too harsh to openly embarrass him. Instead, Confucius used a lie (that he was ill) to save the person's "face" publicly. At the same time, Confucius wanted Rubei to know that it was a lie so that he would not mistakenly think that Confucius was indeed unable to see him because of illness, and would thereby get the clear message that the Master simply did not want to see him.

Confucius's teachings about trustworthiness in words also seem to be inconsistent. On the one hand, he says that "A man not trustworthy in words (*xin* 信) is like a cart without a pin in the yoke-bar" (2.22). His close disciples, Zeng Zi and Zixia, also repeated his teaching of *xin* (see 1.4, 1.7). *Xin* is later even taken as one of the five major Confucian virtues, together with *ren* (human-heartedness), *yi* (appropriateness), *li* (ritual propriety), and *zhi* 智 (wisdom). This is similar in spirit to the biblical commandment, "You shall not bear false witness against your neighbor." It is generally understood in line with virtues such as being honest, keeping promises, seeing actions through to the end, and so forth.

Yet on the other hand, Confucius also says, "A man who insists on keeping his word and seeing his actions through to the end has a stubborn petty mind" (13.20). Following Confucius, Mencius also says that "a great man need not necessarily keep his word, nor does he necessarily see his action through to the end. He aims only at what is right" (*Mencius*, 4B:11).

Confucius and Mencius are not contradicting themselves. For the Confucians, being trustworthy means maintaining an overall consistency between one's words and actions, not a rigid imperative taken at face value. A person should in general be trustworthy with words and with seeing one's actions through to the end. In some cases, however, to tell the truth or even just to remain silent would be morally inappropriate. In the case of treating Rubei, Confucius did convey his unwillingness to see Rubei; he just did it in an indirect way to save the man from the embarrassment of being directly rejected. Seeing the harsh results of being invariably direct or sticking to one's words rigidly, the Master was, again, using the *gongfu* perspective, advising people to begin their practice of *ren* by following the general instruction of being trustworthy in words, but not sticking to it mechanically.

Ultimately people should aim at mastering the art of using discretion (*quan* 权) to determine whether in a particular case one should or should not tell the truth or keep one's word. In fact, this is quite consistent with the morality of common sense. Most people would not tell their dying grandmother the truth: "You look bad!" In a situation like this, a person with good understanding will know that a statement like "You look fine" is not really meant to be a description of her condition, but an encouragement and an action of comforting the dying person. Taken as a description, it would be a lie, but as an action, it is a form of sincere, honest goodwill. German philosopher Immanuel Kant is famous for his view that lying is in no case morally permissible because it is disrespectful for those who are lied to. But as the expression "He does not even care to lie to me!" shows, lying can sometimes be the very act of respecting a person. The complexities of real life require people to have a higher level of truthfulness than the simple kind that Kant advocates.

Later Confucians used the word *cheng* 诚, "sincerity/genuineness" to capture this higher level of truthfulness. If *xin* or trustworthiness is a feature of one's conduct, *cheng* is more a feature of one's disposition and motivation behind one's conduct. A person of *cheng* could be sincere when not telling the truth. The person of *cheng* is different from what Confucius calls a *xiangyuan* 乡原, "village worthy" or "village honest," who the Master condemned as the "enemy of virtue" (17.13). A *xiangyuan*, explains Mencius, is a hypocrite who tries to look good in front of everyone. The person may not have evil intentions but is more dangerous to true virtue because

> if you want to censure him, you cannot find anything; if you want to find fault with him, you cannot find anything either. He shares with others the practices of the day and is in conformity with the sordid world. He appears to be conscientious and faithful, and looks like he has integrity in his conduct. He is likened by the multitude and is self-righteous. (*Mencius*, 7B:37)

Indeed, the person may even be seen as a role model because he appears to be right all the time, but his "virtuous" deeds are merely in conformity with (and hence "honest to" or "faithful to") what is deemed "good" by the majority, and there is nothing virtuous from inside the person.

Compared to *xin* (trustworthy in words), *cheng* is like an advanced *gongfu*, which requires more ability for discerning what is truly good in concrete situations and acting accordingly. Correspondingly, it requires the perceivers to have the ability to properly interpret actions done out of sincerity, or lack thereof. Philosophers often say that one's senses are deceptive and not reliable. They use examples such as "A straight stick may look bent when half immersed in water," or "A big mountain may look small from a distance," to prove the point. However, in doing this they are accusing the innocent. A half-immersed stick *does* look bent; a mountain seen from afar *does* appear small. It is our ability to make sound judgments about what we sense that can be wrong (see Reid, 194).

Similarly, an action that appears to be a lie but is in fact sincere requires good judgment in order to see the higher level of truthfulness in it. On the other hand, a true statement may come from a "village honest" who knows nothing about true virtue or excellence. This is why when Zigong asked, "What do you think about someone who is loved by everyone in his village?" Confucius replied, "It is not enough." "What if everyone in the village despises a person?" asked Zigong. "It is not enough either," said the Master. "It would be better if those who are good like the person and those who are bad despise the person" (13.24).

Whether others have this ability or not, one should try to cultivate sincerity and master the art of discretion to cope with complicated interpersonal relationships. As Ziyou puts it, "If in serving your lord you are unrelenting, you will bring on disgrace; if in your friendships you are unrelenting, you will find yourself estranged" (4.26). In his response to Zilu's question about what an educated person (*shi* 士) should be like, Confucius replied, "Those who are earnest and keen yet amicable can be called educated persons." As if that was not accurate enough, he added, "They are earnest and keen with their friends, and amicable with their brothers" (13.28). The recorders of the *Analects* were careful enough to include this subtle but significant detail. The reason that there should be a difference in how one treats one's friends and one's brothers is that the latter is closer to the "root" of family love, and therefore should be more carefully protected. This idea was later developed by Mencius. Citing the tradition that "In antiquity people taught one another's sons," Mencius says, "Father and son should not demand goodness from each other. To do so will estrange them, and there is nothing more inauspicious than estrangement between father and son" (4A:18).

These teachings, again, have to be understood more as instructions for enabling a person to make the right choices than rigid rules for constraining behaviors. Confucius did not mean that one does not need to be amicable to friends or be critical to one's siblings. The point is only a matter of degree: In comparison, one should be more amicable to one's siblings than to one's friends. In actual application of the instruction, one still has to discern the particularities in a given situation in order to respond appropriately.

The exercise of this kind of art is not easy, and the flexibility of the principle can be misused as an excuse for inappropriate maneuvers. Since Confucius could not tell people exactly when and where one can rightfully make a false statement or conceal a truth, it is left to each individual to decide as one sees fit. Consequently, the people influenced by the Confucian tradition have less hesitation in making an untruthful statement than those influenced by the Judeo-Christian tradition, even when the lie is not clearly necessary. We may presumably blame Confucius for not having set the principle of *xin* as a rigid rule, but the fault is more in the interpreters than in the Master, for the Master has instructed that the person is to be cultivated to embody and utilize the principle, and not that a principle should be forced upon the person who does not know how to use it properly.

After All, the Master Is a Human

Thanks to the compilers of the *Analects*, we know quite a few details about Confucius as a person. As we mentioned before, he was a man who was particular about food and clothing. Among these habits were peculiar ones, such as the fact that he would refuse to eat meat that was not properly cut, or when the proper sauce was not available. While he would avoid overeating, he did not limit himself in the case of wine, although he never got drunk (10.8). He also had other particular habits, such as he would not sit unless the mat was straight (10.12); while eating, he would not converse (10.10); and when sleeping, he would not lie like a corpse (10.24).

The *Analects* also shows that he was fond of music, and quite good at it. In hearing a good piece of music, Shao, he could be so moved by it that he would not notice the taste of the meat he was eating (7.14). He had a conversation with the Grand Music Master of Lu in which he demonstrated a good understanding of music composition, saying, "Much can be realized with music if one begins by playing in unison, and then goes on into full swing, with each instrument and voice presented clearly and distinctly and yet in harmony, flowing consistently, thereby bringing all to completion" (3.23). He also liked to sing. "When the Master was singing in the company of others and liked someone else's song, he always asked to hear it again before joining in" (7.32).

The *Analects* also makes it clear that Confucius disliked eloquence. "The ancients were loath to speak because they feel ashamed of not being able to live up to what they said" (4.22). Mencius quotes Confucius as having said, "I have no talent for making speeches" (*Mencius*, 2A:2). In his view, "It is rare for glib speech and an insinuating appearance to accompany human-heartedness" (1.3). "An exemplary person wants to be slow in speech yet quick in action" (4.24).

His way of dealing with Zilu, one of his closest disciples, is particularly interesting. Zilu's personality is a mixture of warmheartedness and simple directness and impulsiveness. On one occasion when Confucius praised his favorite disciple, YAN Hui, Zilu spoke up loudly, "Well, if you were leading an army of combined forces, who would you want to go along with?" Confucius replied, with a tone of mockery, "I would not take along the person who would go to death without regret by wrestling a tiger bare-handed or crossing the Yellow River without a boat. I would want someone who approached difficulties with caution, and preferred to succeed by careful planning" (7.11). On another occasion, the Master laid a trap for Zilu, saying, "If the Way should fail to prevail and I had to take to the high seas on a raft, the one who would follow me would no doubt be Zilu." On hearing this, Zilu was delighted. But the Master added, "Zilu exceeds me in his fondness for courage, yet does not know what to be courageous about" (5.7).

As our experience with different people tells us, some people are conscientious about their own shortcomings and are very sensitive to others' criticism, whereas others are more careless and simpleminded. One needs to be very careful with the former, so as not to hurt their self-esteem; a gentle reminder of their weakness should be enough for them to take heed of their problems. Yan Hui is clearly this kind of person. Confucius did not have to repeat his words to Yan Hui, for Yan Hui would always listen with full attention and take action on it, never making the same mistake twice (9.20, 6.3). The only time Confucius used strong words with Yan Hui was when he said, "Yan Hui is of no help to me. He is pleased with everything I say" (11.4), and this, as we have explained before, was to urge him to be critical of the Master's own words. To the latter kind, however, a stronger dose of "medicine" will be necessary to get the desired effect. That is exactly what the Master did to Zilu. However, when his criticism of Zilu led his other disciples to disrespect Zilu, the Master stopped them. He told them, "Zilu has already ascended the hall; he has only not yet entered the inner chamber" (11.15).

On most occasions, the Master does not hide his love or his hatred. When Ran Boniu was gravely ill, the Master sighed, "Why should such a man be stricken with such a disease? Why should such a man be stricken with such a disease?" (6.10) When Yan Hui died, he cried heartbreakingly that heaven had ruined him (11.9). His followers cautioned, "Master, you are grieving exceedingly." The Master said, "Am I? If I do not grieve exceedingly for this man, for whom else should I do so?" (11.10) But to a disciple who complained, "It is not that I do not like the Way of the Master, but that I do not have the strength to walk it," the Master replied bluntly: "Those who do not have the strength for it collapse somewhere along the Way. But with you, you have drawn your own line before you start!" (6.12)

Usually the Master is cautious not to hurt others' self-esteem, but with Zai Wo, who is glib and lazy, he made an exception. Seeing Zai Wo sleeping during the daytime, the Master said, "You cannot carve rotten wood, and cannot trowel over a wall of manure. What is the use of upbraiding him?" As if that was still not enough, the Master added, "I used to take on trust a man's deeds after having listened to his words. Now having listened to a man's words I will have to observe his deeds. It is Zai Wo who has taught me this!" (5.10)

The Master was ashamed to seek out someone's friendship while concealing his own dislike of the person (5.25), but he did not hesitate to associate himself with someone who was wrongly accused. When the powerful Ji family violated a ritual propriety that is fundamental to the order of the society, he was angry. He proclaimed, "If this can be condoned, what cannot be?" (3.1) But to a person who was put in prison through no fault of his own, he gave his own daughter to marry.

Sometimes the Master could lose his composure. When he was desperate to find opportunities to implement his ideas in politics, he went to see the notorious wife of Duke Ling of Wei, Nanzi, who had the reputation of having multiple extramarital affairs. When he noticed that his disciple Zilu was unhappy about it, the Master was like a child suspected of having done something wrong. He swore to Zilu, "If I have done anything improper, may heaven's curse be on me, may heaven's curse be on me!" (6.28)

Even though the Master swore that he had done nothing wrong, his meeting with Nanzi still triggered criticism that he was not behaving according to traditional ritual propriety that stated men and women should not have encounters outside of marriage. Modern scholar LIN Yutang 林语堂 took up the story and wrote a drama titled "Confucius Meeting with Nanzi" (1928), which was put on stage by college students from Qufu No. 2 Normal College. Confucius's descendants were so upset by this that they accused the president of the college of insulting their ancestor, Confucius. Finally, the government had to intervene and fired the president.

But most of the time the Master treated unfair criticism with a sense of humor. When someone ridiculed him by saying "How grand is Confucius! He is broad in his learning and yet has nothing in particular to make a name for," the Master responded: "What should I specialize in? Perhaps charioteering? Or maybe archery? No. I think I will take charioteering" (9.2). His serious critics were unwilling to see their great sage making a joking reply and tried to interpret the Master as making a modest reply to praise. They even put the opening words of this passage, "How grand is Confucius," in large characters, hanging it on the walls to laud the sage, missing the entire sense of the ironic tone of the critic and the Master's sarcastic treatment of an absurd criticism.

On another occasion, Confucius was separated from his disciples in the state of Zheng, and he stood in front of the eastern city gate alone. Someone said to Zigong, "There is a tall man standing outside of the eastern gate, . . . frustrated like a dog that has lost its way home." When Zigong told Confucius about it later, the Master smiled and said, "A dog that has lost its way home? Was I really like that? Was I really like that?" (Kong Zi Jiayu, 5.22) It is interesting to note that, despite the Master's humorous way of treating such ridicule, his later critics still used the expression "a dog who lost its way home" to mock him.

Occasionally, Confucius also got embarrassed. On traveling to the town of Wu, the Master heard the sound of stringed instruments and singing. He smiled, saying, "Why would one use an ox cleaver to kill a chicken?" Ziyou responded, "In the past I have heard it from you, Master, that 'Exemplary persons who study the Way love others; petty persons who study the Way are easier to employ.'" The Master realized that his remark was inappropriate. He said, "My young friends, what Ziyou has said is right. What I said was only joking." (17.4)

On another occasion, YANG Huo, the chief administrator of the Ji family who became powerful in politics, wanted to see Confucius, but Confucius refused to see him (presumably because Confucius wanted to avoid a situation in which protocol required him to defer to someone he did not hold in high respect). YANG Huo then sent Confucius a steamed piglet as a gift, intending to obligate Confucius to pay a return visit to him in order to acknowledge the gift and to show gratitude. Confucius waited for a time when YANG Huo would not be home to make the visit, but unexpectedly, he happened to meet up with YANG Huo on the road. Taking advantage of the opportunity, YANG Huo said to Confucius, "Come with me! I would like to speak with you." Then he went on, "Can you call someone human-hearted who, while hoarding his treasure, allows the state to go astray? I should say not. Can a man be said to be wise, who, while eager to take part in public life, constantly misses the opportunity? I should say not. The days and months are passing; the years will not wait for us." Confucius replied, "All right, all right. I will serve in office then" (17.1). The story is quite interesting, because here the Master is not portrayed as a supreme sage who only teaches others; instead, he was lectured at by YANG Huo, a person for whom Confucius held no high respect.

Even though we cannot find records of Confucius's personal love life, there is one passage in the *Analects* that might reveal his understanding of love. Commenting on the song in the *Odes*:

> The flowers of the aspen-plum
> flutter and turn.
> How could I not think of you?
> It is just that your home is so far-flung.

The Master said, "He was not really thinking of her. If he did, there is no such thing as being far away" (9.31). Commentators typically take this as the Master's metaphor for *ren* (human-heartedness), for the Master said on another occasion, "Is *ren* far away? No sooner do I seek it than it has arrived"

(7.30). But this is certainly not a conclusive interpretation. It could very well be that the Master had a similar understanding of personal love as well.

It is both interesting and significant that the original compilers of the *Analects*, who were obviously great admirers of their Master, would include all of these passages in the book, as if they deliberately wanted later readers not to forget that the Master was, after all, human. By portraying Confucius as a real person who enjoyed fine food, liked music and singing, had peculiar personal preferences for clothing, and was liable to make mistakes and encounter awkward situations, the greatness of the Master appears so much more real and accessible to everyone.

Note

1. At the time *"furen* 妇人*"* was a more common term for women in general. Refer to Chenyang Li's *The Sage and the Second Sex* for a discussion on the issue of Confucianism and gender. Pages 3 and 4 of the book discuss the specific issue of interpreting the meaning of *nüzi*.

Bibliography

Ames, Roger T., and Henry Rosemont Jr. 1998. *The Analects of Confucius: A Philosophical Translation*. New York: *Ballantine* Books.

CAO Manzhi 曹漫之, ed. 1989. *Tanglü Shuyi Yizhu* 唐律疏议译注 [*Modern Translation of the Commentaries and Explanations of the Tang Law*]. Jilin: Jilin People's Press.

Chan, Wing-tsit. 1963. *A Source Book in Chinese Philosophy*, Princeton, NJ: Princeton University Press.

CHENG Shude 程树德. 1990. *Lunyu Jishi* 论语集释 [*Collected Interpretations of the Analects*]. Beijing: Zhonghua Shuju.

Cook, J. Daniel, and Henry Rosemont Jr. 1994. *Gottfried Wilhelm Leibniz, Writings on China*. Chicago and La Salle, IL: Open Court.

Creel, H. G. 1949. *Confucius and the Chinese Way*. New York: Harper & Brothers.

DAI Xi 戴溪. *Shigu Lunyu Dawen* 石鼓论语答问 [*Shigu Responses to Questions about the Analects*], vol. 2, in *Siku Quanshu* 四库全书, Wenyuange copy, Classics Part, Four Books Section.

Fingarette, Herbert. 1972. *Confucius—The Secular as Sacred*. New York: Harper & Row.

GUO Moluo 郭沫若. 1983. "Gongsun Nizi and His Theory of Music," in *Yueji Lunbian* 《乐记》论辩 [*Study of the Book of Music*]. Beijing: People's Music Press.

Hadot, Pierre. 1995. *Philosophy as a Way of Life*. Malden, MA: Blackwell Publishing.

Hall, David L., and Roger T. Ames. 1987. *Thinking through Confucius*, Albany: State University of New York Press.

Hansen, Chad. 1985. "Chinese Language, Chinese Philosophy, and 'Truth'." *Journal of Asian Philosophy*, vol. 44, No. 3: 491–519.

I Ching, The, or Book of Changes. 1967. Translated by Richard Wilhelm and Cary F. Baynes. Princeton: Princeton University Press.

Ivanhoe, P. J. 2002. "Whose Confucius? Which *Analects?*" In *Confucius and the Analects: New Essays*, edited by Bryan Van Norden, 119–33. New York: Oxford University Press.

Jensen, Lionel M. 1997. *Manufacturing Confucianism*. Durham, NC: Duke University Press.

Jullien, François. 1995. *Le Détour et l'accès. Stratégies du sens en Chine, en Grèce*. Paris: Grasset.

Jung, C. G. 1967. Foreword to *The I Ching or Book of Changes*, translated by Richard Wilhelm and Cary F. Baynes, xxi–xxxix. Princeton: Princeton University Press.

Kong Zi Jiayu 孔子家语 [*Confucius Family Discourse*]. 1990. Shanghai: Shanghai Guji Press.

Kupperman, Joel. 1999. *Learning from Asian Philosophy*. New York: Oxford University Press.

Lau, D. C., trans. 1979. *Confucius: The Analects*. New York: Penguin Books.

Levenson, Joseph R. 1968. *Confucian China and Its Modern Fate: A Trilogy*. Berkeley and Los Angeles: University of California Press.

Li, Chenyang 李晨阳. 2000. *The Sage and the Second Sex, Confucianism, Ethics, and Gender*. Chicago and La Salle, IL: Open Court.

Li Ji 礼记. 1967. *Book of Rites (Li Chi)*. Translated by James Legge. New Hyde Park, NY: University Books.

Lü Zuqian 吕祖谦. *Lize Lunshuo* 丽泽论说 [*Discourses of Lize*], vol. 2, in *Siku Quanshu* 四库全书, Wenyuange copy, Masters Part.

Mawangdui Silk Manuscript, Zhou Yi 马王堆帛书周易. In *Wenwu* 文物 (*Cultural Relics*), 1984, 3.

Mencius. 1970. Translated by D. C. Lau. New York: Penguin Books.

Neville, Robert Cummings. 2000. *Boston Confucianism: Portable Tradition in the Late-Modern World*. Albany: State University of New York Press.

Ni, Peimin 倪培民. 1996. "A Qigong Interpretation of Confucianism." In the *Journal of Chinese Philosophy* 23.1: 79–97.

———. 1999. "Confucian Virtues and Personal Health." In *Confucian Bioethics*, edited by Ruiping Fan, 27–44. Dordrecht / Boston: Kluwer Academic Publishers.

Odes, The Book of 诗经. 1817, reprinted in 1980. In *Shi-san Jing Zhu-shu* 十三经注疏 [*Commentaries of the Thirteen Classics*]. Beijing: Zhonghua Shuju.

Reid, Thomas. 1846. *Complete Works of Thomas Reid*. Edited by Sir William Hamilton. Edinburgh: Maclachlan and Stewart.

Rosemont, Henry Jr. 1991. *A Chinese Mirror: Moral Reflections on Political Economy and Society*. La Salle, IL: Open Court.

———. 1998. "Human Rights: A Bill of Worries." In *Confucianism and Human Rights*, edited by William Theodore de Bary and Tu Weiming, 54–66. New York: Columbia University Press.

Russell, Bertrand. 1922. *The Problem of China*. London and New York: The Century Co.

Sartre, Jean-Paul. 1993. *Existentialism and Human Emotions*. New York: Citadel Press.

Shu Jing 书经 [The *Book of Historical Documents*]. 2000. *The Chinese Classics*, vol. 3, *The Shoo King or The Book of Historical Documents*. Translated by James Legge. Taipei: SMC Publishing, Inc.

SIMA Qian. 1959. *Shi Ji* 史记 [the *Historical Records*]. Beijing: Zhonghua Shuju.

Smith, Arthur H. 2001. *Chinese Characteristics*. Safety Harbor, FL: Simon Publications LLC.

SUN Xingyan 孙星衍 & GUO Yi 郭沂. 1998. *Kong Zi Jiyu Jiaobu* 孔子集语校补 [*Collected Sayings of Confucius, Proofread and with New Additions*]. Shangdong: Qi Lu Shu She.

SUN Zhongshan. 1927. *Zhongshan Congshu* 中山丛书 [*Collected Works of Zhongshan*], vol 1. Shanghai: Dahua Shuju.

TU Weiming 杜维明. 1998. "Epilogue: Human Rights as a Confucian Moral Discourse." In *Confucianism and Human Rights*, edited by William Theodore de Bary and Tu Weiming, 297–307. New York: Columbia University Press.

Varela, Francisco. 1999. *Ethical Know-How: Action, Wisdom, and Cognition*. Stanford: Stanford University Press.

WANG Huaiyu. 2012. "Review of Peimin Ni's *Confucius: Making the Way Great*." In the *Journal of Chinese Philosophy*, 39.3 (September 2012): 453–65.

WANG Hui 王晖. 2000. *Shang Zhou wen-hua bi-jiao yan-jiu* 商周文化比较研究 [*Comparative Examination of the Cultures of Shang and Zhou*]. Beijing: People's Press.

WANG Yangming 王阳明. 1996. *WANG Yangming Quanji* 王阳明全集 [*Collected Works of WANG Yangming*], vol. 1. Beijing: Hongqi Press.

WEI Qipeng 魏启鹏. 2005. *Jianbo Wenxian Wuxing Qianzheng* 简帛文献《五行》笺证 [*Examination of the Bamboo and the Silk Scripts of Wuxing*]. Beijing: Zhonghua Shuju.

XIA Guiqi 夏瑰琦, ed. 1996. *Shengchao Poxie Ji* 圣朝破邪集 [*Collected Writings against Heresy during the Current Dynasty*]. Hong Kong: Alliance Bible Seminary 建道神学院.

Xiao Jing 孝经. 2009. *The Chinese Classic of Family Reverence—A Philosophical Translation of the Xiaojing*. Translated by Henry Rosemont Jr. and Roger T. Ames. Honolulu: University of Hawaii Press.

XU Fuguan 徐复观. 1984. *Zhongguo Renxing Lunshi, Xian Qin Pian* 中国人性论史·先秦篇 [*The History of Chinese Theories on Human Nature—Pre-Qin Period*]. Taiwan: Commercial Press, 7th edition.

Xun Zi. 1988–1994. *Xunzi: A Translation and Study of the Complete Works*, 3 vols. Translated by John Knoblock. Stanford: Stanford University Press.

YANG Bojun 杨伯峻. 1958. *Lunyu Yizhu* 论语译注 [*Interpretation and Commentary of the Analects*]. Beijing: Zhonghua Shuju.

ZHANG Xianglong 张祥龙. 2008. *Kongzi de Xianxiangxue Chanshi Jiu Jiang—Liyue yu Zheli* 孔子的现象学阐释九讲——礼乐人生与哲理 [*Nine Lectures on Confucius from a Phenomenological Perspective*]. Shanghai: East China Normal University Press.

ZHANG Xiaolin 张晓林. 2005. *Tianzhu Shiyi yu Zhongguo Xuetong—Wenhua Hudong yu Quanshi* 天主实义与中国学统—文化互动与诠释 [Tianzhu Shiyi *and the Chinese Intellectual Tradition—Cultural Encounter and Interpretation*]. Shanghai: Xuelin Press.

Zhongyong 中庸. 2001. *Focusing the Familiar: A Translation and Philosophical Interpretation of the* Zhongyong. Translated by Roger Ames and David Hall. Honolulu: University of Hawaii Press.

ZHU Xi. 1992. *Lunyu Jizhu* 论语集注 [*Collected Commentaries of the* Analects], in *Sishu Zhangju Jizhu* 四书章句集注 [*Collected Commentaries of the Four Books*]. Shandong: Qilu Shushe.

———. *Du Lunyu Mengzi Fa* 读论语孟子法 [*On Methods of Reading the* Analects *and Mencius*]. In *Siku Quanshu* 四库全书, Wenyuange version, Classics part, Four Books section.

Zhuang Zi. 1961. *Zhuang Zi Jishi* 庄子集释 [*Collected Interpretations of Zhuangzi*]. Compiled and edited by GUO Qingfan 郭庆藩. Beijing: Zhonghua Shuju.

Zuo Zhuan 左传. 1991. *The Chinese Classics*, vol. 5, *The Ch'un Tsew (Chun Qiu) with The Tso Chuen (Zuo Zhuan)*. Translated by James Legge. Taipei: SMC Publishing Inc.

~

Index of Quotes from the *Analects*

Index of Names and Subjects